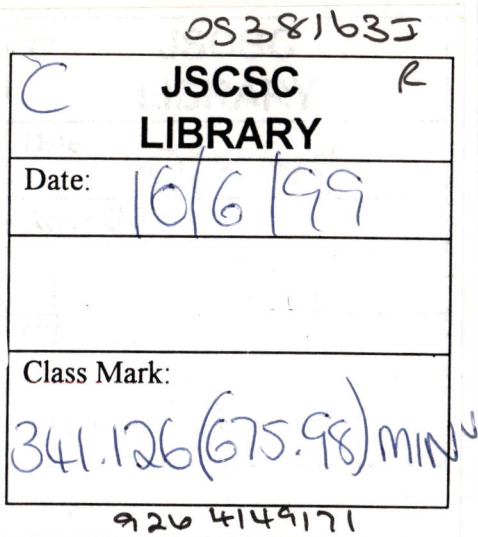

SOLDIERS TO THE RESCUE

Humanitarian Lessons from Rwanda

By
Larry Minear and Philippe Guillot

DEVELOPMENT CENTRE
OF THE ORGANISATION FOR ECONOMIC CO-OPERATION AND DEVELOPMENT

ORGANISATION FOR ECONOMIC CO-OPERATION AND DEVELOPMENT

Pursuant to Article 1 of the Convention signed in Paris on 14th December 1960, and which came into force on 30th September 1961, the Organisation for Economic Co-operation and Development (OECD) shall promote policies designed:

- to achieve the highest sustainable economic growth and employment and a rising standard of living in Member countries, while maintaining financial stability, and thus to contribute to the development of the world economy;
- to contribute to sound economic expansion in Member as well as non-member countries in the process of economic development; and
- to contribute to the expansion of world trade on a multilateral, non-discriminatory basis in accordance with international obligations.

The original Member countries of the OECD are Austria, Belgium, Canada, Denmark, France, Germany, Greece, Iceland, Ireland, Italy, Luxembourg, the Netherlands, Norway, Portugal, Spain, Sweden, Switzerland, Turkey, the United Kingdom and the United States. The following countries became Members subsequently through accession at the dates indicated hereafter: Japan (28th April 1964), Finland (28th January 1969), Australia (7th June 1971), New Zealand (29th May 1973), Mexico (18th May 1994), the Czech Republic (21st December 1995) and Hungary (7th May 1996). The Commission of the European Communities takes part in the work of the OECD (Article 13 of the OECD Convention).

The Development Centre of the Organisation for Economic Co-operation and Development was established by decision of the OECD Council on 23rd October 1962 and comprises twenty-two Member countries of the OECD: Austria, Belgium, Canada, the Czech Republic, Denmark, Finland, France, Germany, Greece, Iceland, Ireland, Italy, Japan, Luxembourg, Mexico, the Netherlands, Norway, Portugal, the United States, Spain, Sweden and Switzerland, as well as the Republic of Korea since April 1992 and Argentina and Brazil from March 1994. The Commission of the European Communities also takes part in the Centre's Advisory Board.

The purpose of the Centre is to bring together the knowledge and experience available in Member countries of both economic development and the formulation and execution of general economic policies; to adapt such knowledge and experience to the actual needs of countries or regions in the process of development and to put the results at the disposal of the countries by appropriate means.

The Centre has a special and autonomous position within the OECD which enables it to enjoy scientific independence in the execution of its task. Nevertheless, the Centre can draw upon the experience and knowledge available in the OECD in the development field.

Publié en français sous le titre :

SOLDATS A LA RESCOUSSE
Les leçons humanitaires des événements du Rwanda

THE OPINIONS EXPRESSED AND ARGUMENTS EMPLOYED IN THIS PUBLICATION ARE THE SOLE RESPONSIBILITY OF THE AUTHORS AND DO NOT NECESSARILY REFLECT THOSE OF THE OECD OR OF THE GOVERNMENTS OF ITS MEMBER COUNTRIES.

*
* *

© OECD 1996
Applications for permission to reproduce or translate all or part of this publication should be made to:
Head of Publications Service, OECD
2, rue André-Pascal, 75775 PARIS CEDEX 16, France.

Foreword

This study, carried out in collaboration with the Thomas J. Watson Jr. Institute for International Studies, forms part of the Development Centre's work on co-operation between states and non-governmental organisations in developing countries, under the auspices of the External Co-operation Programme.

Table of Contents

Acknowledgements 7
Map of Africa 8
Map of Rwanda and Burundi 9
Map of the Great Lakes Region of Africa 9
Preface 11
Executive Summary 13

Chapter 1. **The Historical Moment**

The Passing of the Cold War 17
Impacts on the Military 22
Institutions in Ferment 27
Notes 32

Chapter 2. **Major Policy Issues**

Terms of Engagement 33
Comparative Advantage 35
Cost 37
Institutional Cultures 40
Limiting the Damages of Involving Military Assets 42
Effectiveness 45
Stewardship 47
Notes 50

Chapter 3. **The Rwanda Context**

Historical Background 53
Recent Political-Military Developments 56
Rwandese Military Forces 59
An Overview of the 1994 Humanitarian Effort 63
An Overview of International Military Involvement 68
Notes 71

Chapter 4. **UN Troops: The United Nations Assistance Mission for Rwanda**

The Immediate Background 73
Terms of Engagement and Activities 74
UNAMIR Sectors of Operation and Deployment as of 31 May 1995 81
Assessment 88
Conclusion 92
Notes 93

Chapter 5. **French Troops:** *Opération Turquoise*

Terms of Engagement 95
Activities 97
Assessment 103
Conclusion 107
Notes 109

Chapter 6. US Troops: Operation Support Hope

Terms of Engagement and Activities 111
Assessment 116
Conclusion 125
Notes 126

Chapter 7. Other Troops

Canada 129
The Netherlands 132
Japan 135
Germany 137
New Zealand 138
Australia 139
Israel 139
Ireland 141
Conclusion 142
Notes 144

Chapter 8. Conclusions and Implications

Terms of Engagement 147
Comparative Advantage 149
Cost 152
Institutional Cultures 154
Damage Limitation 156
Effectiveness 159
Stewardship 161
Conclusion 163
Notes 165

Chapter 9. Epilogue

Achieving Security in Camps and Beyond 167
Accelerating the Pace of Reconstruction 170
Addressing the Regional Context 173
The Continuing Dilemmas of International Action 174
Notes 176

Glossary of Acronyms 177

Annex 1: Chronology of Major Events of 1994 in the Rwanda Crisis 179
Annex 2: Excerpts from United Nations Security Council Resolutions
           Related to Rwanda 185
Annex 3: About the Humanitarianism and War Project and the Authors 189

Bibliography 191

Acknowledgements

We wish to acknowledge the support of the sponsors of the Humanitarianism and War Project, listed by name in Annex 3, whose grants have helped make this volume possible. We are also grateful for special contributions to the research on Rwanda from the Irish non-governmental organisation Trocaire and from the American Red Cross.

This work has benefited from the advice and counsel of Giulio Fossi, Jean-Claude Berthélemy, Andrew Goudie, Henny Helmich, and Colm Foy at the Development Centre.

At the Watson Institute in Providence, assistance has come from Sue Miller, Daniel Zalick, and particularly from Juanita Ortiz, whose help in the final production of the manuscript was indispensable. Special thanks are also due to a wider circle of colleagues and friends, including Antonio Donini, Karl Farris, Kate Farnsworth, Jonathan Frerichs, Kaz Kuroda, Charles Petrie, Peter Uvin, and Neill Wright.

Africa

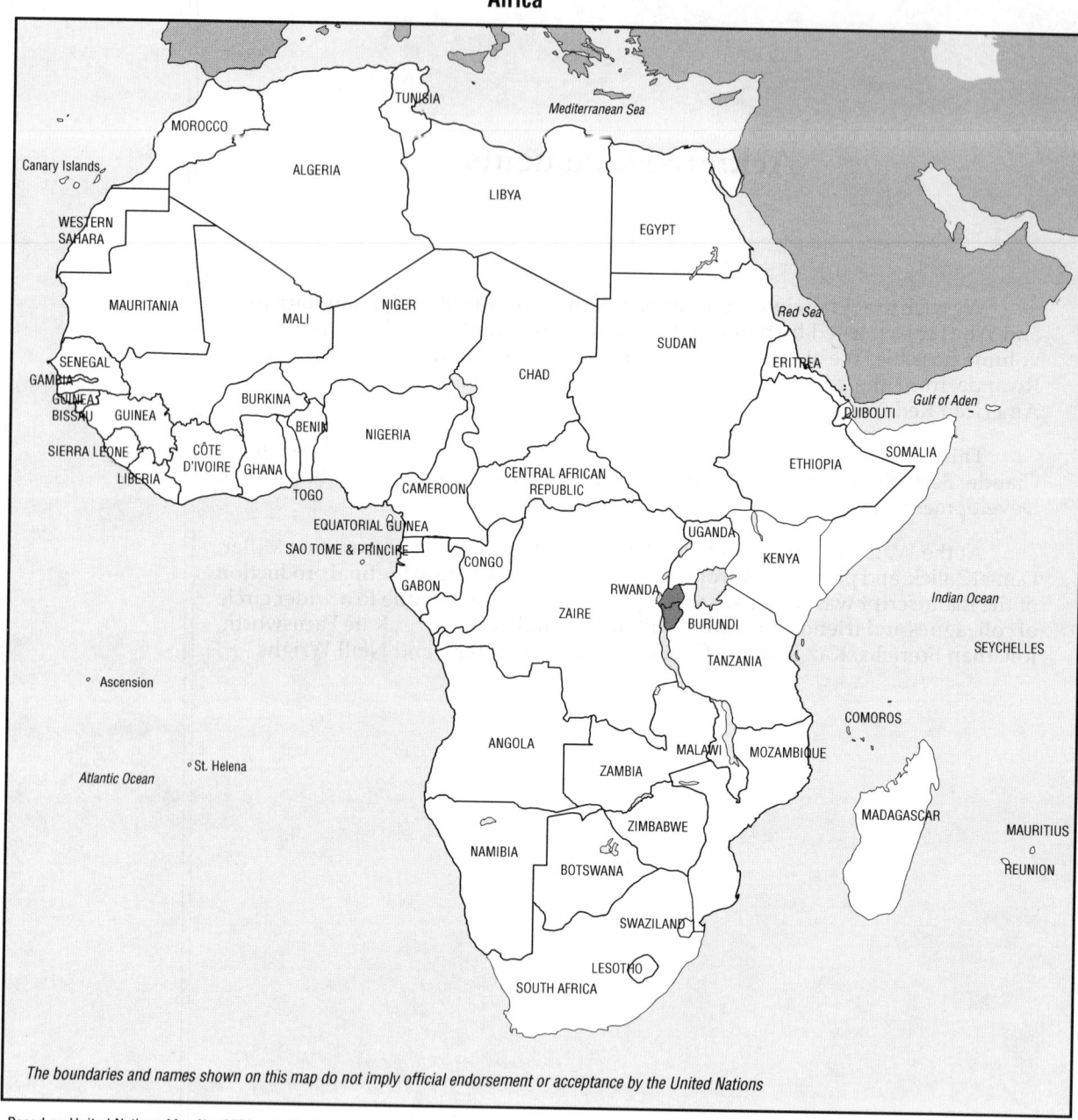

Rwanda and Burundi

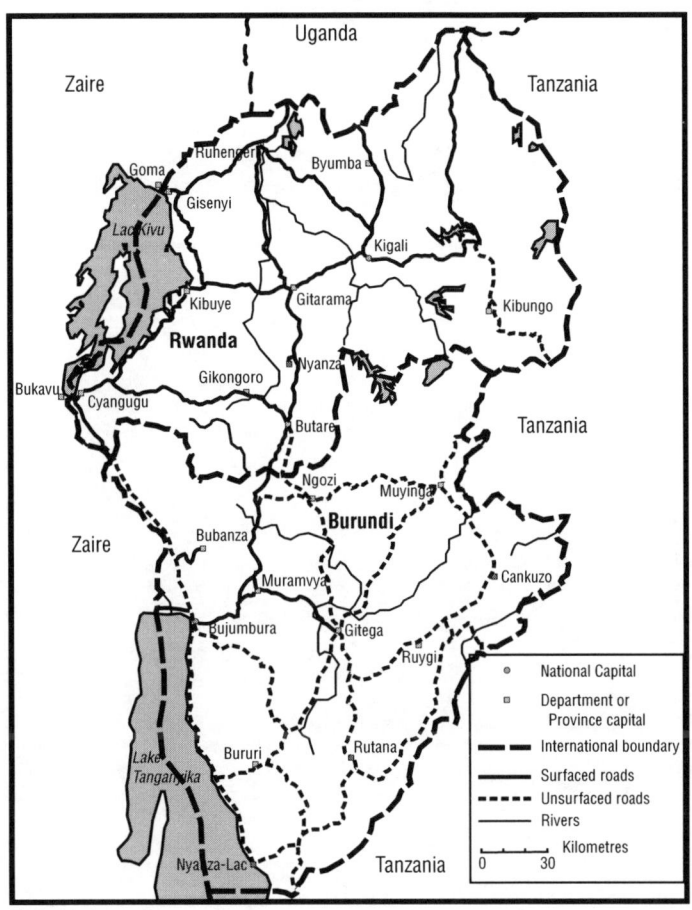

Great Lakes Region of Africa

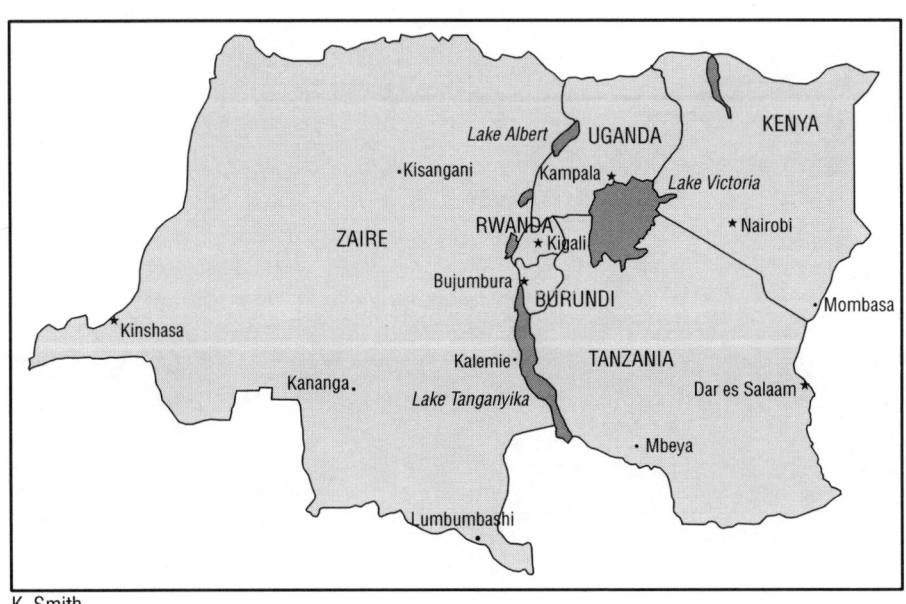

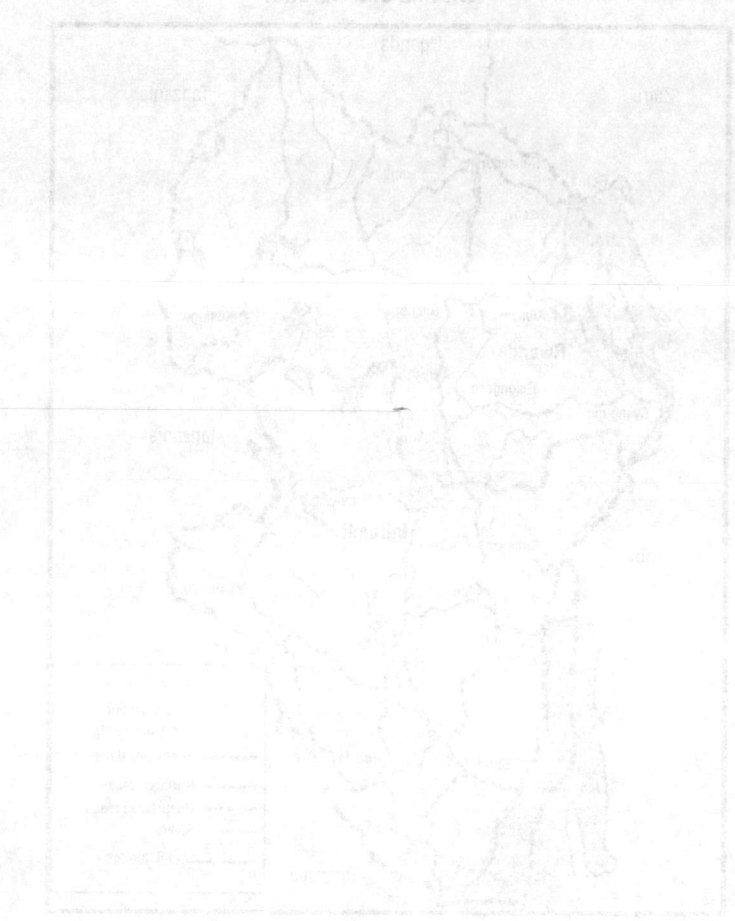

Preface

Among a host of major post-Cold War humanitarian crises such as northern Iraq, Somalia, and the former Yugoslavia, Rwanda will be remembered as the one involving genocide. "Ethnic cleansing" and other assaults against basic humanity have tarnished international norms in other conflicts. The genocide in Rwanda, however, confronted the international community with the stark reality that even the savage and rapid destruction of an entire people is not unthinkable.

This book is about the international response to the Rwanda crisis, and more specifically, about the contribution of international military forces. Rwanda is highly unusual among modern crises in the multiplicity of soldiers who were dispatched to the rescue, both within the United Nations framework and as part of the initiatives of individual governments.

This is not a typical book about humanitarian action. Readers will look in vain for a review of the work of traditional humanitarian organisations such as the United Nations High Commissioner for Refugees or UNICEF, of private relief groups or the International Committee of the Red Cross. The study focuses instead on the activities of what are being called the "New Humanitarians", that is, military personnel sent to the aid of civilian populations. The work of traditional humanitarian organisations surfaces largely as it intersects with efforts by the troops.

The volume is actually two books in one. The analysis of the Rwanda experience is set in the broader context of the growing utilisation of military assets in major humanitarian crises. The debate over use of the military for "operations other than war" thus frames the presentation of the Rwanda experience and the major lessons which may be drawn from it.

We believe that the descriptive and analytical review will prove instructive for a wide range of readers from governments and United Nations organisations, to policy-makers and practitioners, military forces and humanitarian agencies, academics and policy analysts, the media and the concerned international public. There will surely be great interest in Africa, whose experience contributed the notion of "failed state" to the international lexicon and where, in the view of Ethiopia's President Zenawi, "every country is a potential failed state".

The two institutions which have joined together to make this volume possible are no strangers to such issues. In recent years, the Development Centre and its parent Organisation for Economic Co-operation and Development have monitored from Paris trends in military expenditures, economic conversion, and, of course, military and development-assistance flows. Recent publications on such matters by the OECD and in the Development Centre Studies Series are among the items listed in the bibliography.

The Humanitarianism and War Project is an independent research initiative based in Providence, Rhode Island at Brown University's Thomas J. Watson Jr. Institute for International Studies. Co-sponsored by some three dozen UN organisations, governments, private relief groups, and foundations, the Project has interviewed more than two thousand practitioners and others engaged in humanitarian and political-military action in a dozen complex emergencies. Its case studies, handbooks, training materials, and articles are in wide circulation. It is also described further in Annex 3.

The preoccupations of our two institutions are evident in the approach taken by this volume. In reviewing myriad data, the text separates description and assessment. It derives conclusions from evidence gathered in the field rather than from preconceptions or second-hand knowledge. It provides a forum for the roughly 300 persons interviewed by the authors during the course of almost a year to share their particular vantage points and assessments. It is informed by the constraints within which military and humanitarian institutions function, yet challenges them to enhance their effectiveness.

We are well aware of the importance attached by donor governments to understanding better the Rwanda crisis and response. Perhaps the most comprehensive review of a major relief operation ever undertaken is now underway. The Multidonor Evaluation on the Rwanda Crisis provides a vehicle for some 50 sponsoring agencies, many of them Member countries of the OECD and sponsors of the Humanitarianism and War Project, to review this crucial experience. A number of organisations, referenced in the text, have themselves already carried out their own reviews.

The Rwanda story does not have a happy ending — in fact, it does not yet have an ending at all. As of mid-1995, many of the issues analysed here remain unresolved. As the international community charts its future course in Rwanda, the Great Lakes region, and beyond, the story reviewed here needs to be told, the experience savoured. The present volume's focus on events in 1994, updated in an Epilogue through mid-1995, provides an essential ingredient in the ongoing reflection process.

Jean Bonvin	Thomas G. Weiss
President	Brown University's
OECD Development Centre	Thomas J. Watson Jr. Institute
Paris	for International Studies
	Providence

June 1996

Executive Summary

The Rwanda crisis of 1994 took place at a time in the early post-Cold War period when humanitarian crises were on the rise, traditional aid agencies overstretched, and international military forces increasingly used in responding. The historical context at the international level is reviewed in Chapter 1; the context of events in Rwanda and the Great Lakes region of Africa, in Chapter 3.

The use of military assets in recent major crises has confronted the international community with a number of key policy issues. Seven are examined in Chapter 2: the terms of engagement of the military in the humanitarian sphere, their comparative advantage *vis-à-vis* humanitarian organisations, the costs of utilising military assets, cultural differences between military and humanitarian institutions, the possibilities of minimising the often negative effects of military assets, the effectiveness of such assets, and the emerging view that committing troops is a necessary element in responsible global stewardship. The impacts on these issues of the Rwanda experience is reviewed in Chapter 8.

Chapters 4 through 7 focus on the international community's response to the Rwandan crisis in 1994. For analytical purposes, the crisis and the international response are divided into three phases: *genocide*, a three-month period which began April 6 in the wake of the shooting down of the plane carrying the presidents of Rwanda and Burundi; *mass exodus*, the period of roughly six weeks from mid-July involving massive flight by Rwandans, many of them already displaced within their own country, into neighbouring countries, primarily Zaïre; and *reconstruction*, the period from September onward in which the new regime sought to establish its authority, restore basic services, and encourage the return of people to their homes. The focus of the discussion is on activities during 1994, updated by Chapter 9 to include developments through mid-1995.

In reviewing what promises to be a watershed event in the international community's use of military forces in the humanitarian sphere, the book analyses activities by military forces within three different frameworks. The UN Assistance Mission for Rwanda (UNAMIR) was a peace-keeping initiative under Chapter VI of the UN Charter. It was carried out with the consent of the warring parties, with troops allowed to use force only in self-defence. With authorised strength ranging from 270 in the wake of the April 1994 events to 5 500 later in the year, UNAMIR comprised troops, military observers, and civilian police from some 26 nations. Although its initial mandate involved principally diplomatic, political, and military observer functions, UNAMIR over time assumed responsibilities of a humanitarian and rehabilitation nature as well. The contribution of UNAMIR is the subject of Chapter 4.

Troops were also present as part of French and US initiatives. The French-led *Opération Turquoise*, whose mandate under Chapter VII of the UN Security Council conferred a greater degree of force at its disposal, was present in Rwanda and in the Goma region of Zaïre with about 2 500 troops for two months beginning June 22, 1994. Operation Support Hope, a two-month undertaking by the United States military, began July 22 and involved about 3 000 troops. Both initiatives were stand-alone in origin. However, the French received the blessing of the Security Council and enlisted troops from a number of French-speaking West African nations, and US troops worked closely with UN humanitarian organisations and UNAMIR. *Opération Turquoise*, primarily a security initiative with some humanitarian elements, is the subject of Chapter 5; Operation Support Hope, a purely humanitarian effort without a security component, of Chapter 6.

A third set of military forces was comprised of troops associated with the UN High Commissioner for Refugees. A number of countries, including Australia, Canada, Germany, Ireland, Israel, Japan, the Netherlands, and New Zealand, provided military assets to assist in humanitarian activities at UNHCR's request. National governments retained command and control over their troops, although the objectives served and the tasks performed were set by UNHCR. Canada and Australia, in addition to committing troops to UNHCR-related activities, made military assets available to UNAMIR. Ireland seconded troops to aid agencies, in whose employ they functioned as civilians. Most UNHCR-related troop contingents were deployed during the exodus period. None were on hand during the genocide. Some stayed to assist during reconstruction. Their contribution is described and assessed in Chapter 7.

The initial response of the international community to the Rwanda crisis was thus drawn from its existing repertoire of instruments. When the UN peace-keeping operation proved inadequate to the task, two Great Powers became directly engaged: first the French and then the United States, their involvement reflecting a post-Cold War trend for major powers to assert leadership in crises of particular interest such as Georgia, Haiti, and Liberia. New altogether, and most likely to be replicated in major future crises, were the arrangements which facilitated participation of national troops independently of a UN peace-keeping operation in a multilaterally orchestrated response to a major crisis.

Each of the three periods identified had specific humanitarian challenges. Three roles of the military in the humanitarian sphere are analysed: the fostering of a climate of security for civilian populations and humanitarian organisations; the support provided to the work of such agencies; and the provision of direct services to those in need. These roles provide the template used to review the contributions of the military in Chapters 4-7 and to reflect in Chapter 8 on future directions in military-humanitarian co-operation.

The book concludes that while the first of these functions was the most essential and an area of clear comparative advantage, international military forces were least able to foster a secure environment, particularly when it was most needed: during the genocide. Present well in advance of the April events, UNAMIR was largely overwhelmed by the crisis, its numbers reduced at the moment of maximum peril to Rwandan life. *Opération Turquoise* succeeded in providing security in south-western Rwanda for a two-month period, a task assumed thereafter by UNAMIR and then by the new Rwandese authorities. The French also helped provide security in burgeoning refugee camps in the Goma area, a major challenge after their departure. Beyond UNAMIR and *Opération Turquoise*, no troops had a security mandate or mounted activities specifically designed to provide a climate of protection.

With respect to supporting the work of humanitarian organisations, troops operating within each of the three frameworks made major contributions. UNAMIR did so in one form or another from the time of the April 1994 events through the end of its mandate in late 1995. The French and US initiatives did so for periods of eight weeks each in 1994. UNHCR-associated troops were generally on hand for shorter periods — six weeks in the case of the Israeli Defence Forces and the New Zealanders. Reflecting the positive nature of the experience, a number of governments extended their initial commitments. Military activities in this second function were concentrated during the period of the mass exodus.

Troops also provided direct assistance to civilian populations. Within UNAMIR, national contingents such as the British and Canadians had responsibilities of a wholly or partially humanitarian nature. In addition, many UN troops assisted civilians in their off hours. French and US troops also provided direct services, notably in Goma during the exodus period when they joined with aid groups to provide more than a million people with food, shelter, water, and medical care. Troop contingents delivering services for UNHCR also provided relief, most in the exodus but some also in the reconstruction phase. Taken together, the direct relief activities extended significantly the range of what humanitarian organisations could otherwise have done, especially during the genocide and exodus periods.

Assessing the implications of the Rwanda experience for the future use of military assets in the humanitarian sphere, Chapter 8 identifies both positive and negative elements. The Rwanda crisis is likely to distinguish itself not only for the egregious nature of the genocide which triggered it but also for the multiple roles and configurations of international military personnel involved. Troops functioned with great energy and flexibility, putting military assets at the disposal of humanitarian organisations and strengthening them in their tasks. The multiplicity of national troop contingents committed, the variety of authorities under which they functioned, and the nature and extent of their contributions to the humanitarian task are undoubtedly unprecedented.

On the negative side, troops were least available and least effective when most needed. Had international military presence and pressure been more in evidence during the genocide, the exodus of people within Rwanda and into neighbouring countries and the formidable reconstruction task which followed might have been avoided, or at least reduced. Later in the year, the absence of troops to help ensure security in the camps within and outside Rwanda seriously undercut humanitarian efforts and ultimately occasioned the need for even more relief assistance.

The utilisation of the military was also costly, although difficulties in obtaining accurate data combine with differences in how such costs are calculated to render judgements of cost-effectiveness conjectural. Incremental costs of utilising the various militaries to respond to the crisis in 1994 totalled at least $650 million, although they may have exceeded that amount by a factor of two or three. Humanitarian assistance contributions were estimated at $1.3 billion in 1994. As a result, at least 2 per cent of worldwide official development assistance in 1994 went to the Rwanda crisis and its aftermath. At every point during the year, there were more military than humanitarian personnel in theatre.

As Chapter 9 indicates, the Rwanda tragedy is ongoing as of mid-1995, energetic military and humanitarian efforts notwithstanding. The impressive contributions of many soldiers who came to the rescue are thus set in the context of international policies which have not succeeded in assisting the Rwandan government and people to turn the corner from genocide to a more just and sustainable society.

The study underscores that resources, humanitarian and military alike, were triggered less by the genocide than by the subsequent cholera epidemic and other media-mediated events. In this crisis as in others, the approach chosen by the international community was to address familiar problems of uprooted people defined in traditional humanitarian terms rather than to halt genocide or to deal with its underlying causes, challenges of far greater complexity.

While soldiers cannot be faulted for the failures of policies they were deployed to advance, the fact that their presence substituted for, rather than complemented, the necessary political and diplomatic strategies represents a major shortcoming. In this sense, the commitment of military forces runs the risk of serving less as an expression of well-considered international concern than as an indication of the lack of serious and effective commitment. To achieve their full potential, military assets, like humanitarian resources themselves, need to serve effective strategies not only of rescue and relief but also of conflict prevention and conflict resolution, reconstruction and development, reconciliation and peace.

Chapter 1

The Historical Moment

The utilisation of international military forces in responding to the crisis in Rwanda in 1994 took place at a particular historical moment in the early post-Cold War era. A half-decade after the fall of the Berlin Wall and the breakup of the former Soviet Union, military establishments in both East and West were less seized with traditional tasks and newly available for what have come to be called "operations other than war".

At the same time, the increased incidence of major emergencies and a growing willingness to use troops to respond had contributed to the evolution of outside military forces as a significant actor in the humanitarian sphere. A review of changes occasioned by the end of the Cold War thus properly precedes a more detailed look at the contributions of outside military forces to the Rwanda crisis.

This chapter notes the impacts of waning East-West tensions on the incidence of conflict and humanitarian need around the world and on the world's military resources. It also analyses the ferment taking place in both military and humanitarian institutions as they chart their respective future courses of action[1].

The Passing of the Cold War

At the midpoint of this century's final decade, the world finds itself beset by a proliferation of conflicts. Some are taking place in what during the Cold War had come to be called the Third World: that is, in places such as Rwanda and the Sudan, Angola and Mozambique, Afghanistan and Guatemala, Sri Lanka and Kashmir. Others are playing themselves out in the Second World among the erstwhile centrally planned economies of Azjerbaijan and Armenia, Georgia and Chechnya. Long-term tensions also exist in free-market countries of the so-called First World, as residents of Northern Ireland and the Basque region of Spain would attest. Countries such as the former Yugoslavia, something of a bridge among the Worlds during the Cold War era, have themselves been affected.

These conflicts are connected in a variety of ways to the geopolitical tensions which had polarised the world in the aftermath of World War II. As tensions from the bipolar era have receded, some conflicts have proved more susceptible to resolution. Others have been waged even more fiercely. Still others have proceeded without apparent reference to broader geopolitical changes. Some conflicts, it has become more clear, were manufactured and maintained by the superpowers; others had deeper-seated local disputes.

The conventional wisdom is that the passing of the Cold War has led to a new generation of conflicts: internal rather than international, driven by ethnic and communal differences rather than by political ideology, and of unprecedented levels of brutality. There is considerable truth to that perception. Figure 1.1

confirms an increase in the incidence of conflicts and a change in their character. An increasing proportion are now internal rather than international in nature (Wallensteen and Axell, 1994). The accompanying map locates the major conflicts around the world in 1995.

Despite the impression of radical discontinuity between conflicts in the Cold War and post-Cold War eras, there are also little-recognised elements of continuity. Figure 1.1 itself spotlights the remarkable number of internal wars which were taking place during the 1965-85 period, many of them masked by the larger East-West confrontation itself. The element that has changed most, in other words, may be not the existence, the number, or even the brutality of such conflicts. It is rather the wider world's awareness of them, the lack of a single organising principle to render them somehow intelligible, and the world's willingness to try to do something about them (Ayoub, 1995).

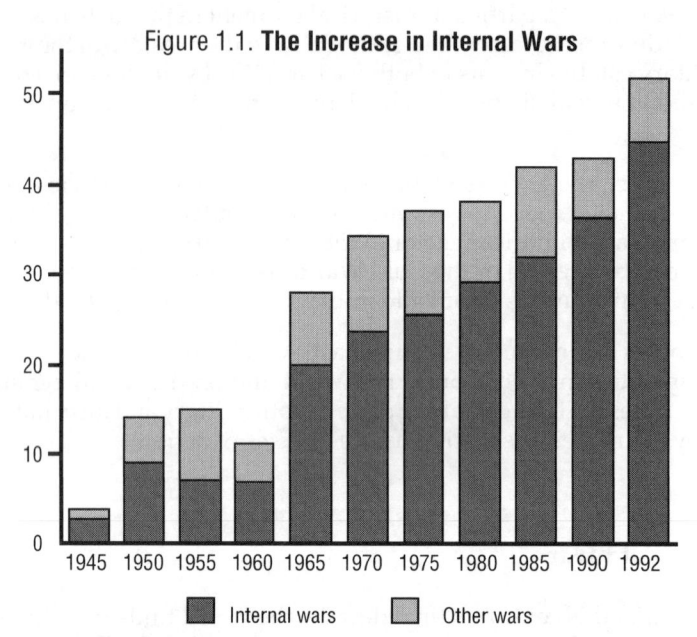

Figure 1.1. **The Increase in Internal Wars**

Source: International Federation of Red Cross and Red Crescent Societies, *World Disasters Report 1995*, Geneva: IFRC, 1995. The data is based on research by K.J.Gantzel.

The ferocity of ethnic cleansing in Bosnia-Herzegovina or the fury of the saturation bombing of Chechnya's Grozny may seem unprecedented. However, such calculated acts of brutality had Cold War era precedents in civil wars in Afghanistan and Angola, in Ethiopia and Cambodia. The internecine struggle in Somalia of the early 1990s recalls the long-lived and only recently abated factional fighting in Lebanon. The civil strife in Sri Lanka has itself been an off-again, on-again reality for decades.

While analysts may differ in explaining the forces behind the upswing in internal armed conflicts, all agree on the consequences of the trend. Post-Cold War conflicts, like their predecessors during the Cold War, are taking a heavy toll on the world's civilian populations. A frequently cited statistic places civilian casualties, which in World War I had represented about 5 per cent of the total, at an estimated 95 per cent in recent conflicts. No longer incidental victims caught in the crossfire, civilian populations have become explicit targets of military operations. One recent survey has placed the figure of all deaths due to armed conflicts for the twelve months beginning July 1, 1994 at some 640 750, with the actual tally perhaps as high as 1 458 750 (Jongman, 1995).

Certainly the pace of economic and social transformation within states is outrunning the capacity of national and international institutions to address the causes of the ferment. "Contemporary forms of insecurity — be they ethnic, human rights or environmentally based — are incompatible with conventional paradigms of international relations theory", observes Kumar Rupesinghe, head of International Alert, a non-governmental organisation founded to promote more effective conflict-prevention and conflict-resolution strategies (Rupesinghe, 1992). His and other non-governmental groups advocate placing internal armed conflicts front and centre on the world's agenda and rethinking traditional concepts of state sovereignty, international responsibility and strategies accordingly.

Indeed, new paradigms are now being elaborated. One emphasizes the obligation, now viewed in some quarters as a right, to intervene in the internal affairs of states when humane values are at stake. "France has taken the initiative as regards the new right, a right that is quite extraordinary in the history of the world", noted President François Mitterrand in comments on the 1991 UN Security Council resolution which authorised military rescue of the Kurds in northern Iraq. It is "a sort of right to interfere inside a country when a portion of its population suffers persecution"[2].

The Minister of Humanitarian Affairs during a period of the Mitterrand presidency, Bernard Kouchner, has elaborated the point. "France's proposal to the Security Council, adopted as Resolution 688, represented a successful example of the right to interfere on humanitarian grounds, and a precedent". (Kouchner, 1991). Kouchner left the International Committee of the Red Cross in 1968 in the wake of the Biafra crisis because he disagreed with its insistence that humanitarian activities receive the consent of the belligerents. He has been a leading and vocal proponent of what he has termed "the duty to interfere".

The growing acknowledgment of a global humanitarian imperative has been accompanied by a concern that such an imperative be not only legitimised but also subjected to groundrules to regularise its use. The Commission on Global Governance, a 28-member group of international luminaries established in 1992, recently proposed amending the UN Charter itself. The Commission argued that a fundamental revision is needed to provide a clear legal basis for intervention in situations within countries in which there is widespread suffering or abuse. The current Charter, strictly construed, limits intervention to circumstances in which international peace and security are threatened. In its 1995 report, *Our Global Neighbourhood*, the Commission proposed altering the Charter to permit such intervention in "cases that constitute a violation of the security of people so gross and extreme that it requires an international response on humanitarian grounds" (Commission on Global Governance, 1995)[3].

Against this evolving global backdrop, the question arises as to whether the response of the international community to the Rwanda crisis in 1994 would have been different had the Cold War still been the dominant fact of international political life. The answer is necessarily conjectural. Yet it seems unlikely that either a Security Council paralysed by the East-West confrontation or military forces caught up in Cold War struggle would have responded. Moreover, a comparison between the Biafran-Nigerian civil war of the late 1960s, in which governments did not provide direct humanitarian assistance, and the Rwanda crisis of the mid-1990s, to which they commited humanitarian and military resources alike, suggests a greater willingness nowadays to tackle complex human problems internal to sovereign states.

World Conflict

Estimated Number of War Deaths in '94/'95

Rwanda	500 000-1 000 000
Angola	>50 000
Chechnya	30 000-40 000
Afghanistan	>10 000
Algeria	>10 000
Azerbaijan / Armenia	>7 000
Yemen	6 000-70 000 *
Bosnia-Herzegovina	>5 000
Turkey	>5 000
Sierra Leone	>3 000
Cambodia	2 000-7 000
Ghana	2 000-5 000 *
Iraq (Kurds)	>2 000
Burundi	>3 000
Pakistan	>1 800
South Africa	>1 600
Sudan	>1 600
Colombia	>1 500
Ethiopia	>1 000
Iraq (Shi'ites)	>1 000
Zaire	>1 000
Chad	>1 000

*terminated in 1994

Estimated Cumulative Number of War Deaths

Afghanistan	1 - 2 000 000
Cambodia	1 - 2 000 000
Sudan	1 - 1 500 000
Ethiopia	1 500 000
Rwanda	500 000-1 000 000
Angola	500 000-900 000
Somalia	350 000
Burundi	200 000-250 000
Bosnia-Herz.	60 000-200 000
Iraq (Kurds)	18 000-250 000
Liberia	150 000
Chad	100 000
Iraq (Shi'ites)	100 000-300 000
Colombia	90 000
Peru	25 000 - 30 000
Tajikistan	30 000-60 000
Algeria	30 000-40 000
Chechnya	30 000-40 000
Azerbaijan	25 000-40 000
India (Kashmir)	17 000-40 000
South Africa	21 000
Turkey	12 000-15 000
Uganda	12 000
Croatia	10 000-50 000
Pakistan	10 000
Sierra Leone	10 000

Lower Intensity Conflicts

Latin America
1. El Salvador
2. Guatemala
3. Haiti
4. Mexico (Chiapas)
5. Nicaragua
6. Peru
7. Peru / Ecuador (border)

West, Central & East Europe
8. Bosnia-Herz. ('Srpska Rep.')
9. Bosnia-Herz. ('Herzeg Bosna Rep.')
10. Croatia
11. Georgia (Abkhazia)
12. Uzbekistan (Fergana Valley)
13. Tajikistan (Gorny-Badakshan)

Africa
14. Angola (Cabinda)
15. Cameroon
16. Congo
17. Liberia
18. Mali
19. Nigeria (Yoruba/Igbo)
20. Uganda (North)
21. Somalia (Somaliland)
22. Somalia (Interclan)

North Africa & Middle East
23. Egypt
24. Iran
25. Israel (Occupied Territories)
26. Lebanon (South)
27. Turkey / Iraq (Kurds)

Central & East Asia
28. India (Assam)
29. India (Maharashtra)
30. India (Manipur)
31. India (Nagaland)
32. India (Punjab)
33. India / Pakistan (Kashmiris)
34. Myanmar (Karen)
35. Myanmar (Shans)
36. Philippines (Moros)
37. Pakistan (Sindh)
38. Sri Lanka (Tamils)

Explanation of Symbols and Definitions

- **UN** United Nations Peacekeeping Operation (PK = Other Peacekeeping Operation)
- **Serious Dispute** (conflict level 3: armed conflict that caused less than 100 deaths in 1994)
- **Lower Intensity Conflict** (conflict level 4: armed conflict that caused 100 to 1 000 deaths in 1994)
- **War** (conflict level 5: major armed conflict that caused more than 1 000 deaths in 1994)

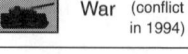

Source: PIOOM Databank, Leiden University, Wassenaarseweg 52, 2333 AK Leiden, the Netherlands, tel.: 31 71 5273861, fax: 31 71 5273788
©1995 - Infographic: Harry Kasemir, Groningen

Map 1994-95

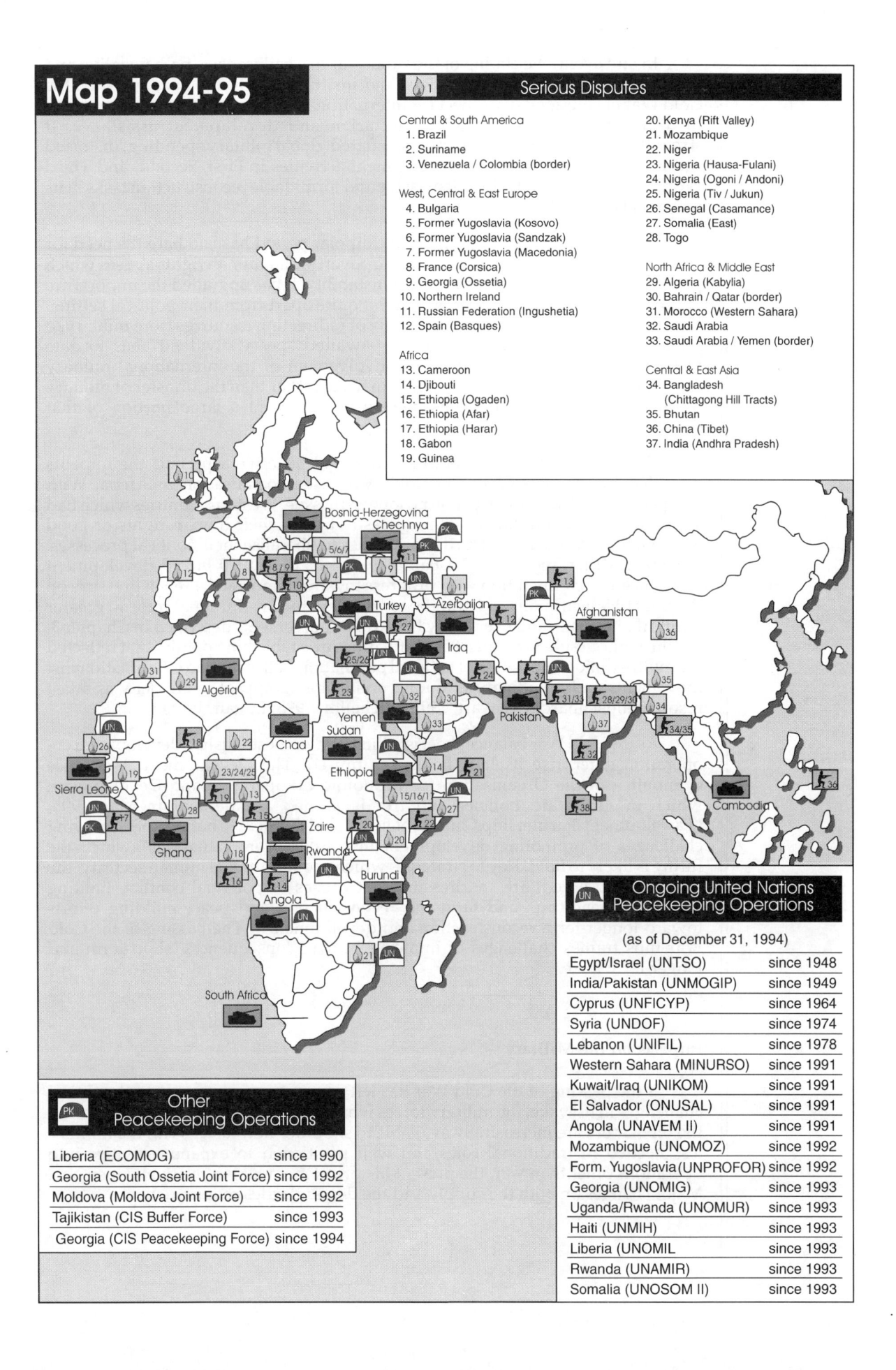

Serious Disputes

Central & South America
1. Brazil
2. Suriname
3. Venezuela / Colombia (border)

West, Central & East Europe
4. Bulgaria
5. Former Yugoslavia (Kosovo)
6. Former Yugoslavia (Sandzak)
7. Former Yugoslavia (Macedonia)
8. France (Corsica)
9. Georgia (Ossetia)
10. Northern Ireland
11. Russian Federation (Ingushetia)
12. Spain (Basques)

Africa
13. Cameroon
14. Djibouti
15. Ethiopia (Ogaden)
16. Ethiopia (Afar)
17. Ethiopia (Harar)
18. Gabon
19. Guinea
20. Kenya (Rift Valley)
21. Mozambique
22. Niger
23. Nigeria (Hausa-Fulani)
24. Nigeria (Ogoni / Andoni)
25. Nigeria (Tiv / Jukun)
26. Senegal (Casamance)
27. Somalia (East)
28. Togo

North Africa & Middle East
29. Algeria (Kabylia)
30. Bahrain / Qatar (border)
31. Morocco (Western Sahara)
32. Saudi Arabia
33. Saudi Arabia / Yemen (border)

Central & East Asia
34. Bangladesh (Chittagong Hill Tracts)
35. Bhutan
36. China (Tibet)
37. India (Andhra Pradesh)

Ongoing United Nations Peacekeeping Operations

(as of December 31, 1994)

Egypt/Israel (UNTSO)	since 1948
India/Pakistan (UNMOGIP)	since 1949
Cyprus (UNFICYP)	since 1964
Syria (UNDOF)	since 1974
Lebanon (UNIFIL)	since 1978
Western Sahara (MINURSO)	since 1991
Kuwait/Iraq (UNIKOM)	since 1991
El Salvador (ONUSAL)	since 1991
Angola (UNAVEM II)	since 1991
Mozambique (UNOMOZ)	since 1992
Form. Yugoslavia (UNPROFOR)	since 1992
Georgia (UNOMIG)	since 1993
Uganda/Rwanda (UNOMUR)	since 1993
Haiti (UNMIH)	since 1993
Liberia (UNOMIL)	since 1993
Rwanda (UNAMIR)	since 1993
Somalia (UNOSOM II)	since 1993

Other Peacekeeping Operations

Liberia (ECOMOG)	since 1990
Georgia (South Ossetia Joint Force)	since 1992
Moldova (Moldova Joint Force)	since 1992
Tajikistan (CIS Buffer Force)	since 1993
Georgia (CIS Peacekeeping Force)	since 1994

In any event, the ebbing of the Cold War has had impacts both negative and positive on humanitarian challenges and institutions. On the negative side, the Cold War encouraged disrespect for international law and politicised many of the institutions which provided humanitarian and development assistance. It strengthened military establishments, inflated global military spending, distorted social priorities, and delayed development activities in First, Second, and Third World countries alike. It also left massive and formidable reconstruction tasks in its wake (Lake *et al.*, 1990).

On the positive side, the end of the bipolar period has laid bare the need for attending to historical inequities, chronic poverty, and human rights abuses which provide a fertile seedbed for continued instability. It has upgraded the importance of humanitarian needs in their own right, quite apart from their political setting. The new era has opened up the possibility of redirecting resources from military to social purposes, even though the long-awaited "peace dividend" has to date proved elusive. In fact, the growing involvement of the international military establishment in the alleviation of human need, rather than the transfer of military resources to civilian institutions, may itself represent a large portion of that dividend.

One development with both positive and negative aspects is the impetus provided by the passing of the Cold War to democratisation in Africa. With competition with the Soviet Union no longer an issue, Western countries which had supported anti-Communist regimes irrespective of their human rights or good governance records urged Third World allies to liberalise their political processes. President Mitterrand in his La Baule speech of June 1990 linked development assistance and co-operation with progress toward democracy. French pressure on President Habyarimana of Rwanda, for one, led to constitutional reform, greater political pluralism, and eventually the Arusha agreements described in Chapter 3. Yet throughout sub-Saharan Africa difficulties in establishing polities that reflected the multi-ethnic composition of national populations led to myriad ethno-nationalist movements and a willingness among politicians to appeal to ethnicity as a last resort against anarchy (Bayart, 1993; Michaïlof, 1993; Lugan, 1995).

As the Cold War balance sheet is tallied, the well-established development co-operation enterprise itself is being scrutinised. The Development Assistance Committee of the Organisation for Economic Co-operation and Development, which monitors aid policies and trends, issued a statement in May 1995, "Development Partnerships in the New Global Context", noting the "growing challenges of promoting development in conflict-prone situations" which the future is likely to hold. Key to strategies which promote global human security, the statement observed, are "addressing root causes of potential conflict, limiting military expenditure, and targeting reconstruction and peace-building efforts toward longer-term reconstruction and development"[4]. The passing of the Cold War thus frames challenges of immense human consequences, short-term and longer-term alike.

Impacts on the Military

If the passing of the Cold War has left major economic, social, and political challenges in its wake, the military forces which achieved such prominence during the bipolar era are increasingly available to shoulder new tasks. With the military less needed in traditional roles and well positioned to expand activities into operations other than war, the present historical moment is a relatively open one. Major changes on both the supply and the demand sides require review.

On the supply side, the waning of the Cold War has meant a decrease in the need for military forces as previously configured. Reflecting a reduction in traditional military threats to existing nation states, global spending on the military during the seven years beginning in 1987 declined by almost a quarter — from $995 billion to an estimated $767 billion. The cumulative amount of the downsizing over seven years was roughly one full year's military expenditures during these years (Renner, 1994).

Of the world's 32 million soldiers under arms in 1990, about 2.2 million were demobilised in the following three years, with further reductions of about the same number still anticipated. During the years 1989-94, government allocations for peace and demilitarisation increased five-fold. An important sign of the times, the increase nevertheless represented still only a single percentage point of military outlays during that five-year period. Military expenditures themselves have totalled some $30-35 trillion since the end of World War II (Renner, 1994). Levels had begun a downward trajectory even before a clear ebb in East-West tensions at the international political level had been widely accepted.

Changes have been substantial in First and Second World military establishments alike. At mid-decade, the US Department of Defense was in the process of closing hundreds of military bases at home and abroad, with about 174 000 troops being recalled from overseas assignments. US military spending was reduced from $303.3 billion in 1990 (the equivalent of $351 billion in 1995 dollars) to $263.5 billion in 1995, a decrease of 13 per cent in current dollars or of 25 per cent in inflation-adjusted terms. Expenditure levels proposed by the administration for the years 1996 through 2001 would result in a further decrease of spending from 1995 levels of 10.7 per cent in real terms. While some in Congress have expressed concern about the impacts of recent reductions on US military readiness and deterrence, their alternative budget would itself only slow the proposed rate of decrease in military spending[5]. Substantial reductions are also taking place in France, where troop strength has been cut from 667 445 in 1990 to 609 902 in 1994, with further decreases to 579 500 expected by the year 2000.

Many of the former Warsaw Pact countries have also experienced steep reductions in military outlays. During the first five years of the decade, the Soviet Union (and, after its collapse, Russia) repatriated some 700 000 troops and 500 000 civilian dependents. Given the absence of resources for conversion and the other tumultuous economic changes taking place, military personnel experienced a rocky re-entry into their respective Second World societies. Outside aid to ease the transition to peacetime economies has been minimal. OECD estimates place such assistance at about $200 million for the years 1991-94.

Third World countries have been less successful in trimming military expenditures. Following a historic high in global military spending in 1987 of $995 billion, military spending worldwide had fallen to $815 billion by 1992. During this period, however, Third World expenditures fell by only 10 per cent, as contrasted with 15 per cent reductions among developed countries. During the years 1960-87, moreover, developing-country spending on the military as a share of global military expenditures had more than doubled — from 7 per cent to 15 per cent (UNDP, 1994; Fontanel, 1994). In some countries, however, a process of "demilitarisation by default" has taken place, reflecting, among other factors, "the large-scale withdrawal of foreign military support following the end of the Cold War" (Luckham, 1995).

Paralleling the downsizing of many military establishments has been the dedication of military assets to a wider array of tasks. In Britain, a 1993 clarification of defense roles included, after protection and defense of the United Kingdom, a third category called "wider security interests". Among the items identified as "without specific defence objective" were humanitarian and disaster-relief activities and operations under international auspices. In Germany and Japan, the military forces in the present decade began, for the first time since the World War II, to participate in international humanitarian operations. In the Netherlands, increased priority was given to participation by Dutch troops in UN peace-keeping activities and support of such efforts by the Ministry of Development Co-operation. For French troops, too, disaster relief and "humanitarian interventions", as well as UN peace-keeping and peace enforcement activities, have become integral parts of their normal tasks.

In June 1992, NATO foreign ministers went on record in support of participation in UN peace-keeping operations. At NATO headquarters in December of that year, NATO General Manfred Worner told a conference on the use of military assets in disaster relief that "Although NATO's function remains centrally that of safe guarding the security of the Alliance, it has enormous resources which must be offered for humanitarian assistance" (Randel, 1994). NATO has subsequently devoted ongoing attention to policy issues relating to the support of humanitarian activities and, in the case of Bosnia, to the support of UN peace-keeping troops themselves engaged in protecting and delivering essential relief assistance.

Although military establishments are showing greater interest in a wider array of tasks, analysts differ on the significance and permanence of such changes. Some hold that they are more cosmetic than structural, designed largely to fend off budgetary cuts from newly cost-conscious parliaments. The "overriding principle of governments' policy", notes Herbert Wulf, director of the Bonn International Center for Conversion, has been "to do a little less of the same" rather than embracing a fundamental rethinking or restructuring of post-Cold War security needs (Renner, 1994). Others analysts view the changes as far more enduring, affecting the basic ongoing missions of the military for the foreseeable future. Even within the ranks of the military there is considerable division of opinion, with some favoring and others opposing dispatching soldiers on humanitarian missions.

Defense expenditures by individual Third World countries have received greater scrutiny among donor governments in allocating Official Development Assistance (ODA)[6]. Some donors — Japan and the Netherlands are examples — have stated that levels of military spending by recipient governments will have a bearing on the size of aid grants. At the same time, NGOs have drawn attention to relationships between the values of arms exports from donor governments to developing countries, on the one hand, and donor levels of ODA, on the other. In 1990, the percentages of ODA represented by arms exports ranged from 38.6 per cent for the US and 37 per cent for the UK on the high side to 0.25 per cent for Sweden and 4.4 per cent for the Netherlands on the low (Randel and German, 1994)[7]. The five Permanent Members of the Security Council account for "80 to 90 per cent of all major armaments exported to developing nations in recent years" (Berthélemy, McNamara and Sen, 1994).

Reductions in military assets on the supply side have been reinforced by a demand-side increase in the incidence of humanitarian emergencies and in the accompanying need for international assistance. One telling indicator of global distress is the series of United Nations consolidated appeals published by the UN's Department of Humanitarian Affairs (DHA). In fact, the creation of DHA itself in early 1992 reflected the growing concern of governments that major complex emergencies be managed more effectively. The series of UN appeals is one of the clearest single statements of the extent of the incidence of need at the global level for humanitarian assistance. Before the advent of DHA it was difficult to derive a comparable picture of global need.

In 1992, DHA launched appeals in the amount of $2.8 billion for six crises with 55.9 million affected persons. In 1993, 22 appeals in the amount of $4 billion were made on behalf of some 60 million affected persons. In 1994, the incidence of need for which funds were requested eased somewhat, with 15 appeals totalling $2.8 million for some 40.9 million persons. By July 1995, there were 11 appeals outstanding, with $2.1 billion requested for assistance to 23.7 million persons.

Reductions in 1995 as against 1994 reflected lower askings for emergency activities in Mozambique, the former Yugoslavia, Kenya, and Yemen (UN Department of Humanitarian Affairs, 1995b).

While figures fluctuate somewhat across the years for which they are available, they are, taken together, significantly higher than during the Cold War. The increased incidence of need is also reflected in the budgets of individual international organisations. The two whose work most closely reflects population displacement flowing from internal armed conflicts are the UN High Commissioner for Refugees and the International Commitee of the Red Cross (ICRC). The UNHCR budget rose from $500-$600 million during the 1980s to upwards of $850 million in 1991 and more than $1 billion in 1992 and each year thereafter (Ogata, 1994). ICRC expenditures worldwide grew from SF 349 million in 1988 to SF 441 million in 1990, SF 778 million in 1992, and SF 748 million in 1994 (ICRC *Annual Reports* 1988, 1990, 1992, 1994).

Humanitarian crises have become so pervasive in the early post-Cold War years that an ever-larger portion of ODA funds is being directed to emergency uses. "Emergency assistance and distress relief, which had constituted less than 3 per cent of bilateral aid until 1990, had come to exceed 8 per cent of the total by 1993", the Chair of the Development Assistance Committee reported in 1994. "Expressed in current dollars, what had been a $300 million item in the early 1980s had become a $3.2 billion claim on bilateral aid budgets in 1993." (Michel, 1995). One early calculation suggested that international assistance to Rwanda alone might total "about 2 per cent of ODA" in 1994, an estimate subsequently confirmed. (Multidonor Evaluation of Emergency Assistance to Rwanda, 1994).

Illustrative of trends at the individual donor level, German expenditures for relief emergencies rose from $36 million in 1988 to $680 million only four years later (Randel and German, 1994). In the Netherlands, government expenditures on emergencies rose from Dfl 180 million in 1988 to Dfl 640 million in 1994, a more than three-fold increase in six years. Figure 1.2 depicts donor government expenditures on emergency relief and refugee programs through their bilateral aid organisations during the waning years of the Cold War and the early years of the post-Cold War period.

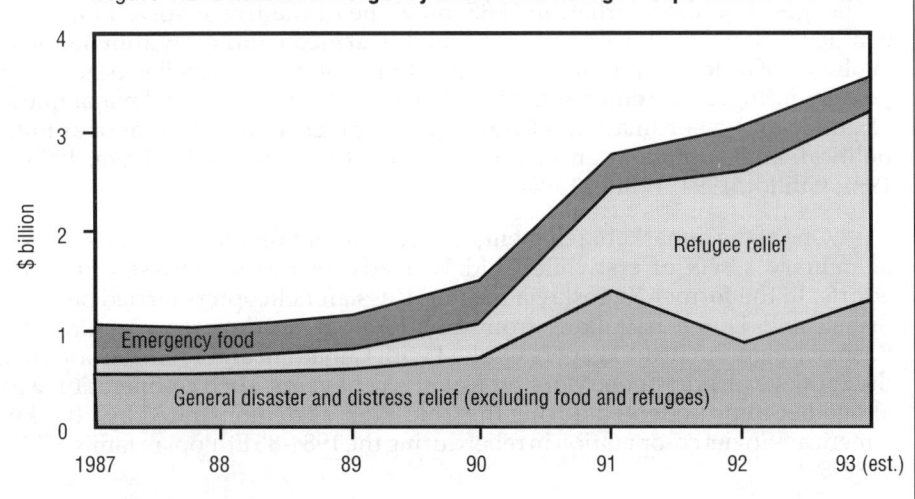

Figure 1.2. **Bilateral Emergency Relief and Refugee Expenditure 1987-93**

Note: DAC member contributions to multilateral and NGO activities showed a similar increase during these years.
Source: James H. Michel, Chair, Development Assistance Commitee of the OECD, *Development Co-operation: Efforts and Policies of the Members of the Development Assistance Committee*, Paris, OECD, 1995.

Since much of the shift to relief allocations has come at the expense of resources otherwise available to address development needs, recent trends are worrisome. Expenditure trends run directly counter to the growing realisation that substantial investment in longer-term development is indispensable for preventing recurring emergencies. Equally worrisome is slippage in ODA levels themselves.

In his 1994 report, the DAC Chairman reported a falling off in aid levels from $60.8 billion in 1992 to $56.0 billion in 1993. This represented an 8 per cent reduction in current dollars (6 per cent in real terms), with the levels in 17 of 21 DAC member countries failing to hold their own. Taking a hopeful view, the DAC report interpreted this development, while troubling, as "a bout of weakness, rather than an incipient collapse" in the fabric of aid co-operation (Michel, 1995). An NGO review was more negative. "In spite of growing prosperity in DAC donor countries, and the consistent support of the OECD public for efforts to help the poor," the analysis concluded, "the era of gradually growing assistance for the poor seems to have come to an end" (Randel and German, 1995).

Paralleling the proliferation of humanitarian need and the tightening of aid availability is the upswing in peace-keeping activities in the early years of the post-Cold War era. As of the end of January 1988, five peace-keeping operations were in place; by mid-December 1994, the number stood at 17. In early 1988, UN peace-keeping troops numbered 9 570; at the end of 1994, there were 73 393 Blue Helmets. During those seven years, the peace-keeping budget had increased from $230.4 million to $3.61 billion (Supplement to an Agenda for Peace, 1995). By 1993 UN peace-keeping expenditures had mushroomed to about one-tenth of ODA (Randel, 1994).

Of importance was not only the increase in peace-keeping operations but also the evolution in the nature of the activities themselves. Traditional peace-keeping initiatives, composed largely of military personnel, had generally interposed UN troops between warring parties or deployed UN observers to monitor cease-fires. In the newer "multifunctional" peace-keeping operations, UN personnel have taken on a wider array of tasks, including overseeing the return of refugees and displaced persons, demobilising belligerents and reintegrating them into society, and supervising or monitoring electoral and human rights reforms (Chopra, 1995).

The five UN peace-keeping operations underway in January 1988 included only one such multifaceted undertaking; eight of the seventeen in December 1994 were of the new type. The operations also demonstrated the changing nature of the challenges described earlier. In 1988, only one of the five involved an intrastate conflict; in 1994, well over half responded to armed conflicts within nations. The evolution of peace operations, including activities variously labelled peace-keeping, peacebuilding, peace enforcement, and peace-making, has raised major questions of policy and co-ordination, of training and practice, for international military, political, and humanitarian institutions alike (Abi-Saab, 1993; Paye, 1993; Goy, 1991; Guillot, 1994; White, 1994).

One of the remarkable elements in recent operations has been the engagement of military assets of erstwhile Cold War adversaries side-by-side in common efforts. In the former Yugoslavia theater, Russian helicopters ferried supplies for British and Dutch battalions from UNPROFOR headquarters in Croatia into Bosnia; Bulgarian peacekeepers worked with Canadian and French troops to keep the Sarajevo airport open. More typical in recent years, such co-operation was not altogether unprecedented during the Cold War, as demonstrated by little-known American-Soviet co-operation in relief during the 1984-86 Ethiopian famine (Minear, 1988-89).

The greater involvement of international military forces in the humanitarian sphere was heralded by Operation Provide Comfort in northern Iraq. Deployed in the spring of 1991, the US-led initiative, blessed by the UN Security Council and joined by the militaries of the United Kingdom, France, and the Netherlands, successfully rescued and returned to their homes hundreds of thousands of Kurds dislocated by Iraqi army. Working under air cover provided from bases in Turkey, Coalition troops initially provided relief and then co-ordinated the work of civilian aid organisations, to whom they eventually turned over all such activities.

Operation Provide Comfort had importance well beyond Iraq. "Successful combined operations such as Provide Comfort have convinced some observers that the gap between humanitarian and military personnel ... may be smaller than it initially appears", concluded one conference which reviewed the broadening role of the military. "The international effort in northern Iraq demonstrated the ability of uniformed and civilian personnel to co-ordinate their efforts in a way which reduced the overall number of personnel required" (US Dept. of State, 1994). Similar conclusions were reached at a conference in Aix-en-Provence in November 1991 on humanitarian aid to the Iraqi Kurds.

Since 1991, military personnel, operating under bilateral, coalitional, regional, or multilateral umbrellas, have been pressed into service in many major humanitarian emergencies. These include Cambodia, Somalia, the former Yugoslavia, Liberia, Georgia, Haiti, and Rwanda. The results have been mixed, tempering the initial euphoria about the application of force in support of humanitarian values and the use of troops to carry out humanitarian missions. At the same time, glimpses have been provided of the potential for expanded collaboration and improved effectiveness.

With the growing deployment of military forces in such operations has come increasing competence in performing the assigned tasks. "The Cold War image of the military as an ugly monolith," writes one analyst, has been "gently replaced by a more realistic appreciation of modern professional armies and their capabilities, which have gradually become the norm in peace support operations." (Mackinlay, 1993). Appreciation among humanitarian professionals for the contributions of the military has in turn ripened, in part reflecting difficulties experienced by aid organisations themselves in such perilous circumstances.

Given the supply of military assets and the demand created by the expanding universe of urgent human need, it is quite possible that what are still "non-traditional" missions of the military may become more traditional. Whether soldiers are deployed regularly or sparingly, however, it is clear that, "In the interests of vulnerable people there is an urgent need for the international community to develop understanding of the most effective mix of military and civilian interventions". (Randel and German, 1994).

Institutions in Ferment

As the world's military and humanitarian institutions contemplate the changing humanitarian landscape, they do so amidst widespread consensus that a basic institutional retooling should be considered in the interest of meeting urgent human need more effectively. Yet the process of conceptualising and implementing changes is proceeding unevenly within each set of institutions and at their interface. As indicated, some in the military see humanitarian tasks as diversionary and ill-advised; others have no such reservations. Some aid agencies see enlisting the military as highly questionable and counterproductive; others see a closer partnership as central to their own future effectiveness.

The changes in process described earlier in the chapter at the global level are strikingly apparent in the operational theatres where both soldiers and civilians are required to respond to human need. Reflecting on the experience of the US Army in Haiti, Lt. Col. Arthur M. Bartell pondered the contribution of the military in restoring the Aristide government to power. "It had never been done before. We had no manual we could follow. There was no template"[8]. While wars have always had elements of unpredictability, improvisation has become standard operating procedure in missions in Haiti and elsewhere. In fact, flexibility and adaptation has had a high correlation with success.

Humanitarian actors, too, have found themselves in largely uncharted waters. In the former Yugoslavia, UN organisations, led by UNHCR, faced challenges previously unencountered. Interviewed in June 1993 at its Zagreb field headquarters, one UNHCR official commented, "It's very hard to run this humanitarian operation according to a book that hasn't been written". Interviewed later in 1993 and again in 1994, the same official confirmed that the template was still in the process of being devised. Absence of flak jackets for HCR staff and lengthy delays in the arrival of bullet-proof landrovers — items not on the standard procurement list of humanitarian organisations — were major staff concerns (Minear et al., 1994).

The necessary changes were attitudinal as well as institutional. "Soldiers are trained to fight, not act as armed international social workers", concluded reporter Chris Black following extensive interviews with the US military in the United States and Haiti[9] "Digging a foxhole, firing a weapon, a young male ego finds a certain satisfaction in that," one official told her. "It's different digging a trench for water or putting a roof on a school". At the institutional level, the reporter concluded, "[W]hile the military's classic warfare mission has changed in these recent deployments to humanitarian relief and peace-keeping, military training has not been adjusted for the new tasks or operational tempo"[10]. Military officials themselves concur with outside analysts in the view that if the shift is to be made from warfare to welfare, training personnel for new-breed assignments will require attention and innovation.

Some countries and organisations have had a head start on tackling the challenge. A number of military and humanitarian institutions worked persistently throughout the Cold War to develop capacities and skills to respond to major international emergencies. Nordic countries, with a long tradition of supplying troops for UN peace-keeping activities, have used special facilities at Niinsalo, Finland and in Sweden and Denmark to train personnel. In 1994, the Canadian government established the Lester B. Pearson Peace-keeping Centre at an otherwise-to-be-closed military facility in Nova Scotia, now the scene of an ambitious training program in peace-keeping and humanitarian activities. The French army has a tradition of its own of using "non-warrior soldiers" to provide critically needed assistance in disasters overseas. On the humanitarian side, organisations such as the International Committee of the Red Cross and various national chapters of Médecins Sans Frontières have fine-tuned their abilities to function in hot-war settings.

Ferment in the field and at national headquarters has paralleled discussions at the international level. In December 1992 NATO hosted a workshop in Brussels at the request of the UN Department of Humanitarian Affairs (DHA) and the International Federation of Red Cross and Red Crescent Societies (IFRC). Participants from the UN, governments, and NGOs agreed on the main elements of a set of voluntary guidelines on the use of Military and Civil Defence Assets (MCDA) in disaster relief. A follow-on conference, again sponsored by DHA and the IFRC, was held in January 1994 in Oslo at the invitation of the Norwegian government and chaired by the Norwegian Minister of Defence, Jørgen Kosmo. The session represented, he said, "the first systematic attempt to develop procedures and conditions for the efficient employment of MCDA". The "Oslo Guidelines", published by DHA in May 1994 and circulated widely since, seek to enlist military assets in filling the "humanitarian gap" between existing needs for relief around the world and the capacity of the current aid system (UNDHA, 1994).

The guidelines are non-binding ground rules "designed to ensure that MCDA are used with full transparency, neutrality and impartiality". They seek to expand and regularise the use of military personnel in relief activities in peace-time emergencies", at the same time recognising that "the use of [MCDA] is an exceptional complement to, not a substitute for, the normal implementing arrangements for humanitarian emergencies"[11]. MCDA personnel, who in principle are to wear military uniforms but to remain unarmed, serve at the request or with the consent of the receiving state. During 1995-96, DHA plans to finalise and distribute a MCDA field operations handbook and encourage training and field exercises.

A set of guidelines specifically for conflict settings was the product of four meetings in 1993 convened by the Task Force on Ethical and Legal Issues in Humanitarian Assistance of the World Conference on Religion and Peace. Published in early 1994, The Mohonk Criteria for Humanitarian Assistance in Complex Emergencies reflect the views of participants from a wide range of humanitarian, diplomatic, legal, and academic institutions. UN peace-keeping officials were on hand, although military personnel from national defense ministries were not.

The Mohonk Criteria are premised on five fundamental humanitarian principles: humanity, impartiality, neutrality, independence, and empowerment. They affirm the right of people throughout the world to request and receive humanitarian assistance and the right of humanitarian agencies to offer and deliver such aid. Military forces, the guidelines specify, should: "*a.* Be used only as a last resort; *b.* Be employed in exceptional circumstances to protect, support and deliver humanitarian relief; *c.* Be used sparingly because of their disproportionate human and financial cost; *d.* Comply with decisions of the appropriate international civilian authority; *e.* Respect the independence and freedom of movement of humanitarian organisations". (Task Force on Ethical and Legal Issues in Humanitarian Assistance, 1994).

UN humanitarian organisations themselves are struggling with these issues. The Department of Humanitarian Affairs has taken the lead in developing a policy paper, The Protection of Humanitarian Mandates in Conflict Situations, which after more than a year of discussion was approved in early 1994 by the InterAgency Standing Committee (UNDHA 1995d). In consultation with the Departments of Political Affairs and Peace-keeping Operations, DHA has encouraged the formulation of interagency guidelines to facilitate interdepartmental co-operation. In 1995, UNHCR in its own right prepared a *Handbook for the Military on Humanitarian Operations*.

Private aid agencies have also sought to identify humanitarian principles and promote a code of conduct among practitioner organisations. In the summer of 1994, eight major international organisations agreed on a self-policing code of conduct for disaster response, featuring ten principles. In the short space of a year, more than 50 organisations or coalitions of agencies from some 20 countries had endorsed the code (International Federation of Red Cross and Red Crescent Societies, 1994). The Humanitarianism and War project, based on its research in conflict situations, has itself identified eight principles and produced a handbook for practitioners which is in wide use (Minear and Weiss, 1993)[12].

Governments, too, have carried out policy reviews and practical exercises to guide the contribution of their military forces in the humanitarian sphere. Particularly seized with the policy issues, the Dutch government, under the lead of Minister for Development Co-operation Jan Pronk, has conducted several major policy reviews. In 1993, *A World of Dispute* articulated greater emphasis on prevention and activities in peace building, peace making, and peace-keeping activities and on the integration of policies among the Development Co-operation, Foreign, and Defense ministries. In 1994, the government's evaluation of its humanitarian assistance to Somalia during 1991-93 identified lessons for the future[13].

Various national military forces have sought to expand their capacity to carry out peace operations, including aid activities, in conflict settings. The US Department of Defense, for example, has staged a series of peace-keeping exercises within which humanitarian challenges have figured prominently. Participants in one such event, a three-week training course at Fort Polk, Louisiana in 1994, included, in addition to 5 000 US troops, an array of UN officials, observers from other governments, and relief-agency personnel. "It's important that people realise that peace-keeping is not just something in the heads of a few goo-goo people interested in saving the world," noted one enthusiastic participant, US Ambassador to the United Nations Madeline Albright. "It's what the American military believes is important"[14].

The delegation from InterAction, the professional association of more than 150 private US relief and development agencies, urged that its members be regularly involved in such Pentagon exercises. "Any debate over the pros and cons of international military involvement in humanitarian relief is at this point an academic exercise," the group's report observed, at the same time acknowledging the reservations held by some members about such collaboration. "Military involvement will, in all likelihood, continue throughout this decade, with or without the co-operation of the relief community" (Interaction, 1993).

One such exercise which attracted more than 250 participants from the military and humanitarian, diplomatic and political worlds was held in April 1995 at Camp Pendleton, California. Like conferences taking place in abundance in the United States and elsewhere, the meeting addressed "Humanitarian Assistance and Peace Operations: Integrating Military and Civilian Efforts". "We see humanitarian tasks as a full-fledged military mission," said Lieutenant General Anthony Zinni of the First Marine Expeditionary Force in opening the conference. "They are not futuristic." In the week which followed, participants examined both the possibilities — and the limitations — in closer collaboration (US Dept. of State and US Marine Corps' First Expeditionary Force, 1995).

InterAction has also served as a forum for discussions among American NGOs on providing aid in wartime settings. Confirming the reality that complex emergencies are not an exclusively post-Cold War phenomenon, InterAction in the mid-1980s sponsored a three-year series of discussions on the impacts of political and military factors on NGO work (Minear, 1988). More recently, a number of individual US NGOs, including the Mennonite Central Committee and Catholic Relief Services, have updated their own policies. In recent years, private agencies such as Lutheran World Relief and UN organisations such as UNICEF have drawn together their own personnel for reflection and strategy sessions.

The Geneva-based International Council of Voluntary Agencies has played a similar role to InterAction's at the global level. ICVA statements over the years to meetings of UNHCR's Executive Committee have articulated NGO concerns. Addressing that body in October 1993, the chair of ICVA's Working Group on Humanitarian Affairs, Trygve G. Nordby, welcomed the new prominence accorded humanitarian values after "decades during which humanitarian imperatives were hedged about by Cold War factors".

He cautioned, however, that "while humanitarian action is coming to enjoy overdue attention in and around conflicts across the globe, the script is often still written by politicians and directed by generals". He urged "wide-ranging debate before patterns are established [determining] the extent to which, and the circumstances within which, humanitarian initiatives in situations of armed conflict will rely on the application of economic and/or military force in the service of humane objectives" (ICVA, 1993).

The interface between humanitarian action and political-military policies has been the subject of numerous international consultations and academic conferences in recent years. An example is provided by the Seminar on International Humanitarian Assistance in Conflict Situations organised by the Swedish Red Cross Society in consultation with the International Federation of Red Cross and Red Crescent Societies. Held at the Swedish Red Cross College May 10-11, 1995, the session was keyed to the fiftieth anniversary of the founding of the United Nations and to the International Red Cross and Red Crescent Conference scheduled for December 1995.

Likewise, the interface between emergency assistance on the one hand and the tasks of conflict resolution and development on the other has been the subject of active debate. One example was a conference in Paris in May/June 1994, hosted by the OECD Development Centre, "Development Within Conflict: the Challenge of Man-made Disasters". In the light of recent experience, the gathering explored the respective comparative advantages of major actors — military and civilian, government, UN organisations, NGOs and the ICRC — in conflict situations (Mooney, 1995).

In short, the international community is reflecting on these issues as its institutions retool for post-Cold War activities. The reflection process is gathering momentum in military and humanitarian institutions, at the international and national levels, in coalitions of humanitarian agencies and within individual organisations, and in academic and policy circles. Some five years into the process, a number of key issues have emerged which are identified in the following chapter. Like the discussion in this chapter, they serve as backdrop for the Rwanda review which forms the core of the book.

Notes

1. Throughout this and later chapters, materials drawn from secondary sources are referenced accordingly. Quotations drawn from interviews conducted by the authors are also noted. In the interest of limiting the numbers of citations, however, some citations derived from the authors' interviews have been omitted. Quotations without citations may be assumed to have been drawn from research conducted by the authors.

2. François Mitterrand, statement of July 14, 1991, quoted in Bettati, 1994.

3. Cf. also Ingvar Carlsson, Commission Co-Chair, "The World Needs Humanitarian Right to Intervene", *International Herald Tribune*, January 25, 1995.

4. Organisation for Economic Co-operation and Development, "Development Partnerships in the New Global Context", Press Release dated May 4, p. 1 point 1 and attachment, item 3.

5. The data are from the President's Budget for Fiscal Year 1996, as interpreted by the National Commission for Economic Conversion and Disarmament in Washington, D.C., a non-governmental organisation.

6. In recent years, Development Assistance Committee discussions and annual reports by the DAC Chairman have demonstrated growing interest in the interrelationships between military and development assistance and in the question of whether donor contributions to peace-keeping activities should be tallied as ODA. Donor government interest in these issues is also reflected in the research activities of the OECD's Development Centre, of which the study referenced in the Bibliography under Berthélemy is one example.

7. These figures were derived from data compiled by SIPRI and the DAC. Published annually since 1994 by a consortium of NGOs. The *Reality of Aid* includes a review of aid trends as well as individually authored reports on relevant developments in donor countries.

8. Quoted in Chris Black, "Army Adapts to Changing World", *Boston Globe*, Jan. 8, 1995.

9. Chris Black, *ibid*.

10. Chris Black, "US Soldiers Battle to Preserve Family Lives", *Boston Globe*, Jan. 9, 1995.

11. Note by DHA on "The Use Of Military and Civilian Defence Assets in UN Humanitarian Operations", (Geneva, August 1995).

12. For a description of the Humanitarianism and War project and its research, cf. Annex 3.

13. The relevant documents are Directorate General of International Co-operation, Netherlands Ministry of Foreign Affairs, *A World of Difference: A New Framework for Development Co-operation in the 1990s* (1990), *A World of Dispute* (1993), and *Humanitarian Aid to Somalia* (1994).

14. Barbara Novovitch, "US Troops Stage Major 'Peace-keeping' Exercise", Reuter, August 14, 1994.

Chapter 2

Major Policy Issues

The passing of the Cold War and the early efforts at institutional retooling described in Chapter 1 have brought to the fore a number of key issues regarding the assumption of tasks in the humanitarian sphere by the military. Seven are examined here: the terms of the military's engagement in the humanitarian sphere, the comparative advantage and cost of utilising the military, the differences in military and humanitarian cultures, the effectiveness of the military and the possibility of limiting the damage it may do, and the commitment of troops as an exercise in global stewardship.

Framed in this chapter, these issues are revisited in Chapter 8 following a review of the Rwanda experience, which has functioned as something of a laboratory for testing new roles for the military.

Terms of Engagement

"The central issue facing the United Nations and international charities is whether force should be used to ensure delivery of humanitarian assistance in a war situation, or whether this will so compromise that mission as to make it unsustainable and endanger those taking part."[1] Thus observed David Pallister, writing in the *Guardian* in mid-1994. In the subsequent year, the increased use of force by UN peacekeepers in support of aid activities in Bosnia has underscored the dilemma. The issue is a fundamental one, involving matters of both theory and practice.

From the standpoint of theory, practitioners take different positions regarding the use of force in support of humanitarian activities. There is broad agreement that humanitarian assistance is a fundamental right, enshrined in the Geneva Conventions of 1949, the Additional Protocols of 1977, and in customary law[2]. Virtually all governments have embraced the Conventions and many, despite some significant holdouts, the two Protocols as well. Even some anti-government insurgent groups have come to see that respect for these legal protections of civilian populations is in their best interest.

Practitioners differ, however, about what to do when belligerents fail to live up to their stated obligations. The ICRC, the only humanitarian agency mentioned by name in the Geneva Conventions and Protocols and their most authoritative institutional interpreter, holds that humanitarian activities are essentially voluntary, requiring the co-operation of the political authorities for their success.

"[E]ven on the basis of United Nations' resolutions", writes the head of the ICRC's division of doctrine Yves Sandoz, "the use of armed force to get relief supplies through cannot be justified by international humanitarian law since ... the obligation to 'ensure respect for' this law rules out the use of force". "The question, therefore", Sandoz reasons, "is not one of implementing international humanitarian law but of the appropriateness of using force to terminate serious and mass breaches of this law" (Sandoz, 1992).

The ICRC's opposition to coerced humanitarian access and imposed aid activities does not mean opposition to the use of force in international relations altogether. In its view, force can be an appropriate instrument for accomplishing political or military — but not humanitarian — objectives. Effective UN peace-keeping operations can have a positive impact on the context within which humanitarian activities are carried out — but not, the argument goes, if troops use force to protect aid operations or if military personnel assume direct humanitarian roles.

Other aid organisations share the ICRC's opposition to direct collaboration with the military. They hold that many of the humanitarian problems in the post-Cold War era have roots in inequities in power, resources, or representation, for which solutions are necessarily political rather than humanitarian. Thus the conflicts in the former Yugoslavia and Georgia are widely held to be "humanitarian problems without humanitarian solutions". While humanitarian activities can facilitate political solutions, as in the Salvadoran civil war in the 1980s, it is counterproductive, the reasoning goes, for humanitarian actors themselves directly to promote such solutions. Maintaining impartiality and neutrality in complex civil wars is difficult enough, quite apart from association with international military forces, which themselves face difficulty maintaining neutrality and addressing knotty root causes (Minear and Weiss, 1995).

Not all humanitarian agencies, however, share the ICRC's philosophical rejection of collaboration with the military. Nor was the ICRC itself fully able to implement its approach in Somalia, where it came to believe that it had no choice other than to employ armed guards to protect its activities from disruption and abuse. Whether to enlist military support for humanitarian activities was an issue which deeply divided aid agencies there.

In November 1992, a dozen NGOs signed a letter to US President George Bush's National Security Advisor expressing the view that "humanitarian agencies cannot work effectively in Somalia without greater security. We believe that appropriate armed UN security forces tasked with protecting emergency supplies and staff may actually decrease the likelihood of conflict"[3]. The appeal figured in the commitment of US troops, who landed two weeks later. That soldiers helped embattled famine relief efforts but proved less than constructive over the longer term further divided an already fractured NGO community.

In fact, a number of NGOs who had been enthusiastic in the early days of the post-Cold War era about the possibility of using force in support of humanitarian activities have moderated their views based on the practical obstacles encountered. "Extraordinary humanitarian crises call for extraordinary action," observed Oxfam UK's Director David Bryer in 1994, "and in 1989 and 1990, as the New World Order dawned, many welcomed the possibility that humanitarian law might at last begin to be enforced". Oxfam, for one, supported the application of force by the international community to open up humanitarian access to the victims, endorsing the Somalia letter.

Yet, Bryer continued, "what's changed for Oxfam as a result of external military intervention in Somalia and Bosnia is that on top of the normal incidental risks of operating in an insecure environment, our aid workers are increasingly seen as targets of violence... indistinguishable from the international governmental intervention effort". Ironically, he concluded, "The very fact of being under UN security umbrellas increases that need for protection!"[4]

UNHCR, too, has entered a cautionary note into the debate, also primarily from the vantagepoint of practice rather than theory. Its 1995 *Handbook for the Military on Humanitarian Operations* affirms in its opening paragraph that in certain circumstances of armed conflict, "military support can ensure the success of humanitarian action". However, in a later section on "How Humanitarian Activities are Affected by the Use of Force", the manual notes that "The use of force under Chapter VII [of the UN Charter] may render untenable the continuation of a United Nations humanitarian operation" (UNHCR, 1995e).

Such observations reflect the hard-won experience of relief workers in armed conflict settings. Many would agree with the view expressed by the UN High Commissioner for Refugees' Special Envoy who headed the UN's humanitarian assistance operation in the former Yugoslavia in 1993-94. "The use or threat of force in support of a humanitarian operation, except in clear self-defence", writes Nicholas Morris, "will gravely prejudice that operation". "Humanitarian action cannot solve problems that are political in nature. ... Where the required political will cannot be mobilised, the humanitarian operation will have a better chance of success when it is clearly separated from the international community's efforts at political containment" (Morris, 1995).

At the same time, other organisations and theorists — particularly those associated with the "right to intervene" school mentioned earlier — welcome the availability of military force to help assure humanitarian access. If and when diplomacy and other sanctions fail, they hold, access should be extracted by force. The international community must be prepared to exercise such force, they argue, and warring parties should expect its exercise. Rather than becoming protagonists in conflicts, aid agencies will benefit from the principled application of force in the service of humane objectives. More humanitarian initiatives fail because of an unwillingness to use force, the argument goes, than because of its use. Soldiers themselves can play a useful humanitarian role, even when serving simulataneously as agents of coercion.

As of mid-1995, clear consensus on the use of military force and military forces in the humanitarian arena has yet to emerge. Necessary distinctions are increasingly being made, however, between the use of military force to accomplish political-military, as against humanitarian, objectives. Distinctions are also being drawn between the use of military forces to carry out military strategies as distinct from their direct involvement in relief activities, with attention now directed to whether the dual roles are inherently contradictory or counterproductive. New data for the debate is provided by each new complex emergency, including the Rwanda experience.

The *first* policy issue, therefore, concerns the appropriateness of enlisting international military assets in major humanitarian crises. Should military force and military forces be used?

Comparative Advantage

The second issue concerns the nature of the tasks that military forces should take on, assuming that they may appropriately be involved in the humanitarian sphere. From the standpoint of a rational division of labour among the various actors, in what areas of such activity do military forces enjoy a comparative advantage?

The issue is a complex one, in part because the term "humanitarian" is used with great looseness and imprecision. "Much of today's international response to a conflict is labeled 'humanitarian' ", observes the ICRC's Director General Peter Fuchs. The term is applied to "purely military" interventions, to troops doing "purely humanitarian work", and to units at borders monitoring embargoes. From Fuchs' vantagepoint, imprecision in nomenclature creates confusion on the ground. "Troops are meant for peacekeeping and peace enforcement. ... Humanitarian work needs a different kind of expertise and should be done by humanitarian organisations"[5]. Even those who disagree with Fuchs' conclusion concur that greater clarity regarding who does what best is essential.

The Olso guidelines on the use of Military and Civil Defence Assets (MCDA) referenced earlier contain an illustrative list of 11 military and civil defence capabilities in disaster relief. These include needs assessment, communications and ground logistics support, airlift/airdrop capacity, and assistance in the fields of medicine, transport, power, water purification, and feeding. The guidelines apply only to disasters in times of peace, although these basic functions need to be performed in conflict settings as well (UNDHA, 1994).

This particular listing of tasks corresponds to the proverbial wisdom that heavy lifting and direct assistance to civilians in distress represent the military's unique contributions. The promotional literature of international military forces — be it of UN peacekeepers or of national military contingents such as those pictured in this volume — reinforces the prevailing public perception. Yet posters and emblems beg the tough questions of comparative advantage and may even convey a misimpression of the relative priority of such tasks.

In actual practice, the situation is considerably different from picture-book descriptions of what the military does in the humanitarian sphere. Military forces are most prominently associated with massive airlifts, as those in Sarajevo or, as will be examined later, in Rwanda. The Sarajevo initiative, history's longest-sustained airlift ever, is widely credited with having kept the airport open and the city alive for several years when road access was difficult and basic foodstuffs and other essentials were not otherwise available. Military air transport also ferried local persons in urgent need of medical treatment out of the area and carried aid personnel in and out. However, the circumstances in which the lift capacity of the military has a comparative advantage and, as will be noted, the costs of utilising that advantage are quite specific and narrow (Natsios, 1994).

The direct involvement of the military in aid activities is also more limited and less advantageous than is generally understood. During the first year of UNPROFOR peace-keeping operations in Bosnia, for example, where peace-keeping troops had an explicit humanitarian protection mandate, the actual escorting of humanitarian convoys was rare and the tonnage of food and medical services actually distributed to civilian populations by UN troops modest. Such activities increased in late 1993 and 1994, however, in areas where humanitarian personnel were absent or overstretched. Only late in the day, however, did reality catch up with UNPROFOR's descriptions of its work.

Dependent for their operations in Bosnia on the consent of the warring parties, UN peace-keeping troops in actual fact were "often least available where and when they were most needed". Even where and when present, they were generally less prepared to take risks than the humanitarians whom they were there to protect. In many instances, aid agencies were reluctant to request assistance from the military for convoy escorts or for gaining entry into Muslim-held enclaves. "The minute you use force," observed the UNHCR chief of operations in mid-1993, by which time UNPROFOR had largely lost the respect of the belligerents, "you make the entire [aid] operation untenable" (Minear *et al.*, 1994).

A more accurate picture of the chores actually performed for humanitarian agencies by the military emerged from a discussion of the Geneva-based Humanitarian Liaison Working Group, an informal but regular gathering of donor government representatives, with humanitarian organisations involved as observers. The Group concluded from a discussion of military support for humanitarian operations in late 1994 that "The use of troops for direct delivery of supplies is often controversial, expensive and full of political complications. If used, there should always be a strategy to ensure their departure as soon as the situation permits"[6].

At the conference at Camp Pendleton, California on civilian-military co-operation mentioned in Chapter 1, one of the co-hosts, General Anthony Zinni, a veteran of operations in northern Iraq and Somalia, noted with pride of the US armed forces that "We can still kick ass but we can also feed kids"[7]. Some other officials, however, tend to take a more cautious approach. "Generally the military is not the right tool to meet humanitarian concerns", Secretary of Defence William I. Perry told a gathering in late 1994. "We field an army, not a Salvation Army" (Perry, 1995).

At the California exercise and others like it, military and humanitarian professionals thoroughly committed to deeper partnership nevertheless struggle to establish the specific areas and circumstances in which military assets should be the instrument of choice. Perhaps the most central issue concerns whether troops have a comparative advantage in providing what humanitarian organisations most need and lack. Many aid agencies place high priority on maintaining law and order in volatile situations such as refugee camps. However, international military forces, even those equipped with state-of-the-art crowd control techniques, may be reluctant to take on that perilous task.

Aid groups value demining and road repairs, but troops often evidence reluctance there as well, as the slowness of the UN peace-keeping operation to address the problems of mines in Cambodia in 1992 suggests. Moreover, the military's approach to demining often means cutting a path through a given area to allow strategic access. From a humanitarian vantage point, by contrast, entire areas must be cleared before civilians can return to their homes and farmers can once again cultivate their fields.

The comparative advantage of the military may also vary according to the stage of a given conflict. In the heat of battle, troops may be able to do more actual relief deliveries than humanitarian personnel, although here, too, the Bosnia experience counsels caution. In evacuating aid personnel, the resources of the military may be unexcelled. When conflicts are winding down and cease-fires in place, NGOs may have the edge in working with local communities to mount reconstruction activities. For long-haul tasks of reconciliation, economic development, and the building of justice systems which respect fundamental human rights, non-military — and sometimes also non-governmental actors — often have the advantage.

In short, the assumed advantages of military assets are being reviewed in the light of recent experience to determine the specific tasks and situations in which they may best be harnessed. As of mid-1995 the debate is ongoing and consensus yet to be achieved.

The *second* policy issue, therefore, involves identifying the specific tasks and circumstances in which military assets enjoy a comparative advantage and matching these with the needs of humanitarian organisations. Assuming that the military should be involved, what does it do best?

Cost

Closely associated with the question of comparative advantage is the issue of cost. The military may have unparalleled capacity to move humanitarian vehicles, supplies, and personnel quickly to a given catastrophe or to reach civilians with life-saving essentials in hot-war situations. But what are the financial costs of doing so and who pays the bill? Is the military the most cost-effective way to get particular humanitarian tasks performed?

The prevailing assumption is that while the military may be an expensive institution to maintain, the utilisation of military assets in the humanitarian sphere will require payment of only the "incremental" costs — that is, the additional costs incurred by the military as a result of taking on specific humanitarian assignments. The fact that fixed costs, including personnel, equipment, and maintenance costs, are borne by the military rather than by humanitarian accounts makes utilising such assets "a viable option compared to any available alternatives". (UNDHA, 1994). The bargain is even a better one for aid interests in that sometimes even the incremental costs are absorbed by a nation's defence budget.

Recent experience, however, has called into question the assumption that harnessing the military can be a bargain for aid interests. A recent study of the Somalia relief effort carried out for the US Agency for International Development (USAID) by the Refugee Policy Group concluded that the US Defense Department's Operation Provide Relief airlift, which transported foodstuffs from Mombassa to Mogadishu, was considerably more expensive than other airlifts in the same crisis. A commercial contractor engaged by AID to transport food for the UN World Food Programme and the ICRC, the study found, "could haul as much or more with five aircraft as the Department of Defence with fourteen". An airlift by a commercial contractor hired by the Lutheran World Federation was cheaper still (Refugee Policy Group, 1994)[8].

In Somalia and elsewhere, an added constraint on military airlifts has been that the size of the aircraft used and the amount of payload carried may reduce the cost savings that might otherwise exist. A senior private aid agency official in Bosnia noted that the UN peace-keeping operation "loaded their Hercules transports with between 6 and 10 tons in order to assure easy handling". In contrast, the official's agency, which utilised similar aircraft, "would never allow itself to use less than the maximum capacity, i.e. 18 tons"[9].

Generally speaking, responses to emergencies that use the military tend to be more expensive than those which do not. As in Somalia, the use of military assets in other theatres such as Bosnia and Cambodia, and, as will be seen in Rwanda, have also had high price tags. As a result, some analysts are concluding that the costs of military assets may be greater than their value[10].

Cost comparisons, whether of individual tasks such as airlifts or of more general tasks such as the deployment of forces to maintain security for humanitarian operations, require caution and precision. Since not all of the costs of using military aircraft are charged against aid accounts, there is generally some genuine additionality involved. In the instance of the Operation Provide Relief airlift, the Defence Department bore the full costs — which amounted to only $20 million above what the Pentagon would have paid in the absence of any involvement whatsoever in Somalia. Even where aid budgets contribute some or all of the incremental costs, there may be offsetting benefits. In a number of humanitarian emergencies, the use of the military has generated additional public interest and resources.

In one sense, no price is too high to pay when human lives are at stake. Thus Aengus Finucane of Concern Worldwide in London, distancing himself from "the chorus of glib critical comment" which holds that the UN operation in Somalia was "virtually a total failure, as well as an astronomically costly one", praised the undertaking for what it accomplished. "Many people in Somalia would not be alive but for the intervention of the US, the UN and so many aid agencies"[11]. From another perspective, however, given limited resources, other humanitarian crises which require action, and alternative approaches to preventing starvation, considerations of comparative cost-effectiveness are increasingly germane.

> The military has two unique advantages compared with other actors in the relief community. One is its ability to move an enormous number of people, weapons, equipment, and commodities such as food and medicine over very long distances at short notice by means of its air, sea and ground-based assets. The other is its combat capability, by which it can provide security. In those complex emergencies where speed and security are essential, the military should be the lead agency in carrying out these tasks. Some emergencies require neither, however — or at least not as a top priority.
>
> Andrew S. Natsios

The use of the military also involves opportunity costs which need to be added to the financial balance sheet. Military activities in the humanitarian sphere may divert funds otherwise available to humanitarian and development activities. Thus the government of the Netherlands transferred from its Development Co-operation budget to the Ministry of Defence for peace-keeping activities some 30 million guilders in 1992, 121 million guilders in 1993, and 111 million guilders in 1994 (Randel and German, 1994). Proponents of such transfers suggest that the value of the services provided may well exceed the amounts by which aid accounts are debited. Opponents, including a number of NGOs, believe otherwise[12].

Many humanitarian organisations believe that with government budgets for international affairs increasingly tight, outlays for the military constrict resources otherwise available to humanitarian organisations. That conviction affected the reaction of UNDP and several NGOs who were approached in Somalia by UN peace-keeping troops seeking funds for projects the soldiers hoped to carry out. While aid personnel were pleased with the expressed interest in assisting local populations, they were incensed that given expenditures on military forces in Somalia which already exceeded humanitarian assistance by a factor of ten to one, additional transfers would even be contemplated.

As noted in the previous chapter, the broader issue of whether outlays for peacekeeping should be counted as official development assistance is a matter of current debate. That proposal, made by the Belgian Minister of Defence at an NGO meeting in December 1993, triggered heated debate. "NGOs responded quickly, stating that military intervention — even if it was humanitarian — could never be considered as development co-operation" (Randel and German, 1995).

Whatever the views of humanitarian organisations about the costs of involving the military, military planners themselves are concerned about the financial costs of operations other than war and the opportunity costs of involvement in "peripheral" missions. A 1995 review by the US General Accounting Office of participation by the US military in peace operations concluded that however valuable to the personnel and services involved, participation in international peace-keeping and humanitarian activities could delay the timely responses to major regional conflicts in the future (US GAO, 1995a and US GAO, 1995c).

To date, much of the evidence is anecdotal regarding whether the ability of a nation's military to protect and defend its country is compromised by the participation of troops in peace operations. Proponents of missions other than war cite significant benefits. One recent review of the US army's experience in Haiti found that "humanitarian and peace-keeping missions honed skills, boosted pride and unit cohesion, and enhanced the combat readiness of the light infantry division"[13]. The enthusiasm of the troops assisting Kurdish civilians in northern Iraq also had a positive impact on military morale.

At the same time, opponents cite examples from a 1994 US government report to buttress their view that the fighting edge of the military is likely to be sacrificed. President Clinton has been chided for "wearing out the [US fighting] force by deploying it all over the world in support of operations of questionable national interest"[14]. A commanding officer in Finland recently complained about the lengthy retraining for his troops needed before they could be reintegrated into the normal ranks following UN peace-keeping duty. Even proponents of utilising troops for tasks in the humanitarian sphere concede that doing so may require different force configurations than would otherwise exist, clearly a financial and administrative burden to the military.

Issues of cost and cost-effectiveness, therefore, range from the specific to the general, intersecting with matters of comparative advantage and opportunity costs. They are often difficult to address because of the unevenness of the data available. Moreover, rigorous policy analysis notwithstanding, cost considerations may not prove determinative in the choice of strategies when high-visibility humanitarian emergencies strike.

The *third* policy issue, therefore, concerns the costs, financial and otherwise, to the military and to humanitarian interests — of involving military assets in operations other than war. What are the costs?

Institutional Cultures

The use of military assets to assist in the humanitarian sphere, most observers agree, is designed to supplement rather than supplant the work of traditional humanitarian agencies. "Military and civil defence assets should be seen as a tool complementing existing relief mechanisms," affirm the Oslo Guidelines, "in order to provide specific support to specific requirements, in response to the acknowledged 'humanitarian gap' between the disaster needs that the relief community is being asked to satisfy and the resources available to meet them". (UNDHA, 1994). Not even the most unabashed enthusiasts envision the military itself becoming the hub of the humanitarian aid regime of the future.

The prevailing assumption is that civilian humanitarian organisations — which often precede the military at the scene of a crisis, stay behind after the troops have departed, and work side-by-side with soldiers for as long as the military are on hand — will continue to do so. This assumption places a premium on effective collaboration between the two sets of institutions while both are present. One of the major issues of the current policy debate thus concerns how the two different institutional cultures that are involved may be accommodated.

That very different cultures exist is widely acknowledged. Cedric Thornberry, a senior UN official with responsibilities for the political aspects of UN peace-keeping missions in theatres such as Cyprus, Namibia, and, most recently, the former Yugoslavia, has observed that "the problems that exist between humanitarian workers and the military stem from a lack of familiarity with one another, and with the new kind of tasks they are having to undertake, jointly and severally". He has described "an attitudinal abyss which frequently separates aid workers from the military" (Thornberry, 1996, p. 230)[15].

Discussions at the headquarters level, in operational theatres, and among policy analysts frequently highlight the existence of such a "culture clash". "Principles of military leadership emphasize structure, hierarchy and the importance of maintaining command and control," note the proceedings of one recent conference, making institutional collaboration and mutuality difficult. "Humanitarian organisations frequently are characterised by informal, improvisational and egalitarian styles which operate on consensus. Military units are much more self-sufficient and logistically independent; their humanitarian colleagues are acutely aware of their dependence on donations and a whole host of material support"[16].

In the handbook recently published by UNHCR to acquaint the military with itself as an organisation, the UN refugee organisation devoted an entire section to its own organisational culture. A subsection on "cultural issues" examines areas of major differences with the military, including decision making, command structure, age, flexibility, and accountability. The guide notes that "UNHCR counterparts to military officers — and especially NGO counterparts to military officers — tend to receive decision-making authority at a younger age than do military decision makers". UNHCR also notes that "Civilian flexibility and military precision often conflict in joint operations". (UNHCR, 1995e).

Problems of different structures and personnel responsibilities which separate military and humanitarian institutions are compounded by deeply held views of practitioners on both sides. Some humanitarians view the military as insensitive to the basic problems faced by societies in crisis, perhaps even implicated in their exacerbation. They suspect that the military are more interested in fending off post-Cold War budget cuts than in providing real assistance to the needy. Conversely, some in the military see humanitarian organisations as disorganised in their activities and unprofessional in their conduct, driven by the need for publicity and shameless in their self-promotion. Particularly objectionable is the perceived naiveté of NGOs in dealing with political and military authorities, although aid agencies themselves criticize what they consider to be the political naiveté of the military.

The clash of cultures, varying in intensity according to circumstance, organisations, and personalities, is moderated by the real-life situations encountered. In Operation Provide Comfort in northern Iraq, the presence of large numbers of soldiers drawn from US national guard units, many of them with specialties paralleling skills found in the ranks of the humanitarians, fostered positive working relationships. Medical personnel in the French military have a long tradition of working collegially with NGOs (Falandry, 1994). Canadian peace-keeping troops and Canadian NGOs have co-operated closely in a variety of settings.

The secundment in recent years of significant numbers of retired or active military and intelligence officials into the ranks of humanitarian organisations — UN agencies, donor governments, and NGOs alike — has also helped bridge the cultural divide. Of particular value has been their assistance on matters related to the demobilisation of soldiers, the demining of ordnance, security matters, and aid strategies and tactics.

As a result, the breadth of the earlier cultural abyss has narrowed. Some of the larger NGOs, having adapted to the logistical, security, and organisational requirements of complex emergencies, now have more in common with military organisations than with smaller NGOs. Conversely, the training and experience represented in some of the national military contingents with a history of involvement in UN peace-keeping activities has helped to establish their bona fides in such matters as humanitarian and human rights law and refugee camp management. As militaries have learned to differentiate among NGOs, NGOs have come to acknowledge variations in the professionalism of the military contingents of various nations.

Narrowing the cultural divide has also confronted both sets of institutions with the implications of more structured collaboration for each. As a result, humanitarian organisations worry about the erosion of their independence and flexibility under the sheer weight of military bureaucracy and presence. They see collaboration requiring connections with the military at every level in its hierarchical chain well in excess of their own resources and interest. They are concerned lest the transparency inherent in humanitarian action be undercut by the military's need for secrecy.

For their part, military officials ponder the implications of becoming partners with the aid community, which often appears maddeningly multifarious and decentralised. Some who know aid organisations best question whether collaboration with such a highly improvisational and free-wheeling group of agencies and personnel is either possible or desirable. More specifically, providing security for such a risk-taking group might compromise the military's own procedures and undercut its traditional approach to force protection.

Paradoxically, it is precisely the progress in cross-cultural understanding and institutional adaptation achieved in recent years which highlights the structural differences which are likely to continue to exist. Still unresolved at mid-decade is a question of fundamental orientation and values: is there not an inherent contradiction in expecting structured collaboration between institutions which function on the basis of command and control vested in political authorities and institutions whose task, the rendering of assistance and protection to victims, is ultimately not political but moral in character?

The *fourth* policy issue, therefore, concerns coming to terms with the cultural differences between military and humanitarian institutions. In view of such differences, can military-humanitarian co-operation be enhanced?

Limiting the Damages of Involving Military Assets

Humanitarian organisations have only in recent years become aware that the ways in which emergency assistance is provided may have negative impacts on disaster-affected communities and their ability to prevent future crises. Earlier generations of practitioners, stressing the well-intentioned nature of their objectives, accentuated the positive results of their activities. The culture of relief agencies, which has traditionally placed a premium on responding and assisting at the expense of planning and evaluation, has made for a reluctance to acknowledge and assess the unintended consequences of aid activities.

In more recent years, however, the negative fallout from aid interventions throughout the prevailing political, economic, and social structures has become better understood. A pivotal contribution to understanding the complex dynamics of interventions on indigenous communities was a 1989 study of NGO projects that established correlations between the ways in which emergency assistance had been provided and the ability of disaster-affected communities to prevent later crises and build more sustainable and peaceful futures (Anderson and Woodrow, 1989).

Post-Cold War emergencies have dramatised how outside interventions can have even more complex and negative repercussions in situations of internal armed conflict than in natural disasters (Deng and Minear, 1992). Injected from outside into conflict situations, aid becomes highly sought-after by warring parties, who also desire the international imprimatur on their cause which aid appears to confer. In wars, where accountability is generally minimal, aid is often abused with impunity. Providing succor to those in distress may prolong and even sharpen conflicts. A humanitarian community chastened by recent experience is therefore now contemplating as its watchword the Hippocratic oath, "Do no harm". New attention is being directed toward finding ways, even under the worst of circumstances, of making a positive contribution, at the same time avoiding the harm that well-meaning outside interventions can cause[17].

If damage limitation is an issue which increasingly troubles humanitarian groups in the normal course of their activities, it is also a major policy concern when international military assets are involved. The question is whether such resources can be deployed in ways which minimise, or avoid altogether, negative consequences in the receiving countries. While the issue is a difficult one — some would place it well beyond reasonable expectations for military involvement — it requires examination.

The issue is complex for a number of reasons. First, the scale of outside military interventions frequently overwhelms local structures and preempts indigenous leadership and decision making. One advantage of military assets — their quick, massive and efficient deployment — may represent a liability from the perspective of local resources and impacts. The military's take-charge mode may work against the engagement of local leadership, obscuring the reality that in disaster after disaster, "people's self-help efforts are cumulatively more important than external aid" (de Waal and Omaar, 1994). In fact, the military itself may need even larger scale presence in order to accomplish its task. "Experience in Somalia, Bosnia and Angola has demonstrated", concluded one NGO study, "that a much greater ratio of force to benefit is needed than many expected" (Actionaid, 1995).

Second, in mounting emergency relief efforts, outside actors normally seek out local interlocutors. For many UN organisations and donor governments, this means working with ministries of health and education and with interministerial committees of relief and rehabilitation. In civil war settings, the logical points of contacts include counterparts in armed opposition groups, although managing such relationships is often problematic. In insurgent and government-controlled areas alike, the opposite numbers of NGOs are typically community leaders and institutions at the local level.

In contrast, the natural counterparts of international military forces are national militaries. In many countries, however, national armies and paramilitaries — and insurgent armed groups — are implicated in the very violence that requires humanitarian relief. Leaders of such groups are often not committed to democratic traditions, civilian structures, or local leadership. If stronger and more accountable civilian institutions are an essential element in a more secure future for disaster-prone nations, international military presence may not represent a positive influence.

Some military contingents which now seek humanitarian roles were involved during the Cold War in "civic action" projects. Unlike humanitarian aid, which is devoid of political, religious, or other extraneous objectives, such projects had controlling political agendas. Thus, forced resettlement of civilian populations by US military forces in Vietnam, working in concert with USAID and non-governmental organisation partners, was driven by political and military agendas while presented to the public as "humanitarian". As a result, "a distrust of the United States military as a humanitarian force can be expected in some countries as a legacy of the Cold War" (Gaydos and Luz, 1994). Unlike aid organisations for whom humanitarian objectives are by definition primary, military forces have multiple objectives, the humanitarian rarely preeminent.

Such concerns provide the context within which Nobel Prize Laureate Rigoberta Menchu has pleaded for an end to US military assistance and civic action in her native Guatemala. "While they say the troops are in Guatemala for social projects, like road construction", she observes, "their presence is perceived as support for the repressive policies of the Guatemalan army". Although civic action projects there and elsewhere were a feature of the Cold War, the downsizing of US military forces and budgets are said to make "weekend warriors" and "uniformed do-gooder projects" an even more attractive instrument to Pentagon planners (Watrous, 1994).

Third, international troops, quite apart from their particular agenda in a given country, are not known for expertise in the humanitarian sphere, including "nation building". They are often unfamiliar with basic principles of international humanitarian and human rights law, popular participation and community development. The debacle in Somalia is widely perceived as reflecting the expansion of a military mission, originally framed in terms of protecting aid activities, into fields where the military was out of its element.

The fallout from lack of competence in such matters, whether in high-level UN policy or in individual national troop contingents, can be sizeable. Human rights, to mention one specific area, "have been treated as a dispensable luxury, not as a central element in the success of UN peace-keeping and humanitarian operations" (Human Rights Watch, 1993). That judgement by Human Rights Watch, based on a review of five major recent operations, is shared by others as well. To be sure, some national contingents serving in UN peace operations have greater expertise in these matters than others, and multilateral and national training is on the rise. For the time being, however, the gaps in expertise must be filled by humanitarian agencies.

Fourth, quite apart from the expertise of troops, activities by the military have their own rationale and timetable. "Humanitarian agencies primarily are concerned with the long-term needs of a target population; military personnel tend to focus on short-term mission objectives", observes the report of one conference. "The former's main concern is with the immediate survival needs of the affected population; the latter place greater emphasis on the immediate need to establish security". Moreover, at the level of policy, "the decision to commit and deploy military units is driven almost exclusively by a determination of the intervening country's national interests", rather than by humanitarian concerns in and of themselves[18].

In considering intervention, military planners and their political masters are careful to describe not only the objectives of a given mission but the "end state" for its termination. Reflecting the deaths of US troops in Somalia, Presidential Decision Directive 25, approved by President Clinton in May 1994, specifies that engagement will not be approved apart from stipulation of criteria for disengagement. Such end-state criteria may vary among nations. In fact, US planners suggest that since other governments are more relaxed about exit dates, their troops may provide ongoing presence after US forces have been withdrawn.

The limited duration of military involvement and the forced-pace tempo of activities while troops are on the ground mean that a knowledge of the local dynamics is often lacking, along with a concern for the long-term effects of military presence. As indicated above, troops come into most crises once they have erupted and leave at the first possible moment, unlike some aid groups who are there beforehand and stay on after the military have left. As a result, "the demands made upon Western armies by politicians and constituents at home for quick fixes and low casualties" may call into question whether troops are likely to be allowed to become serious contributors to the humanitarian task. Contributing to positive social change, an even more tricky task, will require a still different approach (de Waal and Omaar, 1994)[19].

Military activities also develop their own momentum, often changing the situation on the ground as a result. Troops committed to Bosnia to protect humanitarian operations soon needed protection of their own, while by their presence deterring more forceful military action from outside. Soldiers committed to protect humanitarian operations there may, as in Somalia, require additional troops to accomplish their evacuation. As for the impact of military presence on aid efforts, there is reason to conclude that, as in Somalia, "military intervention does not make the job of fighting famine any easier; it merely makes it different" (de Waal and Omaar, 1994).

If damage limitation seems too modest an objective for international military forces, expecting a more positive result such as contributing to the processes of sustainable development and peace may be too great an expectation. Yet even if the commitment of troops from the outset is known to be severely time-limited — or more accurately, precisely because their days are numbered — considerations of sustainability become critical.

Even if the military assets lack a comparative advantage in facilitating the process of local self-reliance and institution-building, troops need to understand the importance of such activities and to facilitate the work of agencies whose primary tasks they are. As expressed in the Mohonk guidelines mentioned earlier, "Humanitarian assistance should strive to revitalise local institutions, enabling them to provide for the needs of the affected community. [It] should provide a solid first step on the continuum of emergency relief, rehabilitation, reconstruction, and development"[20].

For all of these reasons, damage limitation, among the seven issues identified, may be one of the more difficult for the military to address.

The *fifth* policy issue, therefore, concerns minimising the often-overpowering impacts of military assets on countries and societies in crisis. How can the potential damages be limited?

Effectiveness

In order to justify missions other than war, the military need not only to avoid doing harm but also to make a positive contribution. How should the effectiveness of the military in the humanitarian sphere be judged? What are the criteria for assessing its impact? The issue is complex for several reasons.

First, effectiveness is a function of the time-frame involved. When deployed to Cyprus 30 years ago, UN blue helmets were credited with having defused an explosive situation. Today, it is difficult to escape the conclusion that what looked like a success in the near term has become a longer-term problem. The presence of troops has not encouraged the belligerents to find a political solution to the impasse. Similarly, the passage of time in the former Yugoslavia has lent credence to the view that the presence of UN peacekeepers has eased the responsibility of the warring parties for coming to terms with each other. In northern Iraq, the situation of the rescued Kurds is less perilous, but basically unresolved.

Establishing the relative importance of short-term and longer-term effectiveness, it is evident, will affect the judgements reached. While the shorter time horizons of troops point toward the appropriateness of more delimited benchmarks of effectiveness, military forces themselves have a clear stake in what happens after their departure, and in proceeding in ways which promote longer-term success.

Second, the settings into which military — and for that matter humanitarian — assets are deployed are ones in which international actors frequently do not control events. Intervenors from outside, however formidable or astute, constitute only one variable. While outside actors should work to minimise the extent to which they produce reactions which undermine their objectives, there are limits on the extent to which they can be held responsible for factors they do not control. Judgments of effectiveness need to take into account the degree of difficulty of the intervention involved. Most complex emergencies, for humanitarian and military actors alike, will be at the high end of the scale.

In Somalia, for example, four interventions during the years 1992-95 — UNOSOM I, UNITAF, UNOSOM II, and Operation United Shield — inserted international troops into an active civil war. Each deserves to be judged on its merits, including the extent to which each triggered counterproductive reactions. However, the fact that the civil war had a life of its own makes it more difficult to reach firm judgements on the respective international strategies adopted.

Third, if some of the challenges are more demanding than others, some of the initiatives mounted are also necessarily more complex. Military interventions vary from unilateral to coalitional and multilateral, each with differing degrees of difficulty for the troops involved. Initiatives led by a single government — for example, the US in Haiti, the French in Rwanda, the Russians in Georgia — may be more effective from the standpoint of command and control but less effective as expressions of the will of the international determination, even when blessed by the UN Security Council.

Regional initiatives — for example, the ECOMOG peace-keeping force in Liberia or the Commonwealth of Independent States' troops in Georgia — have advantages that flow from the assumption of responsibility by those close at hand. However, they run the risk of entanglement in regional politics. UN operations may be less quick off the mark and less efficient, but their multilateral character may give them greater acceptability. Accountability also varies, from more clearcut responsibility in unilateral undertakings to more diffused responsibility in regional and multilateral ones.

Judgements about effectiveness also require clarity about the responsibilities of respective actors. In a narrow sense, it may be unfair to hold outside actors — humanitarian or military — accountable for the continuation of conflicts to which they respond. Yet while conflict resolution may be outside their mandate, they may legitimately be expected to take a comprehensive view of the problem and of their own role in it.

Aid organisations that teamed up to make Operation Lifeline Sudan a success during its initial six months in 1989 have been increasingly criticized for continuing operations five years later as the bloodletting proceeds and peace grows ever more distant. The response that as deliverers of aid they do not have conflict resolution and peace in their mandates is, over time, ever less satisfying. The Sudan's civil war has undermined their effectiveness in reaching distressed populations while the belligerents have expropriated much relief assistance (Minear *et al.*, 1991).

In settings of the complexity of post-Cold War conflicts, even establishing success and failure and identifying lessons from past activities can prove difficult. The strategies that led to UN success in El Salvador may not prove effective in Angola. The regional initiative taken by the Economic Council of West African States in creating a military observer group might have been more successful in a situation other than Liberia's. At issue, moreover, is not just how well the military performed but how suitable their mandate was to the given circumstances.

That said, it is also true that many militaries pursue activities in the humanitarian sphere with more willingness to learn from experience than is exhibited by humanitarian agencies. The US military sent military historians along with the troops into Somalia and Rwanda. It has held conferences to identify lessons to be learned and worked to incorporate the results into doctrine, training, and practice. Broadly speaking, international military forces appear more results-oriented than their humanitarian counterparts, even if criteria for measuring their effectiveness remain elusive.

The *sixth* policy issue, therefore, concerns establishing benchmarks for evaluating the effectiveness of military assets in the humanitarian sphere. How can their performance be measured?

Stewardship

Providing military assets has become, in the view of governments and international public opinion, an important element in the responsible exercise of global stewardship in the post-Cold War era. The final issue, therefore, concerns whether, given the humanitarian imperative to address urgent and widespread human need, it would not be irresponsible to fail to utilise such assets.

As noted earlier, the present historical moment involves a massive challenge posed by the human damage and debris from the Cold War. Local and regional conflicts, some of them ongoing, have left in their wake enormous unfinished business in conflict resolution, economic reconstruction, and political and social reconciliation. In the view of many, the international community as a whole — and the erstwhile superpowers in particular — bear major responsibility for helping to wind down associated conflicts and pick up the pieces.

"The cold-war superpowers who once used our differences in their proxy battles are now trying to forget their old differences", wrote Jose Eduardo dos Santos, President of Angola. "But they must not forget old obligations. We look to them now as partners" with us in reconstruction. "The national healing process must begin with caring for the hurt, the hungry, and the homeless." The Angolan president's counterparts in other Cold War trouble spots would agree that "The cost of providing peacekeepers and launching national reconciliation is only a fraction of the cost of making war and caring for the victims"[21]. Leaders in the former Soviet republics make a strong plea for applying the global peace dividend specifically to nations and regions such as Georgia and Chechnya which have borne the brunt of priorities skewed by decades of superpower conflict (MacFarlane, Minear and Shenfield, 1995).

Responsibility for peacekeeping is now much more widely shared among the world's militaries than during the Cold War. The 5 operations in place at the end of January 1988 involved troops contributed by 26 nations; the 17 operations underway in late 1994 drew on troop contributions from fully 76 countries. The fact that revenues from peacekeeping were a source of much needed foreign exchange to many troop-contributing nations does not alter the fact that they had committed troops. For a variety of reasons, peacekeeping has become a vehicle by which a wider array of countries paid their international dues.

The growing involvement of Germany in recent years in UN peace-keeping activities offers a case in point. While German forces had participated in a variety of humanitarian activities around the world in recent decades, it was not until the 1990s that troops were provided to UN undertakings. In the last several years, Germany has participated in UN operations in Cambodia, Somalia, former Yugoslavia, Georgia, and Rwanda. Participation in UN peacekeeping has emerged as an item of "enormous importance", the government has said. As a result of its involvement, "Germany has proven herself a reliable partner in the community of peoples", concluded a recent review by the German Ministry of Defence (Bundesministerium der Verteidigung, 1995).

There is also now a widely perceived convergence between the tasks for which military assets are contributed and the national interest of contributing countries. For some nations the connection is anything but new. Many with long traditions of supporting UN peace-keeping efforts — Canada and Pakistan, the Nordics and the Netherlands, Nepal and Bangladesh, for example — have done so as a means of playing a constructive role in international affairs.

With almost 3 000 Canadian troops participating in some 15 peace-keeping missions in late 1993, support of such international efforts represented one of the primary reasons for maintaining Canada's military forces themselves. That tradition served as an anchor against heightened pressures on the Canadian government to reduce its involvement following the verdict of a court-martial which found a Canadian soldier guilty of having killed a Somali civilian in the course of UN peace-keeping duty. (The unit in which he served was subsequently disbanded.)

The solid consensus among "middle powers" in favour of supporting international peace operations and their humanitarian components is less present and less steady among some of the more powerful nations. In France, for example, participation in UN peacekeeping was initially seen as a supportable exercise in global stewardship. However, the negative experience in Bosnia, where France has been the largest troop contributor but has advocated more assertive terms of engagement than the UN has approved, has led to a popular backlash against participation in UN operations. The more positive experience of the French military in Rwanda, described in Chapter 5, seems to have placed French exercise of a leadership role in "humanitarian intervention" back in popular favour (Bettati, 1993; Guillot, 1994).

Debate is also under way in the United States about how the world's sole remaining superpower should understand is leadership role. At issue are how its responsibilities as global policeman and world humanitarian should be viewed and the extent to which leadership should be exercised bilaterally or through regional or multilateral institutions. In the ascendancy in 1995 were voices seeking to frame US action in ways which, for reasons of both policy and cost, would restrict the level of its engagement in collaborative problem solving through multilateral bodies (Randel and German, 1995; Bread for the World, 1995).

Views differ from nation to nation and institution to institution about the extent to which participation in international peace operations and, more specifically, the use of military assets to provide humanitarian assistance constitute a fundamental national interest. In the United States, Secretary of Defence William I. Perry relegates humanitarian concerns to a third category after "vital interests" and "important interests" (Perry, 1995). His typology converges with the viewpoint of US Marine Corps General Bernard Trainor (ret.), currently director of the national security program at Harvard University's Kennedy School of Government. In Trainor's eyes, "You have to question whether a humanitarian imperative constitutes a vital interest"[22].

An alternative view, and one more keyed to active engagement in international humanitarian issues, is articulated by Andrew Natsios, a former USAID official currently an executive of the NGO World Vision. "We need to redefine national interest in the post-Cold War world to include complex emergencies even when there is no geo-strategic interest". Such an approach attaches greater importance to addressing major international human need, using military assets among all other available resources (Natsios, 1994).

In other countries, a new and broader understanding of "international interests" is farther advanced in supplanting traditional preoccupations with narrowly conceived "national interests". At the global level, however, while sovereignty is now less sacrosanct and national borders more porous to humanitarian penetration, a compelling new vision of international interests remains to be articulated and institutionalised. That debate will influence the shape of future humanitarian activities and the extent to which military assets play a prominent role in them.

The *final* policy issue, therefore, concerns the extent to which providing military assets represents a key element in the responsible exercise of global citizenship. Given the humanitarian imperative to address urgent and widespread human need, would it not be irresponsible to fail to utilise such assets?

After a review in Chapters 3-7 of the Rwanda crisis and the roles of international military assets in responding to it, Chapter 8 revisits these *seven* policy issues. As the intervening chapters demonstrate, the experience of sending soldiers to the rescue was so richly variegated that its implications for the future are wide-ranging indeed.

Notes

1. David Pallister, "When Food Relief Comes out of the Barrel of a Gun", *The Guardian*, May 7, 1994.

2. Cf., for example, Articles 23, 55, 59-62 of the Fourth Geneva Convention (Protection of Civilian Persons in Time of War); Articles 68-71 of Additional Protocol I, and Article 18 of Additional Protocol II. *The Geneva Conventions of August 12, 1949*, and *Protocols Additional to the Geneva Conventions of August 12, 1949*, International Committee of the Red Cross, Geneva, 1989.

3. InterAction, Letter to General Brent Scowcroft, Nov. 19, 1992. See also Sapir and Deconinck, 1995, which terms the initiative the first request for armed support in the history of the signatories.

4. David Bryer, "Humanitarian Intervention: Military and Non-military Responses to Global Emergencies: An NGO View," Remarks at the Wilton Park Conference, March 1, 1994.

5. Peter Fuchs, "Conflict Management: A Multidisciplinary Approach, Address to the Nordic Council Conference on the Nordic Countries in the UN — for Peace and Development, Jan. 10-12, 1995, Helsinki.

6. Humanitarian Liaison Working Group, "Ideas Raised During the Discussion", Nov. 21, 1994.

7. Quoted in Larry Minear, "A Role for the New Humanitarians", *International Herald Tribune*, June 14, 1995.

8. The Dutch government study referred to in the previous chapter makes the further point that additional economies might have been realised in the LWF operation itself. See also (Netherlands Ministry of Foreign Affairs, 1994).

9. Private correspondence with the authors dated July 7, 1995.

10. Reviewing the cost data for Somalia, Sapir and Deconinck conclude that "the financial implication of military involvement demands a cautious approach and justifies a better examination of the opportunity costs" (*op.cit.*).

11. "Life-saving Role Played by US Troops in Somalia", Letter to the Editor, *The Manchester Guardian Weekly*, March [13], 1995.

12. For an elaboration of the concern, cf. Randel and German, 1994 (p.91).

13. Chris Black, "Army Adapts Changing World," *Boston Globe*, Jan. 8, 1995, p.1

14. *Ibid.*, p. 12.

15. For an illuminating elaboration of the conflict between the cultures of peacekeeping and of develoment in Mozambique, cf. Ajello, 1996.

16. Bureau of Intelligence and Research, US Department of State, "Improving Coordination of Humanitarian and Military Operations", Conference Report, June 23, 1994, US Government, Washington, D.C., 1994.

17. These issues are currently being reviewed by the "Local Capacities for Peace Project", a research undertaking by Mary B. Anderson of the Collaborative for Development Action in Cambridge, Mass.

18. Bureau of Intelligence and Research, US Department of State, "Improving Coordination of Humanitarian and Military Operations", Conference Report, June 23, 1994, US Government, Washington, D.C., 1994.

19. The authors conclude that "Radical changes in military doctrine and training will be needed if armies are to carry out humanitarian tasks".

20. Task Force on Ethical and Legal Issues in Humanitarian Assistance, World Conference on Religion and Peace, New York, 1994.

21. Jose Eduardo dos Santos, "Angola Needs the World's Help in Making Peace Triumph", *The Christian Science Monitor*, Jan. 25, 1995.

22. Quoted in "Going In," a compilation of views on whether a US military invasion of Haiti was in the US national interest, *Boston Globe*, Sept. 18, 1994.

Chapter 3

The Rwanda Context

Shifting from the focus of Part One on the post-Cold War moment and attendant policy issues surrounding the use of military assets, Part Two reviews the contribution of outside military forces to the international response to the crisis. Chapter 3 describes the historical and political context of the Rwanda crisis, examines the role of Rwandese military forces, and provides an overview of the humanitarian effort at the time of the authors' visit to the region in October 1994 and through the end of the year. The activities of international military forces form the subject of the balance of Part Two.

Historical Background

Rwanda and Burundi were "discovered" by Europeans only a century ago. At the time, the two nations evidenced many similarities. The populations of each shared the same mixed ethnic composition, with substantial numbers of both Hutus and Tutsis in each. According to some analysts, the distinction between Hutus and Tutsis represented an ethnic division predating colonisation (Newbury, 1988; Reyntjens, 1994; Del Perugia, 1994). According to others, the distinctions between the two groups were not ethnic but rather based on social status and economic activities (Chrétien, 1981; Guichaoua, 1992; *Le Temps Stratégique*, 1994; Braeckman, 1994)[1].

The term "ethnic conflict" is used in this text without making a judgement about the validity of alternative explanations of the nature and history of the differences. Since the murder of Tutsis by Hutu Power extremists reflected what they had come to believe — that Tutsis were from a different ethnic group or even from a different race — ethnicity was a question of perception, whatever the historical realities. That said, historical and political events constitute a necessary element in understanding the events of 1994.

Since the sixteenth century, Rwanda and Burundi had each been ruled by a king (*mwami*). Each relied on a type of feudal system based on land tenure and property in the form of cattle. The two states were joined together in 1899 to form German East Africa, with Germany ruling indirectly through the mechanism of local élites. Applying theories in vogue at the time, the Germans used ethnic classifications to distinguish groups within the region's population. They described Hutus as short, dark skinned, and "docile" Bantu people; Tutsis as tall, lighter skinned Hamitic people whom they termed the "Lord's race"; and Twa pygmees as "subhuman dwarfs".

The German approach gave unwarranted importance to the place in society enjoyed by Tutsis, which in reality was but one factor in a complex feudal system. "The ethnic divide", observed one writer, "was in reality more of a political divide, although based on ancestry" (McCullum, 1995). The approach taken by the Germans downplayed other variables, including differences in geographical origins. North-western Rwanda's Hutus were also part of the nobility, while some Twas played prominent roles in the king's court (Lemarchand, 1970; Louis, 1963; Vansina, 1965; D'Hertefelt, 1964; Honke, 1990).

Such historical factors had a direct bearing on events that played themselves out a century later. Rwandese political cleavages are still organised along so-called ethnic lines, which have in fact deepened over time. Geographical cleavages exist as well, even within the Hutu community, reflecting in part the former kingdoms of Kinyaga and Bufundu (in the south-west), Mulera, Bugara, and Bushiru (in the north-west), and Nduga and Buganza (in central and eastern areas). Such fissures are very real even though some groups in the region's political and social scene have downplayed or refused to accept them.

During the early twentieth century, European nations continued to exercise a major influence on the area. In 1916 Belgian troops, entering from the neighbouring Congo (now Zaire), seized the two German colonies. Belgium was given a mandate for Ruanda-Urundi under Article 22(3) of the Covenant of the League of Nations. Belgium received a level of responsibility for the area less than was provided by the League for South West Africa but more than was granted for Middle East countries. Reinforcing the favouritism shown by the Germans, Belgian colonial administrators gave preference to Tutsis, granting them special access to education and jobs (Vinacke, 1934; Nguyen Quoc, Dallier and Pellet, 1994; Linden, 1977; Rumiya, 1992; Gahama, 1983). As a consequence, Hutus felt victimised by a double colonialism. The main Hutu political party, *Parti du mouvement de l'émancipation des Bahutu* (Parmehutu), declared in its manifesto that true independence required getting rid not only of European masters but also "colonisation of Black people [i.e., Hutu] by Black people [i.e., Tutsi]" (de Heusch, 1994)[2].

In the late 1950s, Belgian colonial administrators and missionaries reversed themselves and their established policies in an effort to promote Hutu social mobility. The Christian-Democratic Party then in power in Belgium preferred a docile Hutu majority to the Tutsi-dominated *Union nationale rwandaise* (Rwandese National Union, or UNAR), which was perceived as a left-wing nationalist group. Reflecting the changes, a Hutu peasant revolt, referred to as "the Social Revolution", broke out in 1959 in which the Rwandese king, a Tutsi, was overthrown by Hutu elements. The first of numerous waves of Tutsi refugees was unleashed (Williame, 1995).

The republic of Rwanda was proclaimed in 1961, with a Hutu from southern Rwanda, Grégoire Kayibanda, its first president. On July 1 of that year, the change was ratified by Belgium which, in conjunction with local leaders, formally divided *Ruanda-Urundi* into two states. Alongside the Rwandese republic was established the Kingdom of Burundi, which became a republic in 1965. Both countries were soon ruled by single parties but with opposite results. In Rwanda, the *Mouvement démocratique républicain-Parti du mouvement de l'émancipation des Bahutu* (MDR-Parmehutu, later called the National Party) established an exclusive Hutu state. In Burundi, the *Union pour le progrès national* (UPRONA) reinforced Tutsi dominance.

Each country thus came to mirror in reverse the ethnic composition of the other. In Burundi, the Tutsi minority monopolised power and oppressed the Hutu majority. In Rwanda, a dictatorship by the Hutu majority was imposed on the Tutsi minority. Joined at birth, neither twin recovered from the surgery performed by outsiders when the pair had reached an advanced age. Each nation used the other to justify policies of discrimination and control. Ethnically related frictions and, in extreme cases, massacres in one nation raised levels of political and social tension in the other. Thus for the Hutu élite in Rwanda, the political marginalisation of Tutsis was seen as a means of preventing the indignities suffered by Hutus at the hands of a Tutsi minority in Burundi.

In fact, social and political tensions involving Rwanda became a source of instability for the entire Great Lakes region. Between 1959 and 1963, some 200 000 Rwandese Tutsis fled into Burundi, Uganda, and Zaire. Their presence added a combustible element to Uganda's violent political evolution and introduced an unsettling factor in Burundi and Zaire as well. The Rwandan social revolution created the oldest group of refugees in Africa. Beyond the personal tragedy of so many involuntarily exiled people, the upheaval further destabilized an already unstable region. The Tutsis in Uganda were the so-called "old refugees" who, returning to their Rwandese homeland in 1994 after three decades of exile, would create a special set of problems for the new authorities.

In December 1963, exiled Tutsis unsuccessfully attempted to destabilize Rwanda through guerrilla operations mounted from Uganda, Burundi, and Congo (now Zaire). Mass reprisals by the Hutu government in Rwanda followed. Tutsis who remained in Rwanda were politically marginalised, although their educational and other assets afforded them a certain protection. Rwandan society included poor Tutsis and wealthy Hutus as well.

A new round of mass murders of Rwandese Tutsis was launched by activists from the MDR-Parmehutu party in February 1973, unleashing another wave of Tutsi refugees into neighbouring countries, especially Uganda and Burundi. On July 5, President Kayibanda was overthrown by his Defence Secretary, Major-General Juvénal Habyarimana. The MDR-Parmehutu was abolished and later replaced by a single new party, the *Mouvement républicain national pour le développement* (MRND). A new constitution was adopted in 1978. Although the new régime remained committed to Hutu supremacy, it changed the geographical base of the country's social and political élite. Where President Kayibanda relied on Southerners, President Habyarimana favoured North-westerners.

Meanwhile, the largely Tutsi Rwandese National Union (UNAR) was recreated in Kenya by exiled Rwandans. The leadership, both Tutsi and Hutu in origin, was committed to restore the king to his throne. In the late 1960s the monarchist party became a republican party. In the 1980s, a new movement took shape in Kampala, Uganda: the Rwandese Alliance for National Unity (RANU). RANU initially dealt with the problems of refugees but soon became a political forum for the Banyarwanda of Uganda (that is, for Hutu and Tutsi exiles from Rwanda). In December 1987 RANU became the Rwandese Patriotic Front (RPF), the group which would successfully challenge the largely Hutu regime in Kigali (Prunier, 1993).

Throughout these years, Rwandan refugees across the Great Lakes diaspora constituted a major threat to regional security. In Burundi, Rwandese Tutsis tended to back the UPRONA party's quasi-apartheid policy. Some Rwandese Tutsis dreamed not only of returning home but also of exacting revenge for the Hutu social revolution which had forced them into exile. Conversely, exiled Rwandan Hutus tended to support the programmes of Hutu political leaders in Burundi. In either event, Burundese authorities found the presence of refugees detrimental to internal security and to relations with Rwanda.

In Zaire, Banyarwandas from the Kivu region formed a single "group", regardless of the Hutu/Tutsi divide. Sharing their nationality and the kinyarwanda language, they were perceived as the same people by Zairean nationals, who rejected them as foreigners. Consequently, Banyarwandas share the feeling of belonging to the same nation. However, in Goma itself Tutsis and Hutus have existed for generations as two different and opposing ethnic groups (Reyntjens, 1994). In Uganda, exiled Rwandans joined the Museveni guerrilla group which was committed to overthrow the Ugandan regime.

> Many outside observers, especially in the early days of the slaughter, have tended to dismiss what has happened in Rwanda as African mayhem-as-usual. They saw the Hutu-Tutsi conflict as little more than a savage tribal freak show. While the violence was certainly savage, it was not normal and it was not exclusively tribal. The killings were neither random nor spontaneous. Nor were most of the victims killed as a result of the country's civil war. The slaughter of civilians took place simultaneously with the war — sometimes in the same regions as the combat between the government and the RPF armies — but it was completely separate from the war.
>
> Robert Block, The Tragedy of Rwanda, *New York Review*, October 20, 1994.

From time to time, refugees did return to Rwanda. In August 1988 following an international conference held in Washington D.C., approximately 60 000 returnees arrived from Burundi in Butaré *préfecture*. Between January and March 1990, several thousand illegal Rwandan migrants who did not meet the provisions of the 1951 Convention on Refugees were expelled from Tanzania and returned to Rwanda.

The existence of a Rwanda diaspora was used for political purposes by both sides. The RPF became a strong advocate of the right of refugees to return while Hutu ideologists depicted the RPF as a foreign-inspired reactionary (that is, royalist) political force. Ethnic differences were also magnified by Hutu ideologists close to President Habyarimana, who described the RPF as a Tutsi party, Tutsis — in exile — as enemies of the Rwandan state, and Hutu participation in the Tutsi-dominated RPF as cosmetic.

Ethnic differences politicised by ideologues thus fuelled the Rwandan civil war and the genocide which accompanied it. Ethnic tensions, of course, do not always result in genocide. In the particular circumstances of Rwanda, however, the politicisation of ethnic divisions, particularly by Hutu extremists, fed an organised campaign to eliminate Tutsis and Hutu moderates. After the eruption of violence in April 1994, ideologues succeeded for some time in using the civil war to mask the genocide[3].

Recent Political-Military Developments

On October 1, 1990 the Rwandese Patriotic Front (RPF) from within Ugandese borders launched an offensive against the Rwandan government and the Rwandan Armed Forces (RwAF). As a consequence of the ensuing war, famine broke out in the Rwandese countryside and a great outflow of displaced persons reached Kigali. Some 10 000 Tutsis and political opponents were arrested by Rwandan authorities in the capital. In one incident, the RwAF killed more than 500 Himas, an ethnic group close to the Tutsis. In another, approximately 400 Tutsis were murdered by MRND militias. France and Belgium intervened militarily, with Belgian troops exiting after having evacuated expatriates. Under an agreement between Paris and Kigali, French Marines remained to assist and train the RwAF.

In January 1991, the RPF, continuing their military pressure on the Kigali regime, attacked the Byumba area. Hutu militias retaliated throughout the country against Tutsis and moderate Hutus. A new attack by the RPF was thwarted by the RwAF, reinforced by the French military, whose intervention was credited with having helped prevent the capture of Kigali by the RPF. A number of RPF violations of humanitarian law, including the murders of civilians, were reported. On the government side, violations of human rights were ongoing. A number of persons were sentenced to death for alleged collusion with the RPF, although some detainees accused of complicity were later released.

On June 10, 1991, a new Rwandese constitution was adopted, providing for freedom of speech and the right to organise political parties. Several opposition parties were soon formed: the *Mouvement démocratique républicain* (MDR), the Liberal Party (PL), the Social-Democratic Party (PSD), and the Christian Democratic Party (PDC). An extremist Hutu Power party was also created: the Coalition for the Defence of the Republic (CDR). The following April, a coalition government was formed which included the MRND and opposition parties (with the exception of the RPF). Dismas Nsengiyaremye served as premier.

The following month saw violent demonstrations and attempts by terrorists to overthrow the regime. The youth branch of the MRND organised its own militia, called the *Interahamwe*, or "the ones who work and fight together", which would become a major perpetrator of violence. On a more positive note, officials of various opposition parties met with RPF representatives in Brussels and Paris, where a common front in favour of the Arusha peace accords was created.

Arusha, Tanzania became the scene of a series of agreements designed to find a political accommodation for the ongoing tensions. On July 12, 1992, a cease-fire agreement was signed there between the Rwandan Government and the RPF, followed on October 18 by a protocol of agreement on the rule of law. Two weeks later, the first part of a protocol on power-sharing within the framework of a broad-based transitional government (BBTG) was signed. A second part followed on January 9, 1993. Six months later, a protocol on refugee repatriation and the resettlement of displaced persons was finalised. On August 3, two protocols relating to the integration of the armed forces and other legal matters were concluded. The Arusha process was capped August 4, 1993 with agreement on a peace accord. The Arusha agreements provided the context within which the UN peace-keeping operation began deployment November 1, 1993.

The accord represented a signal accomplishment for the major Rwandan actors, the OAU, and others who had promoted it. However, the process and results were far from harmonious. The appointment July 17 of Mrs. Agathe Uwilingiyimana, a leading Hutu moderate, as interim Prime Minister was designed to facilitate agreement with the RPF. Instead, it caused a serious split in the MDR, whose President, Faustin Twagiramungu, a presumptive prime minister, was excluded from the party. A victory by the *Parmehutu* wing of the MDR over its more moderate wing represented a setback for advocates of national reconciliation.

The Arusha agreements themselves were not implemented due to opposition by Hutu Power activists to RPF participation in the broad-based transitional government. Hutu Power was an unofficial and clandestine political and social movement of Hutu activists committed to one-party rule. It was composed of an inner circle known as *Akazu*, made up of Mrs. Agathe Habyarimana's immediate family and friends. A second circle, Network Zero, was composed of MRND die-hards, including death squads and *interahamwe* militias. A third circle of extremists from the CDR's *impuzamugambi* militia rounded out the structure.

Hutu Power ideology, developed in the years preceding 1994, has been described as racism or "tropical nazism" (Chrétien, 1994). Ideologues and activists believed Tutsis to be Hamitic invaders who centuries ago had reduced Hutus to slavery. They feared that an RPF victory would mean a restoration of the Tutsi monarchy. Exercising great political influence, Hutu Power succeeded in impeding implementation of the Arusha provisions regarding a broad-based transitional government. An ally in the process were radio broadcasts of Hutu Power ideology that spurred the atrocities which erupted in April 1994.

Pursuant to the Arusha agreement, RPF representatives, escorted by 600 RPF fighters, arrived in Kigali on December 28, 1993 to participate in the transitional cabinet and national assembly provided for in the agreements. Hard-line Hutu parties mobilised opposition to following the process specified in the agreement. For its part, the RPF was reluctant to share power with the MRND when a military victory seemed achievable and a democratic election would likely have resulted in the marginalisation of what was a perceived as Tutsi political group. That, in fact, had been the upshot of recent elections in Burundi.

As a result of historical factors and political developments such as these, Rwanda by early 1994 was poised for disaster. On April 6 1994, Rwandan President Habyarimana and his Burundese counterpart, Cyprien Ntaryamira, were killed when their plane was shot down by a ground-to-air missile as they returned to Kigali from Tanzania. Selected and pre-planned murders of Tutsis and moderate Hutus began within hours. Prime Minister Agathe Uwilingiyimana was assassinated by the Presidential Guard. The speaker of the National Assembly and the president of the Supreme Court, both Hutus, were killed. Many moderate government ministers and also democratic opposition party members were also murdered, creating a political vacuum.

According to a protocol on power sharing of October 30, 1992, the broad-based transitional government should have brought the succession issue before the Supreme Court and a new president should have been elected by a joint session of the transitional government and assembly. Since these institutions did not exist at the time, a political solution in the spirit of the Arusha agreements should have been found. Instead, a "crisis committee" — a military junta, headed by Colonel Bagosora — filled the constitutional vacuum and declared as acting President the former Parliament speaker, Théodore Sindikubwabo. He, in turn, appointed as Prime Minister Jean Kambanda, a member of the 'Parmehutu' wing of MDR. These decisions were grounded on provisions in the lapsed 1991 Constitution (Reyntjens, 1994).

The resulting interim government, however unconstitutional in character, was thereby in a position to pursue a campaign of genocide. In fact, that campaign had been organised well in advance of April 6, 1994 and depended for its execution on the participation of a large segment of the Hutu population. The UN Commission of Experts, which later in the year would conclude that "every provision laid out in Article III of the Genocide Convention has been violated in Rwanda in the period from 6 April to 15 July 1994" also found "abundant and compelling evidence [that] supports the conclusion that prior to 6 April Hutu elements conspired to commit genocide." (UN, 1994a; Destexhe, 1994; Ternon, 1995; Sounalet, 1994; Vaiter, 1995; Poincaré, 1995). Rwanda at the time held a seat on the UN Security Council, the body which would respond to the abuses the Kigali authorities were perpetrating

With the acquiescence of Rwandese authorities, France on April 9 launched *Opération Amaryllis*, and Belgium and Italy Operation Silver Back to rescue their nationals and others Westerners. The paratroopers were to extricate their fellow nationals, not to stop the atrocities by Hutu Power. Within five days, 2 000 Europeans had been evacuated, along with the family of President Habyarimana which was taken by French aircraft to Bangui and then Paris. Endangered Rwandan personnel employed by embassies and NGOs, most of them Tutsis, were left behind. With the backing of the United States and the United Kingdom, France and Belgium argued that these operations were not humanitarian interventions but rather exercises of the right of states to rescue nationals abroad and thus of no concern to the Security Council[4].

On June 16, French Minister of Foreign Affairs Alain Juppé declared that France was ready to intervene militarily. Six days later, the UN Security Council authorised *Opération Turquoise*. A month later, RPF was in control of most of the country, with the exception of the south-west, where French troops had established a protected zone. Under Pasteur Bizimungu's presidency, a national union government was formed, with Faustin Twagiramungu as Prime Minister. Major-General Paul Kagame, who headed the RPF military, became Vice-President (a post which did not exist in Arusha agreements on power-sharing) and Minister of Defence.

In the wake of the RPF take-over, exiled Tutsis — many of them the "old refugees" described above — arrived from Burundi and Uganda in large numbers. By July, fully 40 per cent of Kigali's inhabitants were said to be former refugees, many occupying properties owned or rented by people who had sought asylum in the French-protected zone or in neighbouring countries. Those who had fled feared returning home because summary settlements of property disputes rather than legal proceedings were taking place. While the new regime sought to adjudicate such disputes and to work toward meaningful national reconciliation, lack of resources among refugees and within the new government slowed effective resettlement.

Rwandese Military Forces

While Rwandan soldiers are not the subject of this study, which focuses instead on international military forces, they represented the original military actors in the drama of 1994 and a key element in the context into which outside military assets were inserted. For analytical purposes, Rwandan military forces are grouped according to their affiliation with the *"ancien régime"*, the Hutu government in power through July 1994, or with the new regime which assumed power thereafter.

> For the refugees, as for any Rwandan today, one's politics is determined by the place where one sought shelter from the holocaust. During the genocide there was no neutral position between the rebels and the government. Afterward, whether implicated, innocent or apolitical, place defines politics for each individual — either one is in the camps and hence on the side of the deposed regime, or at home in Rwanda and on the side of the new government. To move now is to declare oneself regarding the cataclysmic events of 1994. So to avoid further problems one stays where one is, surviving but also deepening the impasse.
>
> Jonathan Frerichs, "In the Camps, the Rwanda Crisis Goes On", *Christian Century*, Feb., 1995.

As for the *ancien régime*, the Rwandese Armed Forces (RwAF) were the government's army and gendarmerie, composed predominantly of Hutus from northern Rwanda. Their strength in early 1994 was estimated at 35 000 including 1 500 Presidential Guards, élite troops recruited from President Habyarimana's home area of Bushiru (Africa Watch, 1992; Human Rights Watch, 1994; Guichaoua, 1995). Like many African armies, the RwAF were used less for national defence than to enforce domestic order. Under defence agreements with France, they received material and training in 1990-94, including the use of sophisticated weapons. They suffered from indiscipline and corruption and in early 1994 were a source of insecurity for local people and NGOs. RwAF members, especially the Presidential Guards, were accused of torturing people suspected of being RPF spies (Braeckman, 1994).

In spite of clear superiority in men and material. RwAF troops were unable to repel the RPF offensive, even with assistance from France and Zaire. However, their retreat, reflecting to be sure a shortage of ammunition, was less a rout than a tactical manœuvre to provide cover for a Hutu exodus from the north-west. Entire villages moved to Zaire under the guidance of their *bourgmestres* and *chefs de cellule*, with exiting civilians serving at the same time as a human shield for the RwAF[5]. Fear of reprisals by the ascendant Tutsis spurred the exodus, both among those who had and those who had not participated in acts of genocide.

While the RwAF was a stronghold of Hutu Power sentiment, some of its members chose not to participate in the post-April violence against civilians. "General Gatsinzi, General Rusatira and seven senior RwAF officers called for national reconciliation and condemned the *ancien régime* as corrupted by genocidal extremists" (Munyarugerero, 1995)[6]. A significant number of officers and soldiers, perhaps as many as several thousand, chose to surrender rather than to go into exile in Zaire. Some RwAF members refused to participate in the killings, although how many remains unclear (African Rights, 1994, Ch. 15; McCullum, 1995, Ch. 4). Non-co-operators were sent to political re-education camps in southeastern Rwanda, where journalists under escort were allowed to visit them, prior to reintegration into Rwandese society. While some rank-and-file RwAF soldiers were implicated in the genocide, many atrocities were committed by the Presidential Guard and by civilians, acting as militia members in their own right.

The situation was confused in part because during the months following the shooting down of the presidential plane, two different kinds of events were taking place simultaneously. In addition to the campaign of genocide, another chapter in the ongoing civil war was playing itself out, pitting incumbent RwAF forces against the insurgent RPF. While RwAF troops were not invariably murderers, most who fled to Zaire were suspected by the new authorities of having blood on their hands.

According to a variety of sources, between 12 000 and 15 000 RwAF were present in or near refugee camps in Zaire at the end of December 1994. Fears of a resurgent RwAF were expressed not only by the new regime but also by diplomats and aid officials. The possibility of an assault was bolstered because former governmental troops had not been effectively disarmed by Zairean soldiers. While certain arms had been confiscated at the border, some were sold back to the RwAF once they were inside. Before the end of 1994, sporadic cross-border attacks were already being mounted by the members of the former Hutu army and militias.

Forces of the *ancien régime* also included, in addition to the RwAF, Hutu Power militias. The UN Secretary-General reported that "each of the 147 communes in Rwanda had between 100 and 150 organised militia, which would represent a total of between 14 700 and 22 050 personnel". (UN, 1994d, Para. 10). Hutu Power militias were divided into two principal branches. Most numerous were the *Interahamwe*, self-defence bands mainly of jobless youth who constituted the activist vanguard of the MRND party. Operating often with the explicit encouragement of the Interim Government but often also on their own, they were the main perpetrators of the genocide. They answered Rwandan government radio broadcasts calling upon citizens to take up arms against "the [Tutsi] enemy all over Rwanda"[7].

The extremist Hutu Power party, the Coalition for the Defence of the Republic, had its own militia, the *Impuzamugambi*, or "The ones who have only one goal". That goal was to prevent a return to Tutsi dominance. This militia was geared to fight against Rwanda's enemies, whether external ones in the form of the RPF or internal ones such as Tutsis or Hutus who favoured moderate political stances. More radical than the *Interahamwe*, the *Impuzamugambi* constituted the most extreme of the Hutu Power militias, compared by some analysts to the *Khmers rouges*. With several thousand in their ranks, their actions were encouraged by broadcasts of *Radio-télévision libre des mille collines* (RTLM), a private radio station in Kigali which incited Hutus to kill "internal enemies".

While the two militias were largely separate entities serving separate political factions, they had much in common. Both were committed to Hutu supremacy. Both were armed and trained by the Presidential Guard. Both did the bidding of government authorities, though without specific accountability to them. Both fled to Zaire, where they posed a major problem to the local political authorities, to the relief agencies, and to more disciplined elements within the exiled Hutu political and military leadership. From Zaire, both waged an effective campaign of intimidation against both Hutus and Tutsis who wished to return home. Over time, the term *Interahamwe* became a shorthand for all elements of the Hutu Power militias.

The military forces of the new regime were initially guerrillas operating from across the border. After the government changed hands, these elements were transformed into the new Rwandan army. The troops which comprised the backbone of the Rwandese Patriotic Front, the military challengers of the old Rwandan army, were known as *Inkontanyi*, or the *Invincible Ones*. They were, for the most part, young refugees in Uganda from Rwanda, Hutu and Tutsi alike, who had joined Yoweri Musuveni's National Resistance Army in large numbers, having fought from 1981 onward in the bush against Milton Obote's regime.

Following victory over the official Ugandan army and the replacement of Obote by Museveni in January 1986, Rwandans assumed positions of leadership in Ugandan civilian and military structures. Major-General Fred Rwigema became deputy chief of staff and vice-secretary of defence. Major-General Paul Kagamé became deputy head of intelligence services. These two officers created the RPF and headed its armed branch, the *Inkontanyi*.

Seasoned by almost a decade of guerrilla and army experience in Uganda, the *Inkontanyi* represented a formidable fighting force. Some 13 000 strong, they were able to face and to rout, if not to defeat, a national army in Rwanda with superior strength, infrastructure, and international backing. The RPF's seizure of the Rwandan capital and of provincial strongholds such as Butaré reflected hard-won experience and discipline.

Following RPF victory and the installation of a new Rwandan régime, the *Inkontanyi* became the core of the new Rwandese Patriotic Army (RPA). Over 25 000 in number as of early 1995, fully 40 per cent of whom were Hutus, the RPA was composed largely of *Inkontanyi* and of young people who joined RPF fighters on their sweep in mid-1994 into Kigali (Guichaoua, 1995). Many of the rank and file were orphans or "unaccompanied minors" with personal reasons to oppose Hutu Power. As elsewhere in Africa, their involvement was a clear violation of the UN Convention on the Rights of the Child, to which the state of Rwanda was a signatory, and became a sensitive political issue for the new regime.

Even though the initial recruits of the *Inkontanyi* in Uganda and many of those who came on board later were predominantly Tutsi, the RPA was not an exclusively Tutsi army. Moreover, it served a government which was a coalition that included, in addition to the RPF, the moderate wing of the MDR, the Liberal Party, the Christian Democratic Party, and the Social-Democratic Party. Government officials included Hutus in key positions such as president, prime minister, and ministers of justice and the interior. While critics derided the appointments of non-Tutsis as token, Hutu involvement suggested an effort to reach a broader constituency.

Major-General Kagamé imposed severe discipline on his troops, including 600 lashes for robbery and the death penalty for rape or murder. During the early phase of the RPF offensive, however, the *Inkontanyi* performed a variety of atrocities, including mass murders. "If [Hutu] people ran away, it was not because of the RPF's kindness", commented an NGO official. "They fled because of the murders. There were thousands of displaced persons escaping RPF strongholds".

Expatriate aid personnel working in those parts of Rwanda controlled by the RPF before its take-over of Kigali, however, were generally allowed access to civilians, except on occasion for security reasons. As of October 1994, the RPA had its own humanitarian unit, although inquiries were unable to determine its size or activities.

Some Rwandese and other observers alleged a pattern of incidents of retaliation by the army against persons suspected of genocide. Some suspected the RPF of wanting to establish an authoritarian regime and therefore encouraging reprisals by *uncontrolled elements*. Such suspicions were fuelled because the army was in charge of the tasks of *gendarmérie*, police, and administration of prisons, wherein some abuses were known to have taken place.

Evidence suggested, however, that while soldiers may have committed individual acts of revenge, the army as such did not have a policy or encourage the practice of reprisals. Moreover, the new government lacked the wherewithal, either from its own resources or from the international community, to establish and pay a civilian police force and prison administration. In fact, to reassure a concerned international public, the new authorities encouraged outside monitoring of its performance in these sensitive areas. "We are talking about a country in which everything has been destroyed", observed the then Minister of the Internal Affairs M. Seth Serdashonga in October 1994. "Give us the means and test our good will"[8].

In the fall of 1994, the attitude of the new authorities toward the humanitarian community changed. Relationships became more tense. The Ministry of Rehabilitation sent NGOs a charter of rights and duties which imposed a certain control on their activities[9]. Governmental attitudes also hardened with respect to internally displaced persons as well. In November 1994, personnel from the Rwandese Patriotic Army were reported to have committed the first harassment of those camps, presaging the April 1995 events in Kibeho described in Chapter 9.

The military forces of the old and new regimes illustrated the interlocking and regional nature of the political and humanitarian problems of Rwanda. The majority Hutu regime in Rwanda used the situation in Burundi, where the Hutus comprised the dominated group, to generate fears about the RPF. Indeed, Burundi was a preferred sanctuary for Rwandan Tutsis when political tensions escalated at home. Tutsi returnees from Burundi were also said to be among RPF die-hards, although RPF members were historically drawn from refugee camps in Uganda. Uganda was also accused by Hutu Power of attempting to recreate an empire of Hima (i.e. "Hamitic") people which would include Uganda, Rwanda, Burundi and parts of Kenya and Zaire.

For their part, Hutus developed ties to their own communities in Tanzania and Zaire, where they sought refuge as the situation required. The planned nature of the exodus in mid-1994 from Rwanda to both countries reinforced the suspicion that these represented bases for a potential two-front offensive to retake power. Initial forays back into Rwanda by Hutu militia in late 1994 and early 1995 lent credence to the suspicion. At the time, the Hutu population in the major camps in Tanzania and Zaire remained under the control of RwAF and Hutu Power militias.

Interconnections between Rwandan forces and the militaries of other countries were also apparent. The French-trained RwAF could rely on assistance from Zaire, whose President Mobutu Sese Seko provided aid to his Rwandese counterpart. On the other hand, it was unlikely that Tanzania, a regional power with a strong interest in seeing the Arusha Accords prevail, would back any attempted revenge by Hutu Power. Uganda's President Musuveni, who had reasons for wanting to see Banyarwanda exiles who had fled into Uganda resettled in their country of origin, could probably be counted on to support his former "comrades in arms" as he did in 1990. Yet Burundi, whose army shared a common ethnic origin with most of the RPF, seemed unlikely to help the new Rwandan authorities in case of a Hutu Power attack.

Thus the Rwandan military forces within the country in 1994 and those scattered around the region illuminated the complexity of the issues to be faced. At the time of the April events, there were some 55 000 in the then-Rwandan army including the Presidential Guard and the militias, and some 17 000 in the opposition forces. By the end of the year, the former Hutu army numbered some 15 000 in exile in Zaire and probably about 10 000 in the *Opération Turquoise* safe zone. At that time, the army of the new regime itself totalled an estimated 25 000.

Numbers aside, however, Rwandan forces — governmental and insurgent, uniformed militaries and more informal militias, armed personnel outside the country and within — had histories and ideologies, agendas and grievances to be reckoned with. They represented players — and complicating factors — in the international effort to provide humanitarian assistance and protection to the region's civilian populations. International military forces would need to assess their strengths and weaknesses. International humanitarian activities would need to take these forces into account as well.

An Overview of the 1994 Humanitarian Effort

The downing of the presidential plane on April 6, 1994 unleashed a concatenation of events which, for analytical purposes, may be grouped into three broad periods. The period of **genocide** spanned the three months from April 6 through the take-over of the RPF in Kigali in early July. The period of **mass exodus**, a stretch of roughly six weeks beginning in mid-July, featured the flight of persons, many of them already displaced within Rwanda, across the borders into neighbouring countries, primarily Zaire. The period of **reconstruction**, which began roughly in September and continued haltingly through the end of the year and into 1995, encompassed efforts by the new regime to establish its authority, restore basic services, and encourage people's return to their homes. Each period had its own humanitarian challenges and international military involvement[10].

As of mid-October 1994 when the authors carried out on-site research in the region, the Rwandan emergency had been largely stabilized. The human upheaval had been extraordinarily massive, even for a country and region with a history of recurrent tension, violence, and displacement. In the six months since the outbreak of violence, genocide by the Hutu government and associated military elements had claimed at least half-million lives, with some estimates placing the figure as high as one million. The victims were largely Tutsis, although moderate Hutus were also killed. Others had died in the civil war before it ended in victory by the Tutsi-dominated Rwandese Patriotic Front (RPF).

Of Rwanda's estimated pre-April population of about 8 million, some 2 million fled genocide and civil war into neighbouring Zaire, Tanzania, Uganda, and Burundi. The initial upheaval saw Rwandans cross into Tanzania on April 28 at the rate of some 10 000 per hour; the two-day total was placed at some 500 000, many of whom sought shelter in the refugee camp at Benaco. The April-May wave was followed by an even more massive refugee flow in July as advancing RPF troops consolidated their hold on the country, took the capital of Kigali, declared a unilateral cease-fire July 20, and installed a new government the following day.

On July 14-15 alone, some 1 million persons, mostly Hutus, crossed into Zaire at Goma fearing reprisals by the advancing Rwandese Patriotic Army in what was described as "the largest and swiftest mass exodus of people" in recent memory. At about the same time, some 200 000 Rwandans crossed into Zaire at Bukavu and a similar number into Burundi. In September, the UN tallied 2 129 200 Rwandans in neighbouring contries: 1 332 200 in Zaire, 510 000 in Tanzania, 277 000 in Burundi, and 10 000 in Uganda (UNREO, 1994a). With some 2 million refugees and about 1.8 million internally displaced persons, almost half of all Rwandans were uprooted by the events of 1994. Virtually no Rwandan family remained unaffected.

Overwhelmed by the crisis during the genocide and mass exodus, the international community by October 1994 seemed better prepared for future eventualities. During the intervening six months, aid supply lines had been re-established, although food inventories in some warehouses were adequate for only a few days. Basic health and sanitation needs were being met; vaccines for livestock as well as for people were being provided in some areas. Relief efforts were giving priority to seed distribution for fall planting. More adequate data was becoming available on the needs and movements of refugees and the internally displaced. Way stations had been established to assist their return home. A degree of normalcy was evident.

By October, co-ordination of relief activities was also going reasonably well. The UN Department of Humanitarian Affairs (DHA), which on April 9 had constituted a situation room in Geneva and an emergency relief team, on April 18 established the United Nations Rwanda Emergency Office (UNREO), with support from UNDP and involvement of other UN agencies. UNREO was based in Nairobi until early August, when it moved to Kigali. With offices early in the crisis in Goma, Zaire, Bujumbura, Burundi, and Kabale, Uganda as well, UNREO by September was opening field offices within Rwanda at Byumba, Cyangugu, Gikongoro, Gisenyi, and Kibungo. The operation received an innovative boost from a Swedish Support Team, which provided a self-contained package of communications and administrative support that allowed UNREO as soon as the Team set up shop to become the nexus of Kigali-based humanitarian activities.

In October, UNREO was convening twice-weekly meetings in Kigali that were well attended by personnel from UN humanitarian and peace-keeping agencies, NGOs, donor governments, and Rwandan government officials. The sessions provided useful updates on recent developments, reviewed unmet needs, and served as a venue for sharing programme initiatives and common concerns. Working groups in health, nutrition, and sanitation drew together interested parties for detailed discussions. UN personnel also conferred regularly among themselves in separate meetings, as did NGOs.

UNREO also provided a productive forum for briefings of, and discussions with, high-level visitors and delegations. On a trip to the region in October, Ireland's President Mary Robinson was given an overview of the situation by agency representatives and shared her own perceptions. The meeting was attended by a standing-room-only group of international military and humanitarian personnel and Rwandan government and NGO officials.

In earlier emergencies, DHA had concentrated on information collection and dissemination in Geneva and New York. In the Rwanda crisis, DHA efforts achieved greater effectiveness on the ground and a new level of respect among aid agencies, donors, and host government authorities. A focal point of its co-ordinating efforts involved not only UNAMIR but also the US military, which located its civilian-military operations centre for Rwanda on the UNREO premises.

The scale of the international response to the crisis was impressive. The initial UN-consolidated appeal, launched April 25, 1994 and calling for $11.6 million, was followed by individual appeals by UNHCR, the ICRC, and various NGOs. Of the $590.4 million in resources eventually requested by UN organisations for the latter half of 1994, $423.6 million (71.8 per cent) had been pledged or contributed by October. By November, pledges totalled $539.4 million (91.5 per cent) and the end of the year, $562.7 million (95.3 per cent), unusually high percentages for such appeals.

The total of international resources available for use in the Rwanda crisis, however, was higher still. In addition to the $562.7 million, another $646.9 million was reported to DHA for activities outside the framework of the consolidated appeal. Among the additional funds were costs associated with Operation Support Hope. A total of $1.209 billion was thus available. The grand total, however, may be larger still since, as DHA points out, the $1.209 billion figures reflects only donations reported to DHA "and hence does not encompass all of the funding received by the organisations active in the region"[11].

The order of magnitude of such sums is suggested by comparing them to the total development assistance flows. Early estimates for 1994 placed worldwide ODA at about $50 billion. The conclusion drawn in many quarters — that 2 per cent of ODA was allocated in 1994 to the Rwanda crisis and its aftermath — seems therefore, if anything, too modest a percentage figure.

As of October 1994, the immediate crisis past, international agencies were settling in for the long haul. Many emergency personnel who had arrived in Kigali among the first wave of relief personnel in late July and early August were winding up tours and being replaced by colleagues with reconstruction skills and portfolios. Consultants retained for the short term were giving way to regular agency staffs with ongoing responsibilities. In this particular crisis, aid personnel, particularly within UN ranks, were characterised by a high degree of specialisation: for example, in the problems of unaccompanied children, malaria, and nutrition.

As the scene shifted to reconstruction, it was thus unusual to find people who had been in Rwanda for more than three or four weeks, or for that matter, who had prior experience in the region. Only a few veteran UN humanitarian and peace-keeping personnel dated back to the period of genocide; a few more had been present at the time of the mass exodus. As of early October, 108 NGOs were registered with UNREO, including 11 Rwandan agencies. Some of the more relief-oriented groups were winding up operations and leaving the scene altogether.

Looming over all activities, however, was the ever present issue of insecurity, with ominous rumblings from both outside Rwanda and within. From camps in Zaire and Tanzania, temporary home to tens of thousands of soldiers and militia from the previous Hutu regime, came increasing reports of violence against refugees who sought, or might seek, to return. Even asserting international control of the camps was proving difficult. A UNHCR plan to conduct a census in October was abandoned because the situation was too volatile and the registration process too explosive; the camp population was not tallied until well into 1995.

Insecurity also took its toll on the international relief effort. Reacting to harassment of aid workers, some NGOs withdrew personnel and eventually suspended operations in the Zaire camps altogether. When one NGO opted out in early October, explaining to UNHCR that it was no longer prepared to risk the safety and lives of its staff, UNHCR managed to find another willing to step into the breach and accept the risk. The perilous nature of aid activities was a regular agenda item in co-ordination meetings in Goma and in conversations among international and national staff.

Back in Rwanda, the new authorities by October had arrested and detained some 7 000 people implicated in acts of genocide, some of whom had died while in custody. The regime published a list, complete with photographs, of others also implicated in the killings. In late September, a UN consultant alleged a pattern of fresh killings implicating the new government. The issue proved so sensitive — the charges were strenuously disputed by the authorities — that the study was never released, its accuracy a matter of dispute even within the UN's own ranks. The discovery in early October of newly laid mines in the Rwandan capital underscored the fragility of security and the tenuousness of international presence and activities.

Reflecting pressures within and outside Rwanda, the total number of refugees who had returned to their homes as of mid-October stood at well under 100 000, or less than 5 per cent of the number that had fled. In fact, more people were still fleeing Rwanda than returning, becalming an international resettlement effort for which careful preparations had by then been made. Having been taken by surprise by the earlier outflows, agencies now sought to assist people back to their homes, only to find few takers.

Serious uncertainties loomed about the future. "We can't tell whether we are now in the eye of the storm", commented one aid worker from the European Community's Humanitarian Office, "or have come through the storm altogether". Those who were most knowledgeable about the history of the Great Lakes region and most informed about the current political tensions seemed to be most pessimistic about what the future might hold.

Two contrasting realities were evident as attention shifted from assisting the uprooted to reversing the exodus. The first was the positive attitude of the new regime toward international presence and assistance. Realising the need to re-establish confidence both among Hutus and the international donor community, Rwandan officials welcomed international involvement — and oversight — in the formidable task of reconstruction. In sharp contrast to other governments in Africa and elsewhere which have resisted such monitoring, the regime pledged to grant to as many human rights watchdogs as the UN wished to deploy "free and unrestricted access to all parts of Rwanda to conduct their work". A total of 147 monitors were requested and pledged, one for each of the country's administration jurisdictions.

The second reality, however, was the lethargy of the international response. Of the 147 human rights monitors promised in August, only 26 were on the scene as of mid-October — all of them in Kigali, none of them stationed in outlying areas where serious abuses were said to be taking place. Investigators had yet to begin the painstaking task of compiling evidence for an international genocide tribunal, urged by many relief and human rights groups and approved by the Security Council several weeks later. Discussions of accountability for war crimes were complicated by Hutu insistence that actions committed since 1990 by Tutsis in the civil war be scrutinised along with post-April 6 bloodletting[12].

Meanwhile, the machinery of government was in shambles: offices in disrepair, the national treasury empty, civil servants unpaid, administrative connections to the hinterlands severed. Having provided substantial levels of emergency assistance during the exodus, most donor governments were holding back on major infusions of funding for reconstruction until the new regime had established its credibility. "Failure by the international community to support the formation of a functioning government and the regeneration of civil society adds to the risk of authoritarianism", a UN report warned (Donini and Niland, 1994)[13].

The picture in October was of a tangled skein of interconnected problems that the government was seeking to address with mixed results and an indifferent level of outside assistance. The prevailing consensus was that positive changes were not being introduced quickly enough to avoid a recurrence of violence. In the absence of prompt progress in human rights and in re-establishing a functioning government, it seemed likely that, in the words of one seasoned relief expert, "the situation could get ugly again".

The picture at year's end was no more reassuring. In requesting funds for 1995, the UN Consolidated Appeal stressed what remained to be done rather than what had already been accomplished. The largest group of returnees to their homes in Rwanda were not those displaced by the events of 1994 but some 600 000 long-term refugees who had fled the country in earlier decades. Of the 2 million refugees who had crossed into neighbouring countries since April, only an estimated

200 000 were thought to have returned. Of the 1.8 million internally displaced, some 147 000 had received international help in returning to their communes, many of them as the government moved late in the year to close their camps (UNDHA, 1995a)[14].

The major issues of international concern at year's end were twofold: the continuing insecurity in the camps outside Rwanda, and, within the country, the slowness of the government in re-establishing the due process of law, including the protection of the human rights of all citizens. The absence of decisive progress in either respect, compounded by an evident falling off of international interest and support, made the situation appear bleak.

With respect to camp security, Hutu military and militia personnel in the Zaire camps late in the year had tightened their hold, effectively deterring those who wished to return to Rwanda from doing so. None of several plans for reasserting international control of the camps had been implemented, including separating Hutu military elements from civilians and giving the task of maintaining order to UNAMIR or outside military contingents. In late January, the Secretary-General announced that none of sixty governments contacted had been willing to provide troops for camp security purposes. By then, a number of aid groups had suspended activities, arguing that feeding programmes were simply fortifying Hutus for a seizure of power and rekindled killings.

Progress was also slow in reinvigorating government and civil society. UN officials spoke of a "growing lag" in the ability of the new regime to reassert effective authority and meet the needs of its civilian population. Government departments were still struggling to resume operations, although stopgap payments to civil servants in selected ministries had been arranged. The basic infrastructure of government — typewriters, telephones, consumable supplies — was still largely lacking. Prison conditions remained degrading, with a growing toll of daily deaths of detainees continuing to undermine government credibility. If a secure future for Rwanda required the orderly review of allegations of participation in the genocide — and there were those who doubted that such would ever be possible — the judicial system showed no signs of readying itself for the challenge.

At the same time, criticism by the new authorities and some aid agencies themselves of the lethargic pace of outside assistance continued. Of the 147 human rights monitors pledged, only 80 were in place by year's end. Yet in a demonstration of the connection between international presence and the incentive to return, human rights personnel were reporting a higher rate of resettlement in those areas in which they had been deployed. Meanwhile, help from outside to train an interim civilian police force, restaff the criminal justice system, and restart judicial processes was materialising slowly. A modest increase in NGO presence was reported, with 134 agencies operating within Rwanda in November (UNDHA, 1995a).

Thus at the close of a year characterised by horrific genocide, mass exodus, and languishing reconstruction, Rwanda's devastation remained enormous, its unfinished business staggering. "With 13 per cent of Rwanda's resident population dead, 2 million living as refugees in neighbouring countries, half a million displaced within the country, and 150 000 children orphaned or left on their own", a UN document observed, "the Rwandese people are in a state of shock and almost total deprivation"[15].

In fact, the nation seemed entrapped in a vicious cycle. "Without effective and rapid rehabilitation, there can be no reconciliation", observed the Special Representative of the Secretary-General, "and without reconciliation, the need for humanitarian assistance can only increase as the number of refugees and displaced is likely to grow with the persistence of tension and conflict". Surveying the situation at the turn of the year, he observed ominously that "The recent violent incidents in Rwanda's border areas are a strong reminder of the potential conflict which still prevails"[16].

An Overview of International Military Involvement

Into the historical, political, and humanitarian context described above were inserted outside military forces. Their contribution to the international response to the Rwandan emergency was notable in the diversity of the national contingents involved, the variety of their terms of reference and relationships to UNAMIR, and the array of tasks performed. This final section of Chapter 3 sketches the broad outlines of activities by international military forces described in greater detail in Chapters 4-7.

During the period under review — from the eruption of the emergency in April 1994 through the end of that year — the most durable and sustained military presence, although not always the most numerous, was provided by UNAMIR, a UN peace-keeping initiative. Authorised in October 1993 under Chapter VI of the UN Charter, UNAMIR's original task was to monitor implementation of the August 1993 Arusha Accords. With the advent of the violence in April 1994, UNAMIR sought to provide assistance and protection within the limits of its 2 548 military personnel, a number soon reduced by the Security Council to 270.

With Resolution 918 on May 17, 1994, the Security Council launched UNAMIR II with an expanded mandate and approved troop strength of 5 500, although that number was not reached until October 1994. Troops were provided by Argentina, Australia, Austria, Bangladesh, Belgium, Canada, Congo, Ecuador, Egypt, Fiji, Ghana, Malawi, Mali, Nigeria, Pakistan, the Russian Federation, Senegal, Tanzania, Togo, Tunisia, the United Kingdom, Uruguay, and Zimbabwe.

UNAMIR evolved over time. In the period from April 1994 onward, its activities included deploying military observers and conducting regular patrols, protecting minority populations and aid personnel, providing administrative and security support for humanitarian activities, and assisting in the transport and distribution of relief supplies. As the security situation improved and with the arrival of larger numbers of humanitarian personnel in August and September, UNAMIR shifted to a predominantly back-up role. UNAMIR included civilian as well as military personnel, numbering some 100 in early October. In all, UNAMIR personnel were drawn from some 26 countries.

Among UN peace-keeping missions, UNAMIR was unusual in that it had several units — contingents from the United Kingdom and Canada with medical specialisiation — whose full-time tasks involved providing assistance to civilian populations and to humanitarian assistance organisations. As in other peace-keeping operations, other UNAMIR troops — the Australians are an example — carried out such activities either as an offshoot of their principal tasks or in their off-hours. All activities associated with UNAMIR took place within Rwanda proper.

International military troops were present in a second framework separate and distinct from the UN peace-keeping presence. That was provided in the form of initiatives taken by the French and US governments. On June 23-24, France deployed some 2 500 troops in *Opération Turquoise*. Operating from a base in Goma, they established a security zone in the south-west part of Rwanda providing protection for a largely Hutu population fleeing the advancing troops of the Rwandan Patriotic Front. A month later, 3 000 US troops took part in Operation

Support Hope. They provided water purification and logistics support in Goma and operated an airlift of relief supplies into and within the region. The French left on schedule August 22, US troops departed as planned by the end of September.

Although both undertakings had the blessing of the UN Security Council, neither was under UN command or control. *Opération Turquoise* was primarily a security initiative, although containing some humanitarian elements; Operation Support Hope, a purely humanitarian effort without a security component. Both worked supportively *vis-à-vis* UNAMIR; the aid activities of the US troops were, over time, part of a larger complement of military support services orchestrated by UNHCR.

The service packages organised by UNHCR, in fact, constituted the third framework within which international military assets were contributed to the Rwanda crisis. Although their contributions were less attention getting at the time than French or American activities and remain less widely known a year later, troops from Australia, Canada, Germany, Ireland, Israel, Japan, the Netherlands, and New Zealand were an essential element in the larger responses by the international community.

Military contingents from each country carried out activities according to service packages negotiated by their governments with UNHCR. The tasks performed in various locations included airport services, logistics base services, road services and road security, site preparation, provision of domestic fuel, sanitation facilities, water management, and airhead management. Governments also responded to a UNHCR appeal for health items, with their troops themselves involved in setting up and providing emergency medical services. Contributions in the form of non-military assets were also solicited.

The UNHCR-associated activities took place during the period between mid-July and the end of 1994, both within Rwanda and outside. An alternative to committing troops to the tougher security tasks within the UNAMIR framework, the UNHCR association was attractive to many governments, particularly its stress on high visibility humanitarian duties, lessened exposure to danger, and undiluted national command and control authority. In short, the service package approach is one of the several innovative elements in the Rwanda crisis and perhaps the most likely to be replicated in the future.

The world's response to the Rwandan crisis was unique in the scale and multiplicity of military assets brought to bear on humanitarian need. Some of the military personnel were uniformed and armed; others were neither. Some took their orders from the UN, others from their own defence ministries. Some were contributed at no cost to the UN; others were reimbursed for services rendered, whether by their defence departments or aid co-operation ministries. The array of military assets involved made the Rwanda response something of a laboratory for various configurations and approaches.

From a functional standpoint, military assets — whether UNAMIR troops, UNHCR-associated troops, or the more stand-alone initiatives of the French and US — made three major kinds of contributions. First, troops worked to foster a protective framework of overall stability within which civilian populations were protected and humanitarian activities carried out. Second, they supported those activities with logistics, personnel, and security counsel. Third, they carried out relief activities themselves.

The activities of the military evolved over time. During the genocide period, when humanitarian organisations for reasons of security had largely left the field, troops worked closely with the aid personnel who remained in Rwanda, tackling a variety of aid activities themselves. During the mass exodus, soldiers assumed a range of aid tasks both within Rwanda and across its borders. As the agencies became better able to manage the crisis in Zaire and with the return of humanitarian personnel to Rwanda to assist in reconstruction, the tasks of the miltary in the humanitarian sphere became more limited, with a reduced number of soldiers involved and more assistance being provided on a behind-the-scenes basis.

If the activities of the military expanded to fill a humanitarian gap early on, there was by the end of 1994 a clear winding down of military involvement. Following the French and American departures in August and September, the UNHCR-associated Canadian troops left October 15, the British UNAMIR contingent a month later. Japanese troops, deploying for the first time in Goma in early October, stayed through year's end. UNAMIR troops as a whole stayed on following the extensions of their mandate on November 30 through June 9, 1995, at which point their mandate was extended, presumably for a final time, until December 8, 1995.

In short, the world's soldiers, having been a major part of a dramatic rescue effort during the mass exodus, were less needed in high-visibility roles following the arrival of the traditional humanitarian organisations and the tapering off of the violence. They were conspicuous by their relative absence, both early in 1994, when they might have prevented the worst of the genocide, and later in 1994 and thereafter, when a lack of security in the camps imperilled refugees and aid personnel alike.

Looking back at the experience, it is clear that the international community's response to the Rwanda crisis relied initially upon a then familiar peace-keeping operation. When the situation outran the ability of UNAMIR to address, first France and then the United States became involved in high-visibility initiatives, reflecting a post-Cold War pattern of major powers asserting leadership in crises of particular interest. Eventually, a new vehicle was devised which enlisted the participation of national military assets in a multilaterally orchestrated response to the crisis.

An analysis of the multiple contributions of this array of military actors to various aspects of the overall humanitarian efforts forms the core of this volume. The activities of UN troops is reviewed in Chapter 4, of French troops in *Opération Turquoise* in Chapter 5, and of US troops in Operation Support Hope in Chapter 6, and of other national contingents in Chapter 7. The activities and analysis seeks to shed light on the broader issues of the use of military personnel, to which the narrative returns in Chapter 8.

Notes

1. See also Marc Sommers (1994), "Healing Rwanda's Nose War", *St. Petersburg (Florida) Times*, August.

2. See also Nahimana, 1993, who argued that a unified Rwanda under Tutsi dominantion was achieved only in 1931. Nahimana was an RTLM speaker accused of having called for the assassination of Tutsis.

3. The Joint Evaluation, scheduled for publication in early 1996, contains a detailed review of the historical background of the crisis, co-ordinated by the Swedish-based Nordic Africa Institute.

4. For distinctions between humanitarian intervention and rescue operations of nationals abroad as an exercise in self-defence, Akehurst, 1986. On armed intervention for the protection of national abroad, Tanca, 1993; Sicilianos, 1990.

5. The retreating RwAF apparently fired mortar rounds into Goma at a time when it contained many Hutus who had fled from Rwanda. The purpose of the shelling was apparently to frighten the refugee population and instill fear of the RPF, who were blamed for the attacks. French soldiers subsequently confirmed the RwAF strategy.

6. See also Robert M. Press, "Rwandans Speak of Openness to Reconciliation", *Christian Science Monitor*, Aug. 17, 1994. Press notes that General Rusatira and some of the other officers, having signed a declaration opposing the killings in April, did so again in July. Rescued by French troops from fellow Hutus unhappy with their stance, they returned to Kigali in late July. Of his decision to return, Rusatira said, "My example can help others. What do farmers have to fear if I, a general, am here?"

7. For example, the report of the UN Commission of Experts notes that in a radio broadcast April 19, President Theodore Sindikubabo called for the killing of "accomplices" in Butaré. UN Document S/1994/1405, Paras. 80 and 85.

8. Interview with the authors, Kigali, October 10, 1994. On August 28, 1995, Prime Minister Twagiramungu, the Minister of Internal Affairs and three other ministers, including the Minister of Justice; all of them Hutus, resigned. According to Rwandan officials interviewed by the authors, their resignaiton does not alter the political or ethnic balance since they were replaced by other MDR members.

9. By January 1995, only 60 NGOs had signed the agreement, while those reluctant to do so faced problems. The French NGO *Equilibre's* trucks and material were seized and a dozen of its 25 expatriate drivers expelled. The drivers of the NGO *Solidarités* were also forced to leave Rwanda, since local drivers were to be given preference. To preclude seizure of its trucks, the NGO *Atlas* terminated operations, withdrawing following the accusation of collusion with *Interahamwe* rather than trying to persuade the government of its good faith.

10. Given the welter of events that took place in 1994, a framework of phases that is fully satisfactory is difficult to devise. The time periods used here may be somewhat misleading insofar as already in April a large-scale exodus of Rwandans had taken place into neighbouring countries while in September reconstruction efforts were only beginning to take shape. The phases identified do correspond, however, to the sequencing of the international military and humanitarian response to the crisis.

11. Figures are taken from regular Rwanda Financial Updates compiled by DHA and from DHA/Geneva correspondence with the authors.

12. For an elaboration of the complexities of moving toward reconciliation in a polarised and traumatised society, Jonathan Frerichs, "In the Camps, the Rwandan Crisis Goes On", *Christian Century*, Feb. 22, 1995.

13. The Report, based on research conducted in September, identified international resources, along with attention by the new regime to the issues of genocide and property ownership, as essential to the survival of a broad-based government and the eventual return of the country's refugees.

14. The 200 000 estimate includes the period through November 3.

15. UNDP Information Note, "Government of Rwanda to Unveil $764 Million Recovery Plan to Donors in Geneva", January 12, 1995.

16. Shaharyar Khan, "Roundtable Conference for Rwanda", January 20, 1995.

Chapter 4

UN Troops: The United Nations Assistance Mission for Rwanda

The United Nations Assistance Mission for Rwanda (UNAMIR) represented something of a barometer of international engagement in the Rwanda emergency. It was a UN peace-keeping operation: a largely non-coercive military presence made up of national troop contingents provided by concerned UN member states. Its personnel included both unarmed military observers and arms-bearing troops, as well as civilian police and other civilians performing political and diplomatic tasks. Authorised under Chapter VI of the UN Charter, it relied on the consent of the warring parties.

After low-profile beginnings in late 1993 and shaky performance following the outbreak of violence in April 1994, the undertaking slowly gained stability and stature. Toward year's end, the Secretary-General reported that "UNAMIR is firmly in place, as a focal point of the international community's effort in Rwanda, to provide the co-ordinated leadership necessary to move forward the overall process of peace and reconciliation". (UN, 1994c, Para. 46). Its mandate throughout was limited to Rwanda proper.

Building on predecessor UN presence, UNAMIR's evolution reflected sharply divergent views of emerging events and international interests and responsibilities among governments on the Security Council. During the period between April 6 and the end of the year, there were more than twenty Security Council meetings on Rwanda, resulting in eight resolutions. The Chronology in Annex 1 notes key Security Council actions; Annex 2 contains excerpts from resolutions bearing on UNAMIR functions in the humanitarian sphere.

The Immediate Background

In the years preceding the eruption of violence in April 1994, tensions throughout the region had been running high. The October 1990 offensive by the Rwandan Patriotic Front (RPF) led to a wave of displaced persons fleeing from northeastern Rwanda to Kigali and of refugees seeking asylum abroad. With the Uganda-based rebels holding large portions of Rwandan territory, the government called for international help. France and Zaire intervened militarily to back the RwAF, making the war no longer simply an internal matter. From 1992 the Organisation of African Unity (OAU) and from 1993 the United Nations were involved as sponsors of the peace process.

Recent UN political-military involvement began in March 1993 when Secretary-General Boutros Boutros-Ghali dispatched a UN goodwill mission to the area, acting in response to a request from the governments of Rwanda and Uganda for assistance in monitoring their border. The mission also observed the peace talks taking place at the time between the Rwandan government and the Rwandese Patriotic Front.

France, supported by Rwanda itself, was pressing the Security Council to approve a more visible UN peace-keeping presence which would create a buffer zone along the border. RPF forces which had crossed the Rwandan border from Uganda were closing in on Kigali. Less seized with a sense of urgency, the United Kingdom and the United States urged that the UN defer to the OAU. Since July 1992 the OAU had monitored an earlier cease-fire in Rwanda with a 50-man Neutral Military Observer Group from various African countries. A March 1993 cease-fire between the Rwandese government and the RPF pledged that RPF troops would be withdrawn and replaced by an international force organised by the OAU and the UN.

On March 12, 1993, Security Council passed Resolution 812 calling on the Government of Rwanda and the RPF to respect the March 7 Dar-es-Salaam cease-fire agreement, resume negotiations, and allow delivery of humanitarian supplies and the return of displaced persons. In August, the OAU sent a second military observer group, augmented to 130 personnel.

At the urging of the French government, Security Council resolution 866 of June 22, 1993 stepped up the level of UN involvement, authorising creation of the United Nations Observer Mission in Uganda-Rwanda (UNOMUR). Supporters of the initiative prevailed over the United States and others who favoured waiting until the completion of peace negotiations in Arusha. UNOMUR was based in Uganda and monitored the Uganda-Rwanda border to check that no military assistance reached Rwanda.

On August 4, 1993, peace agreements were signed by the Rwandese Government and the RPF in Arusha. Several weeks later, a UN reconnaissance mission visited Rwanda to explore deploying personnel there as well as in Uganda. Based on the findings of the mission, the Secretary-General recommended launching a peace-keeping operation as a contribution "to the establishment and maintenance of a climate conducive to the secure installation and subsequent operation of the transitional Government".

On October 5, 1993 Security Council resolution 872 created the UN Assistance Mission for Rwanda (UNAMIR), to which UNOMUR was administratively attached, its mandate unchanged. UNOMUR itself continued until its termination by resolution 928, approved June 20, 1994. Once its military observer group had been subsumed under the United Nations, the OAU became largely invisible (UN Dept. of Public Information, 1994).[1]

Terms of Engagement and Activities

UNAMIR was conceived as a peace-keeping presence with responsibilities for monitoring implementation of the Arusha peace agreement, including provisions for holding a national election and establishing a new government. The transitional processes established by the agreement, however, were soon overwhelmed by events, both the genocide and the wresting of power from the Rwandan government by the Rwandan Patriotic Front. In the changed circumstances, UNAMIR activities in the military-security and humanitarian support spheres came to constitute the most significant elements in its work.

Over time UNAMIR's mandate evolved to reflect not only changes in the situation on the ground but also in the political resolve of Security Council members. At the outset, UNAMIR duties included aiding "in the co-ordination of humanitarian assistance activities in conjunction with relief operations"[2]. UNAMIR was also responsible for demobilisation, elections, security, mine clearance, and mine awareness in Rwanda. Its personnel, including troops, civilian policy, military observers, and political officials were drawn from some 26 contributing countries. The size of its ranks throughout 1994 is indicated on Figure 4.1.

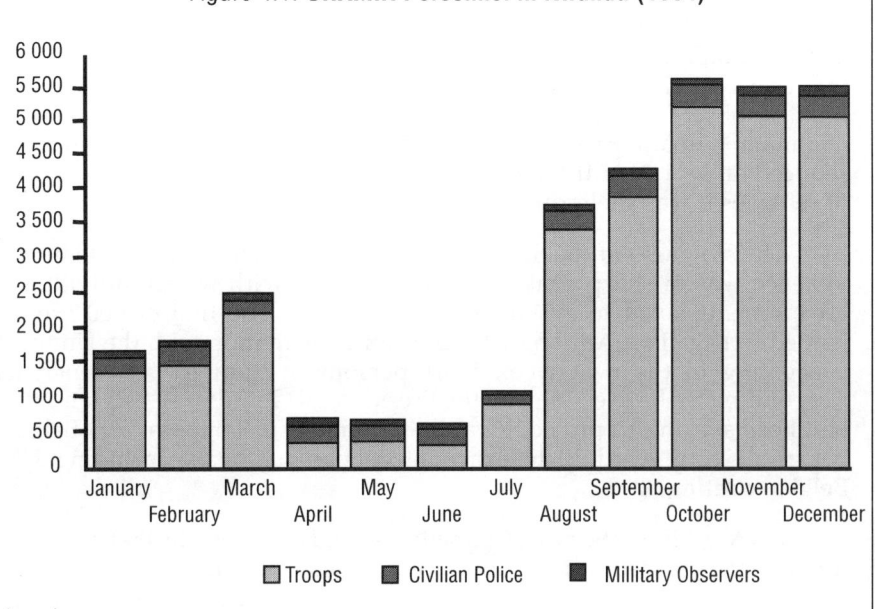

Figure 4.1. **UNAMIR Personnel in Rwanda (1994)**

☐ Troops   ■ Civilian Police   ■ Millitary Observers

Total number
of personnel: (1 614) (2 131) (2 485) (640) (626) (593) (1 077) (3 764) (4 298) (5 645) (5 522) (5 522)

Note: Additional to those tabulated here are civilian UNAMIR personnel, (including the SRSG, humanitarian and reconstruction specialists, and administrative support personnel). Their numbers were generally modest throughout the year, decreasing in April when some were evacuated and augmented later in the year when the security situation improved.

Following the outbreak of violence in Kigali April 6, the Security Council was deeply divided on the best course of action[3]. Nigeria, speaking on behalf of non-aligned nations, favoured expanding UNAMIR's mandate and ranks, as did Russia, the OAU, and France. The United Kingdom favoured reducing UNAMIR presence, maintaining a presence to encourage dialogue. The US initially favoured evacuating UNAMIR troops, although over a period of time came to favour the UK position and eventually supported expansion. Argentina suggested temporarily relocating UNAMIR to a nearby country. Awaiting additional information from the scene, the Security Council did not act until two weeks later on April 21.

On April 14, the UNAMIR Force Commander formulated three options for Secretary-General Boutros Boutros-Ghali. The first was to maintain UNAMIR strength (but not to replace the Belgian contingent, which was about to depart). The second was to reduce UNAMIR strength to 1 000 personnel, with a focus on controlling the airport and key sections of Kigali, supporting relief efforts, and promoting political reconciliation. The third was to cut back to only 200 personnel, maintaining a presence at the airport and a downtown hotel, and supporting the diplomatic work of the Secretary-General's Special Representative.

A week later, with the situation on the ground far worse and UNAMIR largely overwhelmed by events, the Force Commander himself and the Secretary-General's Special Representative, backed by the UN Department of Peace-keeping Operations, recommended cutbacks to about 300 (LaRose-Edwards, 1994). Reporting mortar attacks on civilians under UNAMIR protection and on April 19 a direct hit on UNAMIR headquarters, the Secretary-General observed that "The dedicated personnel of UNAMIR, who have performed courageously in dangerous circumstances, cannot be left at risk indefinitely when there is no possibility of their performing the tasks for which they were dispatched"[4].

In Resolution 912 on April 21, the Security Council approved reductions to 270. Evacuation began the next day, with 1 000 UN troops withdrawn during a two-day period. Remaining behind in UNAMIR were 387 troops and 72 UN military observers, whose tasks were to seek to arrange a cease-fire, assist in resuming humanitarian relief operations, and monitor developments. Despite reduced ranks, UNAMIR hoped to provide continued protection to the thousands of refugees it was sheltering.

The slowness of the Security Council to respond to the widening vortex of violence was in sharp contrast to the dispatch with which individual member governments acted to evacuate their nationals. The first of 600 French troops landed in Kigali on April 8, without prior consultation with the United Nations, evacuating in the next week 1 361 persons, including 450 French nationals. Responding to the execution by the Presidential Guard of 10 Belgian soldiers who had been seeking to protect Rwanda's Prime Minister, some 700 Belgian troops began arriving April 10 to evacuate Belgian nationals, including UNAMIR's Belgian contingent.

On April 29, the Security Council reviewed a proposal by the Secretary-General for more forceful action, including an expanded UNAMIR and an upgraded peace-enforcement mandate. On May 9, the Secretary-General suggested augmenting UNAMIR to 5 500 to protect displaced persons and assist humanitarian agencies more adequately. France, New Zealand, and the non-aligned nations, including Rwanda, lobbied for a Chapter VII mandate, which did not require consent of the warring parties and allowed the use of force other than in self-defence to carry out authorised functions. The US called for a smaller and more focused operation under less assertive Chapter VI ground rules.

On May 17, the Security Council approved Resolution 918 authorising an expansion of UNAMIR to 5 500 personnel. Reversing course in the period of less than a month, the Council created a revamped peace-keeping operation that came to be called "UNAMIR II". Its Resolution also called for an end to mass murders and a cease-fire agreement and spelled out the humanitarian aspects of its mission. UNAMIR II was "to contribute to the security and protection of displaced persons, refugees, and civilians at risk in Rwanda [and] provide security and support for the distribution of relief supplies and humanitarian relief operations"[5].

The resolution recognized that "UNAMIR may be required to take action in self-defence against persons or groups who threaten protected sites and populations, United Nations and other humanitarian personnel or the means of delivery and distribution of humanitarian relief". The fact that UN troops were equipped only with light defensive weapons, however, made the expanded use of force unlikely. UNAMIR II was not a peace-enforcement action, although Resolution 918 referenced Chapter VII of the UN Charter as the basis for the arms embargo it imposed on Rwanda.

On June 8, the Security Council approved resolution 925, extending UNAMIR II's mandate until December 9 1994. To UNAMIR's existing responsibilities were added the tasks of establishing and maintaining secure humanitarian areas "where feasible". On November 29, the Security Council passed resolution 965 extending UNAMIR mission until June 9, 1995, which was in turn extended for another six months through November 29, 1995 by resolution 997 on June 9.

UNAMIR's Force Commander through August 1994 was Canadian Major-General Romeo A. Dallaire, who had also headed UNOMUR from July 1993 onward. He was succeeded by a fellow Canadian, Major-General Guy-Claude Toussignant, who served from August 1994 through 1995. The Force Commanders reported to the UN Department of Peace-keeping Operations in New York and, in Rwanda, to the Special Representative of the Secretary-General (SRSG), a civilian responsible for UNAMIR's political and humanitarian-support functions as well. Cameroonian diplomat Jacques-Roger Booh-Booh served as SRSG from late November 1993 until June 1994, when he was replaced Shaharyar M. Khan of Pakistan, who served through 1995.

UNAMIR's mandate thus evolved in response to emerging events on the ground and reflected an expanding set of humanitarian tasks, detailed in the following section. Protection of civilian population and support of humanitarian activities, elements in the earliest mandate of UNAMIR, were elaborated over time in the light of the worsening situation on the ground. However, that the Security Council acted slowly and took a very guarded approach to the authority of the Force Commander and the roles of UNAMIR had a direct bearing on its capacity and performance.

For analytical purposes, UNAMIR activities may be grouped into three separate but related categories. UNAMIR sought to foster a secure environment within which day-to-day life in Rwanda could be resumed, support the activities of humanitarian organisations, and carry out such activities itself. Each is described in the following three sections and assessed thereafter.

Fostering a Secure Environment

UNAMIR began as a classical peace-keeping mission, supervising the Arusha peace agreements. That mission, as Force Commander Dallaire observed, fell "victim of the larger resumption of the conflict, following political decapitation and the subsequent descent into the maelstrom of genocide" (Dallaire, 1996).

UNAMIR's relative weakness was immediately apparent amid the swirl of violence which commenced on April 6 within hours of the shooting down of the presidential plane. By April 8, reported the NGO *Médecins sans frontières* (MSF), "Movement in the streets had become impossible. Thousands of casualties were counted. The MSF hospital was inundated with several hundreds of injured persons, many of them needing surgical treatment"[6]. A number of local MSF staff had already been killed.

Responding to the violence, UNAMIR tried to restore stability and curb the spread of bloodshed and chaos. The Force "consolidated in a few reasonably defendable sites and opened its doors to those who could reach the sites and who sought protection", recalled its Force Commander. UNAMIR also "continued to negotiate cease-fires and truces, and ultimately kept a UN and international community presence throughout this storm of destruction in order not totally to abandon innocent Rwandans to their fate" (Dallaire, 1996).

When the killings started, Tutsis who found themselves in areas controlled by the Rwandan army and Hutus in RPF-controlled areas sought UN protection. UNAMIR threw up protective cordons around the estimated 10 000 civilians sheltered in Kigali's Amahoro stadium, where the peacekeepers were themselves based, and at the King Faisal Hospital. Yet UN troops were not authorised to establish Kigali as a weapon-secure area and even, under duress, were compelled to return seized weapons to their owners. Rather than intervening to protect civilians, UN troops were reduced to requesting, generally without success, the Rwandese *gendarmerie* to do so.

As the violence worsened, UN troops and military observers stationed outside the capital were recalled, reducing UNAMIR's capacity to monitor events there. Although facing increasing difficulties within the city, UNAMIR carried out daily patrols through areas in which no resident UN presence was possible in order to attempt to deter killings by the militias. UN troops protected convoys which transported some 5-6 000 thousand persons to safer locations. After the capture of Kigali by the RPF on July 4, UNAMIR arranged for the return of Tutsis into the city. It also facilitated the safe departure of Hutu civilians and negotiated prisoner-of-war agreements under which Hutu militia members were turned over to the new regime.

UNAMIR's efforts to foster a more secure environment for Rwanda's vulnerable civilians were encouraged and appreciated by humanitarian organisations. In a reflection of the critical choices which UNAMIR faced in the April maelstrom, one of the few UN aid officials present in Kigali urged the Force Commander to give priority to stopping the genocide rather than to protecting aid activities themselves. UNAMIR's contribution in this regard, he said upon reflection, was "indispensable".

Some UNAMIR troops acted with heroism. Senegalese Captain Mbaye Diagne lost his life protecting others (Guichaoua, 1995). General Dallaire played an active personal role in saving lives and reassuring imperilled UN and other international staff. He also alerted his superiors at UN headquarters in New York to the problems encountered, making no secret of how little credibility the UNAMIR mission was able to muster and how little of the necessary assistance it was able to provide.

Also well regarded for his actions was UNAMIR's Ghanaian deputy force commander. "[I]t was his thankless job to spend many hours trying to negotiate cease-fires which would then allow him to evacuate terrified Rwandese hiding from their killers. More than once, he and his troops were almost killed when one side or the other fired on the canvas-covered lorries with their blue flags and red crosses flying, killing helpless women and children who thought they were safe". (McCullum, 1995).

UN troops were clearly overmatched by the situation and altogether unable to head off the blood bath. The Belgian contingent was quickly withdrawn after ten Belgian blue berets, accused of having shot down the presidential plane, had been tortured and killed by Hutu extremists. "This contingent, the best-equipped in UNAMIR and with significant operational experience from Somalia", General Dallaire recalled, "could have become an effective deterrent force had we been given the appropriate mandate and backing" (Dallaire, 1996). Its departure left UNAMIR even less able to rescue imperiled civilians and prevent the spread of violence.

One of the Rwandans who, with his wife and daughter, looked to UNAMIR for protection was Jean Paul Biramvu, a Kigali resident and secretary-general of the human rights coalition CLADHO. On April 7 he went to the school where Belgian UNAMIR troops were based, only to have them, by his account, leave his family and other civilians who were seeking shelter to their fate at the hands of the surrounding militias. Ghanaian UN troops, too, were reported to have passed by while civilians were under duress.

"We wonder what on earth UNAMIR was doing in Rwanda", Biramvu later stated. "They could not even lift a finger to intervene and prevent the death of tens of thousands of innocent people who were being killed under their very noses. We were there, they were there and they could see what was happening in Rwanda. An institution must have the capacity to be effective. But the UN protects no one". To have been effective, he believed, UNAMIR should have had its mandate changed "as soon as the massacres started, to enable them to protect civilians" (Africa Rights, 1994).

Besieged civilians were not alone in their criticisms. The performance of UNAMIR and the United Nations was so inadequate, commented an editorial in the *Times*, that "It is time to ask a simple question: if it cannot respond adequately to carnage of this magnitude, what is the UN for?"[7] The Security Council's decision to pare UNAMIR ranks at a time of desperate need was a focal point of attack. "MSF is indignant at the decision to reduce the peace-keeping force in Rwanda", declaimed a press release April 22, the day after the Council decision. "The reduction of troops to 270 turned the UN intervention into a real farce", observed MSF, urging reconsideration of the decision (MSF, 1994). A UNHCR official, speaking privately, labelled April 21 "a shameful black day in UN history".

Even after the Security Council had reversed itself in mid-May and increased UN troop strength, UNAMIR struggled to keep pace with fast-moving events and the demands placed upon it. Having lambasted the April troop reduction, MSF doubted the effectiveness of the decision to expand UNAMIR presence. "After five weeks of international indifference", it lamented, "the assembly and deployment of UN troops, which could take more than four weeks, may come too late for the thousands of civilians trapped in the country today"[8].

Such fears were indeed borne out by events. Not one of the 19 governments which had committed themselves to provide troops for the stand-by force for such situations proposed by the Secretary-General in his Agenda for Peace of January 1992 came forward to offer them for Rwanda[9]. "Not a single government with the necessary capacity (except for Ghana)", reported the Secretary-General's spokesman Joe B. Sills in August, "offered to provide fully trained and equipped military units"[10]. Indeed, two full months elapsed before UNAMIR began to benefit appreciably from the increased troop strength approved May 17. In mid-June, France justified its proposal to launch *Opération Turquoise* on the grounds that only 500 blue helmets were then in Rwanda and that reinforcements would take at least three months to arrive.

Between mid-July and mid-August, the Ghanaian battalion was reinforced to 520, Australia sent a 75-person medical team, Canada a 289-strong signals unit, the UK a contingent of 225, and Ethiopia 150 blue helmets. After the windup of *Opération Turquoise* in August, UNAMIR II received a 540-person French-speaking African battalion which had served with the French. Yet as of August 15, more than four months after the outbreak of violence, UNAMIR still had only 1 624 troops out of an approved complement of 5 500 (UNREO, 1994c). By the end of October, it had still not reached its full strength. Figure 4.1 depicts UNAMIR ranks month by month through 1994.

Even with commitments in hand, UNAMIR found arranging transport and then training and integrating newcomers a time-consuming process. Some units arrived in Rwanda with "almost nothing". According to P.J.A. Hornsby, UNAMIR's Chief of Support Services, Ethiopian troops came only with vehicles while "160 Malawi troops came out of the clear blue sky with just their rifles. Tunisians popped up with no equipment at all. Fortunately, the French lent those in the FRAFBAT [the French-speaking African battalion] some equipment". The absence of an effective UN military response capacity spurred discussions of the need to create a UN rapid reaction force which would be on call for such emergencies in the future.

UNAMIR's task of fostering a climate of security had civil as well as military dimensions. The original plan was for its Civilian Police (CIVPOL) unit "to maintain liaison with the local civilian authorities on matters relating to public security". In the wake of the collapse of the country's infrastructure, however, police functions were carried out by members of the new Rwandese armed forces.

Those functions, indispensable to establishing confidence in the regime and encouraging a return to normalcy, were particularly sensitive given the fear of reprisal and the need to address issues of personal property and other legal matters in the wake of the violence.

UNAMIR accepted the invitation to train members for what would eventually become the national police force. As of October, 30 UN CIVPOL officers from Ghana, Mali, and Nigeria were thus engaged, with plans to expand the number and the coverage as soon as governments provided additional police observers. While the assistance provided was significant, the pace was disappointing. By mid-November, only ten of the ninety police observers which had been promised had yet to take up their duties (UN, 1994e, Paras. 38-42; UN, 1994c, Paras. 26-29).

In organising for its military and civilian tasks, UNAMIR divided Rwanda into six operational sectors. Five contained roughly 3 600 square kilometres each; the sixth, around Kigali, encompassed about 900. Operations in each of the sectors were carried out under sector commanders accountable to UNAMIR's Force Commander.

Following the recall of UNAMIR personnel to Kigali in April and the evacuation of some from the country altogether, redeployment took time. The contingents involved included in the northeast a Nigerian infantry company, in the north-west a unit from Tunisia, in the southeast Ghanaian and Nigerian contingents, in the south troops from Malawi and Mali, in the city of Kigali an Indian battalion, and in the south-west, following the departure of the French, soldiers from Ghana, Ethiopia, Zambia, Chad, Congo, Guinea-Bissau, Niger, and Senegal. Some 320 military observers from a score of countries were stationed throughout the country.

The security that UNAMIR was able to provide was uneven. When UN soldiers took over from French troops exiting the south-west in August, the local population initially did not trust the Blue Berets. Over time, however, Rwandans recognized that the zone initially protected by the French would remain safe under the UN and some who had fled into Zaire after the French withdrawal returned to Rwanda.

UNAMIR functioned as an intermediary between the departing French troops and the new government, managing well the transition in a volatile political situation. Under UNAMIR's umbrella, the Kigali regime in early September installed prefects in the towns of Kibuyé, Gikongoro, and Cyangugu and over time deployed troops throughout the sector, first at platoon strength and later augmented to companies and battalions. UNAMIR also collected weapons from troops in the former RwAF who were being encouraged to enlist in the new army. By early October, the Secretary-General reported that "The gradual establishment of the Government's authority in the south-west zone has now been completed without incident" (UN, 1994e, Para. 26).

Over time, UNAMIR established itself in other sectors as well. Six months after the April events, UNAMIR spokesperson Captain Stéphane Grenier noted that UN troops were "deployed to each of the sectors in sufficient numbers to ensure the necessary levels of security, stability, and support required by the UN normalisation process currently under way to assist the present government in rebuilding the country".

UNAMIR also enhanced the climate of security in indirect ways by providing effective liaison with international military forces not attached to the UN. During *Opération Turquoise*, for example, UNAMIR maintained regular contact with a team of French officers in Kigali and facilitated communication between them and RPF leaders, including Major-General Paul Kagamé. UNAMIR also shared information on the security situation with the Japanese military contingent in Goma later in the year.

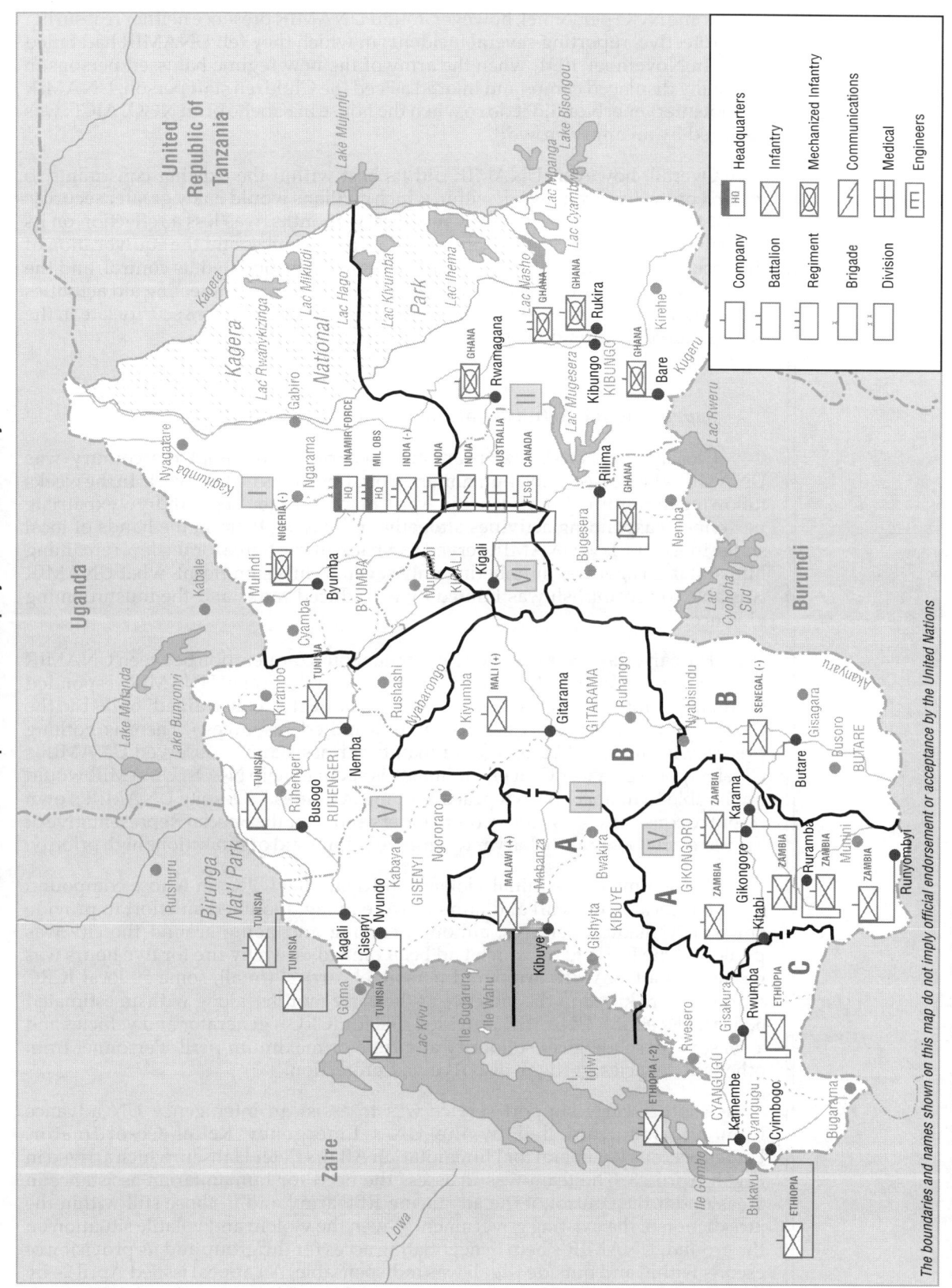

UNAMIR Sectors of Operation and Deployment as of 31 May 1995

Some NGO personnel, however, found UNAMIR presence neither reassuring nor protective, reporting several incidents in which they felt UNAMIR had failed them. In November 1994, when the army of the new regime harassed persons in internally displaced camps and injured a Feed the Children staff person, UNAMIR did not intervene. Nor did it do so when the house in Kibeho of an NGO, AICF, was besieged by an angry crowd[11].

Overall, however, UNAMIR did its best within the existing constraints to foster a protective framework within which civilians would enjoy greater security. That it failed to do so, particularly in the early months, was less a reflection on its personnel than on the chaotic nature of the circumstances and the equivocation of the Security Council. As time passed, the regime consolidated its control, and the situation on the ground stabilized, UNAMIR shifted from protecting aid activities to facilitating their implementation, although a recurrence of insecurity late in the year required its attention as well.

Supporting the Activities of Humanitarian Organisations

Closely connected with promoting security throughout the country was UNAMIR's task of assisting humanitarian organisations in their work. In the weeks following the outbreak of violence in April, many aid agencies withdrew expatriate personnel, suspending activities altogether or leaving them in the hands of local staffs. In April-May, UNAMIR served as a back-up resource for the few remaining humanitarian agencies, numbering only seven. While significant, what UNAMIR was able to accomplish was limited by its reduced ranks and the mushrooming violence.

The early days were marked by spontaneous co-operation between UNAMIR and aid groups. With only a handful of NGOs on the scene, UNAMIR responded to their various requests quickly and effectively, constrained only by the deteriorating circumstances in Kigali and limited resources. "There is nothing precisely in UNAMIR budget for humanitarian assistance", observed UNAMIR's Chief Support Services Officer. "If money is spent to help NGOs, UNAMIR would not be able to finance its own peace-keeping activities." Despite UNAMIR's own resource constraints, its Force Commanders and later the Special Representative of the Secretary-General Shaharyar Khan gave helping aid organisations high priority.

At the time of the initial violence in Kigali, the ICRC, in whose compound some 600 local ICRC staff and families were living, mounted an effort to provide emergency medical services, although coming and going around the city was perilous. One ICRC team which had been pinned down by fire for five hours was rescued by a UNAMIR armoured personnel carrier. (In all, some 50 local ICRC workers were killed in the violence of the early months, along with an estimated 60 local UN staff.) UNAMIR provided fuel for ICRC's generator and vehicles and a sense of pyschological solidarity at a time of maximum peril. Personnel from other aid agencies in Kigali also received protection.

Another early support service was to assist an interagency UN advance humanitarian team, led by the UN's Emergency Relief Co-ordinator, Under-Secretary-General for Humanitarian Affairs Peter Hansen, which arrived in Kigali April 23. The team was to assess the need for humanitarian assistance in areas under the control of the advancing RPF army and in those still within the jurisdiction of the existing government. Given the violent and volatile situation on the ground, UNAMIR's help in negotiating acces for the group and its provision of escorts within and outside Kigali was indispensable. An appeal issued April 24 by DHA based on the team's findings requested $11.6 million for an initial five-week period.

On May 2, UNAMIR provided a military escort for UNICEF staff and vehicles distributing "high-protein biscuits, medical supply kits, soap and jerry cans to some 4 500 persons at a school and three religious institutions in a previously unreached district of Kigali where many militia have been active"[12]. Relief officials reported that the presence of UN troops reduced the danger to aid workers, whose activities were being carried out "at great personal risk"[13]. Major Don MacNeil, a Canadian soldier who served as Operations Officer in UNAMIR's humanitarian cell throughout this period, estimated that during the initial hundred days, fully 25 per cent of UNAMIR's total budget was directed to providing support for humanitarian organisations[14].

UNAMIR was less successful in evacuating UN staff, although for reasons not entirely of its own making. While UNAMIR had responsibility for evacuating UN personnel, the task of drawing up a plan for doing so rested with UNDP. In early April, that plan had yet to be finalised, with the result that individual UN staff lacked instructions on what to do and where to congregate in an emergency.

Expatriate aid workers in Kigali, unable to contact other UN staff or UNAMIR, were hard pressed to protect themselves or their local counterparts as house-to-house searches and killings proceeded. UN staff outside of the capital were even more out of touch. When a UNAMIR-escorted evacuation from Kigali to Nairobi was finally organised, Rwandese national staff of UN organisations were removed by force at roadblocks and killed.

As the situation stabilized over time, the presence of UNAMIR personnel, civilian and military alike, had an even more positive effect on the ability of aid agencies to function. One indicator was the observation of UNAMIR Force Commander Tousignant in October that in the southeast sector where UN soldiers were fewest, there was also a comparative dearth of NGOs. Aid workers confirmed that the presence of, and security provided by, outside military forces did play a role in their decisions about where to site their aid activities.

Throughout Rwanda as a whole, the security situation improved during August and September, a development credited perhaps too facilely by the Secretary-General to the "rapid reinforcement of UNAMIR in early August" (UN, 1994e, Para. 30). By early October, when UNAMIR strength was at 4 270 of 5 500 authorised personnel, he reported that, "As stability in Rwanda improves, emphasis in UNAMIR is shifting from purely military security-related tasks to the support of humanitarian operations aimed at assisting the population in need and facilitating the return of refugees and displaced persons to their homes" (UN, 1994e, Para. 32).

That progression continued well into 1995. Improvement in the security situation decreased the need for physical protection of humanitarian convoys and allowed UNAMIR to devote more attention to other forms of support for the work of humanitarian organisations. For their part, the aid groups themselves were able to devote more attention to co-ordinating their activities with each other and with UNAMIR. It took some time, however, for co-ordination problems to be sorted out.

Within ten days of the outbreak of violence, UNAMIR created a humanitarian assistance cell with a complement of about six officers. On April 18, the UN Department of Humanitarian Affairs (DHA), which co-ordinates UN work in complex emergencies, established a Rwanda Emergency Office (DHA/UNREO), initially in Nairobi. UNDP, whose resident representative generally functions as the senior in-country representative of the UN system, also assumed a co-ordinating role. Other UN operational agencies such as UNHCR and UNICEF co-ordinated activities in their own sectors. It was not until at least August, however — fully four months into the crisis — that the multiple players with co-ordination mandates established a division of labour between and among them. Some major problems between UNAMIR and aid groups were still being addressed in November, as indicated below.

Over time, military, political, and humanitarian actors came to understand each other better. UNAMIR became an integral part of a more co-ordinated response. Its representatives attended the twice-weekly co-ordinating meetings hosted by DHA/UNREO. UN military personnel gave regular updates on information gained from patrols, including recent incidents and emerging patterns of tension. NGOs and other humanitarian organisations "reciprocated by briefing my Force on1996 security risks in specific localities", General Dallaire recalled (Dallaire, 1996). UNAMIR secunded to UNREO a liaison officer who helped facilitate the processing of NGO requests for UNAMIR assistance. UNAMIR staff also participated in various UNREO work groups in sectors such as water and sanitation.

In a co-ordination meeting in Kigali on October 14, for example, UNAMIR alerted aid organisations to the discovery of three mines within Kigali city limits. Whether the mines were newly laid, as claimed by the UN troops, or newly uncovered through the action of the rains, as claimed by the government, was unclear. Coming at a time of relative tranquillity, the news spurred efforts among aid groups to improve radio communications and to give contingency and evacuation plans more serious attention.

A good example of collaboration was a joint operation mounted in mid-August in the town of Ruhango, 80 kilometres south of Kigali. Activities at a centre for unaccompanied children involved provision of oral rehydration salts by UNICEF, supplementary feeding organised by the NGO Concern, and World Food Programme rations transported by UNAMIR. Regular visitors at the centre included Canadian military personnel who, in their spare time, supplied a generator to operate the centre's water pump and raised funds through their families and other contacts in Canada to meet other needs[15].

Improvements in collaboration were evident in relations between UNAMIR and UNHCR, the agency responsible for facilitating the return of refugees to Rwanda from outside the country. "At the beginning", commented a UNHCR field officer, "co-operation was quite chaotic because neither did UNAMIR II know about UNHCR's mandate nor was UNHCR aware of the evolution of UNAMIR's mission". Over time, the interaction became more productive, particularly as "the humanitarian burden" of UNAMIR activities shifted "from relief-effort protection to massive relief delivery".

While UNAMIR did not have a specific mandate extending beyond the borders of Rwanda, it kept a close eye on developments there. By October 1994, insecurity in the refugee camps in Zaire and Tanzania had become a major problem as pressure by Hutu political and military leaders in the camps slowed the flow of refugees back into Rwanda, whose safety UNAMIR was to protect once they returned. Such pressure also undercut the security and the work of aid officials in the camps.

In early October, a UNAMIR technical team went to Zaire as part of a joint Zairean government/UN working group studying the situation. The team sought to determine the conditions, including security guarantees and elections, under which Hutu political and military leaders in exile would be prepared to return to Rwanda and to allow others to return. The team also reviewed more distant sites within Zaire to which troublesome leaders might be temporarily relocated.

One of the proposals was an expansion of UNAMIR's mandate beyond territorial Rwanda. However, UNAMIR officials in Kigali and the Secretary-General himself had serious reservations. Ensuring security in the camps, given the likely resistance of the political-military leadership, would have required acquiescence by the Zairean authorities, a Chapter VII mandate, additional resources, and a different configuration of UN forces — each of which, UN authorities suspected, would not be readily forthcoming. UNAMIR involvement in Zaire might also create confusion with its existing mandate, which was limited to Rwandan territory. The security needs in the camps were not systematically addressed until the following year, as indicated in Chapter 9, and then, paradoxically, by UNHCR rather than UNAMIR.

Humanitarian activities received particular support from UNAMIR in the area of logistics. UNAMIR managed an airlift for relief supplies and personnel, maintained vehicles for aid organisations, and transported returnees home. The airlift was an outgrowth of a small operation already in place at the time of the April events to supply the needs of the peace-keeping mission. During the genocide, the airlift was expanded to transport humanitarian personnel and supplies. The airlift and the military personnel operating it were separate and distinct from the UNHCR-co-ordinated airlift described in Chapter 7.

Another UNAMIR contribution was vehicle maintenance. One beneficiary was the UN Human Rights Centre, a unit without a tradition of stationing personnel outside of Geneva and, in Rwanda, otherwise bereft of logistical support. UNAMIR provided human rights monitors with radios, serviced their vehicles, and passed on information about security problems and alleged human rights abuses. Without such help, the human rights mission would have been even slower off the mark. Some monitors were reluctant to become associated with UN troops, however. "Soldiers are seldom perceived as human-rights advocates, especially in Africa", explained one.

UNAMIR's assistance in transporting people overland back to their homes within Rwanda was more problematic. In the waning months of 1994, an estimated 350 000 Hutus resided in camps in the south-west, which would become the scene of violence in 1995. They presented a sensitive political problem for the government, which viewed them with suspicion as perpetrators of or accomplices in genocide and saw the camps themselves as an affront to its sovereignty. The residents also posed a difficult problem for aid agencies, who, while committed to facilitating their return, differed with the authorities about when and with what safeguards this should be done.

UNAMIR, under pressure from Rwandan authorities to assist and viewed by the regime as pro-Hutu, was also anxious to put its logistics capacity and personnel to work and in fact had done so beginning in August, transporting small numbers of people home. Approaching the issue primarily as a matter of logistics — a "trucking operation" — UNAMIR was prepared to proceed on its own, foregoing discussions with aid agencies more knowledgeable about population movements and attendant protection and other re-entry problems.

In November 1994, the SRSG forwarded a confidential plan for the resettlement of the camp population, Operation Rondaval, to the Secretary-General. That such a plan could be prepared without consultation with the humanitarian organisations was itself indicative of a fundamental lack of co-ordination. Once the aid agencies became aware of the proposal, they enlisted UNAMIR in a more collaborative approach, dubbed Operation Retour. During the first six weeks of 1995, that effort facilitated the move of some 82 000 persons back to their communes (Kent, 1996).

Carrying out Relief Activities

Beyond helping improve the overall security climate and supporting aid organisations, UNAMIR troops carried out emergency relief activities themselves. While it is not uncommon for soldiers in UN peace-keeping operations to engage in direct relief work, doing so was a distinguishing feature of UNAMIR. Such activities were the full-time task of some military units, as illustrated by the British contingent. They were carried out on a time-available basis by others, as UNAMIR's Canadian and Australian units demonstrated. They were tackled by many others on their own free time.

The purpose of the UNAMIR British contingent was explicitly humanitarian. In fact, the term "British contingent", or BRITCON, was chosen to convey a non-military image. The original plan was to have BRITCON, which deployed August 17 and withdrew November 17, concentrate in north-western Rwanda. With refugees slow to return from Zaire and with French troops winding up *Opération Turquoise*, however, much of BRITCON's work took place in the south-west. Its activities, called Operation Gabriel, involved 537 personnel from 6 contingents in the United Kingdom.

The 23rd Parachute Field Ambulance unit, a rapid reaction contingent that specialised in responding to emergencies quickly and in traveling light, provided medical services to some 132 598 refugees, internally displaced, and others who simply lived near its health facilities. Ninety-nine Rwandese lives were lost during the treatment process. However, "many thousands of patients", British officials reported, "would certainly have died had they not received treatment"[16]. BRITCON worked particularly closely with NGO programmes in the health sector such as MSF, Oxfam, Samaritan's Purse, and *Pharmaciens sans frontières*.

The 9th Parachute Squadron, Royal Engineers rebuilt critical roads and bridges following the war, maintained roads against the punishing wear and tear of large aid trucks, and improved access to camps for the internally displaced. Extensive repairs on the Kigali hospital by the troops provided a boost to the work of Australia's military medical contingent and of MSF. Joining with the American NGO Africare, they launched a new rubbish disposal site for the capital. In the Byumba area of the north-west, they repaired ten clinics and put electrical and water systems back into functioning order. In addition to disposing of some 3 000 munitions and mines, they counselled aid agencies on mine awareness and safety.

The 63rd Airborne Close Support Squadron of the Royal Logistics Corps specialised in moving people and relief supplies. It transported more than 20 000 refugees and internally displaced persons and almost 2 100 tons of equipment and supplies. The 10th Airborne Workshop maintained the UNAMIR vehicle fleets, providing vital services to the vehicles of UN and private aid agencies as well.

From start to finish, Operation Gabriel was designed to support the missions of UNAMIR, the UN humanitarian agencies, and the NGOs. The rationale, an official explained, was "to provide a bridge between the immediate need at the end of the war and the point at which the traditional agencies had established themselves enough to take over". That was, in fact, its principal contribution.

Those involved concur with a BRITCON official that "The Contingent gave UNAMIR a sound organisational benchmark, boosted their morale through their efforts, and increased the respect with which the mission is held in Rwanda". The transitional nature of the BRITCON task and the links to civilian aid organisations, it was explained, made broader policy issues of reconstruction and development "irrelevant". The troops were "simply providing humanitarian services".

The costs of Operation Gabriel to the UK Ministry of Defence was an estimated £6 million. Of this, some £4.8 million was recoverable from the UN, the balance representing a UK contribution. That a UN peace-keeping operation had contracted with a national defence ministry for such services, which may well have broken new ground, also raised questions about the division of responsibilities with the UN. At the time, DHA was unaware that the UN was paying for BRITCON services. Their continued provision on a commercial basis after BRITCON's departure by a private, for-profit contractor raised a question of whether more cost-effective arrangements might have been found.

British army officials were enthusiastic about the BRITCON experience. "[T]he deployment was extremely valuable as a demonstration of our ability to respond rapidly to such a humanitarian request", commented Maj. M.W. Hiskett. "The operation demonstrated that it was also possible to make a significant contribution for a specified period and then extract [that is, withdraw] at minimum cost to the taxpayer, other than our annual UN contributions"[17].

Operation Gabriel also provided valuable training to troops, some of whom were building on previous experience in Bosnia and others of whom were being exposed to a major humanitarian crisis for the first time. British troops "were given substantial responsibility and had to cope with pressures that cannot be simulated on exercise and as a result they are better soldiers for their experience"[18]. The wind-up of the tour in Rwanda and the convoy of personnel and materiel to the coast at Mombassa represented "the largest British Army road movement in Africa since World War II".

A second category of direct relief activity — that carried out by soldiers as a complement to their primary tasks — was illustrated by Canadian and Australian troops. The Canadian contingent, deployed to UNAMIR in response to the Security Council's decision in May to expand the size and function of the peace-keeping mission, mounted a variety of activities under the name of Operation Lance.

The main purpose of the unit, numbering 430 at full strength, was to set up and operate a communications network for the UN peace-keeping operation. In addition to a Signals Squadron for the actual communications work, the unit included a Support Squadron for vehicle maintenance, a Medical Platoon for health and logistical support, and an Engineer Support Regiment to handle construction tasks and water purification. Canada was also among the score of countries providing military observers to monitor developments in support of the peace process.

The purpose of Operation Lance was not, strictly speaking, humanitarian. However, when the Signals unit was not relaying messages between UN helicopters and their Kigali base, it worked to improve living conditions at a large orphanage. When the medical platoon was not fulfilling its primary task of caring for Canadian soldiers, it treated Rwandan civilians. When the engineers were not constructing communications facilities, they were disposing of unexploded munitions and operating a water purification unit for local residents. As duty time permitted, military observers also assisted.

The Canadian UNAMIR contingent in Operation Lance was distinct from Canadian troops serving in Rwanda under separate authority in arrangements made with UNHCR. (Those latter activities in air logistics and medical services are reviewed in Chapter 7.) Canada supplied UNAMIR with two Force Commanders and headquarters support staff. The Force Commander's formal authority was limited to Canadian troops in Operation Lance and did not extend to those in the operations associated with UNHCR.

In August 1994, the Australian government committed to UNAMIR the Australian Medical Support Force, a contingent of 308 personnel. The unit's resources include a surgical team, two preventative medical support teams, two dental groups, an air medevac section, and assorted logistic and security personnel (including an infantry rifle company). Upon completion of its six-month tour, the Medical Support Force was replaced by another similar unit, which after a second six months was to conclude Australia's UNAMIR contribution.

Based in Kigali and working out of the central hospital, Australian troops were deployed by the Force Commander around the country as needed. Their primary task was medical care to UNAMIR personnel. However, they also provided services for Rwandan civilians. Costs to the ministry of defence were estimated at

A$ 2 million, some of which were to be reimbursed by the UN. The Australian military also provided air transport and relief supplies as part of a services package agreement with UNHCR, described in Chapter 7. UNAMIR's Australian contingent worked closely with the NGO CARE Australia.

A third category of direct relief activity — and the one most typical of UN peace-keeping operations — involved work undertaken by units or soldiers on their own time. Some troops extended into off-duty time projects begun as part of the working day. Other troops whose routine duties did not allow them to assist in such ways were also involved. Off-duty projects were important not only for what they accomplished in Rwanda but also for the sense of involvement they promoted among people "back home". Soldiers from many troop-providing countries enlisted their families and communities in the broader effort[19].

All in all, the direct relief activities of UNAMIR forces were impressive. In the health sector, British, Canadian, and Australian medical personnel administered some 50 000 anti-meningococcal meningitis vaccines to children in Kibeho area. In social services, the quality of life in various orphanages was demonstrably improved. Technical assistance in telecommunications by the Canadian contingent brought new capacity to a shattered government infrastructure. The perils of civilian life were reduced by activities carried out by various militaries in the area of mine clearance.

UNAMIR involvement in the human needs sector did not stop with the activities of its military. A number of UNAMIR's civilian branches also made contributions, although UNAMIR's mandate was more circumscribed than some of the multifunctional UN undertakings such as those in Cambodia and El Salvador mentioned in Chapter 1.

Beginning in August 1994, the Special Representative of the Secretary-General drafted a Rwanda Emergency Normalisation Plan which established priorities for postwar rehabilitation and reconstruction. The goal of the plan, explained a UNAMIR Political Affairs Officer in October 1994, was "to call attention to priorities which are required to stabilize the country. When the political situation is rather delicate, rapid progress on the development front is needed". Thus, repairs to the electrical grid serving the capital were essential, without which essential work in health facilities such as the Kigali hospital would be stymied.

The Plan was the subject of a roundtable conference held in Geneva in January, at which some $634 million were pledged. The conference also provided an opportunity for discussions between the new regime and donors, who were raising questions about its effectiveness and commitment to human rights. For its part, the regime used the plan as a vehicle for shifting priorities from relief to reconstruction and for articulating its concern at being denied the international resources necessary to restore services and confidence.

The Plan also illuminated confusion within the UN system. The SRSG at the time, a relative outsider to the UN system, viewed his responsibilities as the ranking UN official to include reconstruction. UNDP viewed the Plan as encroaching on its traditional responsibilities. In other UN peace-keeping operations, too, there has been a lack of clarity about the division of labour between the UN's political-military and its humanitarian and development arms.

Assessment

UNAMIR's performance in the humanitarian sphere was paradoxical. UN military assets were least available when most needed: in fostering protection and preventing wider bloodshed during the genocide period. They were most available later in the year when traditional humanitarian organisations were once again on hand, making significant contributions in supporting the work of aid groups and in carrying out relief activities themselves.

UNAMIR's greatest challenge — and its most obvious failing — was to stop the killings and prevent the spread of violence. UNAMIR I was overtaken by events during the period of the genocide and, despite the best efforts of troops on the ground, was patently and painfully unable to protect those vulnerable to attacks. "Throughout most of this carnage", recalled General Dallaire, "UNAMIR's hands essentially remained tied" (Dallaire, 1996). Fully five or six months elapsed before UNAMIR II, with an expanded mandate and more troops, had established its presence and authority throughout the country.

UNAMIR's ability to provide the necessary security for Rwandese civilians and aid operations was undercut by the lack of timely political, financial, and material support from the UN Security Council and UN member governments. UNAMIR I's terms of engagement, formulated in October 1993 when the main task was to monitor the cease-fire agreement, were not revised for seven weeks after the conflict resumed in April 1994. Monitoring the process of repatriation of Rwandese refugees and the resettlement of displaced persons, a task identified in October 1993, was not what was most needed as the bloodbath commenced.

In retrospect, most observers believe — and, as noted, some expressed the view at the time — that promptly revised terms of reference and additional resources would have allowed UNAMIR more successfully to meet the challenge. "If I had the mandate, the men and the equipment, hundreds of thousands of people would be alive today", Dallaire commented after the fact in a radio interview on the Australian Broadcasting Corporation (African Rights, 1994). Similarly, UN Under-Secretary-General Kofi Annan, who headed the Department of Peace-keeping Operations, observed that "the timely presence of a mechanised brigade deployed in Kigali within seven to fourteen days might have stabilized the situation", quite possibly preventing as many as a half-million deaths[20].

A more well-resourced UNAMIR might also have maintained presence outside Kigali, provided more adequate intelligence, reassured civilian populations, discouraged human rights violations, and moved quickly to put Radio Mille Collines off the air (LaRose-Edwards, 1995). The military forces of the warring parties, whose make-up and numbers were described in the previous chapter, should not have posed an insuperable challenge. The insurgent Rwandan Patriotic Front, while associated with some atrocities, was seeking to exercise firm discipline over its ranks. The defending Rwandan army contained significant numbers who did not support genocide. Much of the actual killing of Tutsis and moderate Hutus, committed by militias and a network of civilians enlisted in advance, might have been nipped in the bud by swift action.

Instances of successful protection and prevention by UNAMIR cited above highlight what might have been done with a broader mandate and more personnel. UN troops did protect civilians and rescue aid workers; their presence did deter violence, albeit temporarily. In the final analysis, however, the numbers of troops were probably a more critical liability than their mandate[21]. In fact, senior UNAMIR officers wished for additional troops which, positioned more firmly around vulnerable populations, could have offered more effective protection — utilising weapons, if necessary. They spoke off the record of being prepared to rationalise such an application of force as undertaken to protect UN troops themselves rather than Rwandese civilians, for whom their mandate at the time was less clear.

If UN troops were least available when their preventive and protective presence was most needed, they were more available later in the year when traditional humanitarian organisations were themselves once again on hand. The small complement of UNAMIR troops that had joined with the tiny band of humanitarian organisations to assist civilians during the genocide was eventually augmented — as were the numbers of aid personnel themselves. Roughly six months into the crisis, the direct relief role of UNAMIR was reduced as humanitarian organisations became more able to respond to the challenge.

UNAMIR accomplishments throughout in supporting the work of those agencies and in carrying out direct relief activities themselves were exemplary. By their own accounts, humanitarian organisations benefited greatly from UNAMIR support in the areas of logistics, vehicle maintenance, and security counsel. The hands-on accomplishments of the troops in the medical, communications, and transport sectors were also outstanding. They reflected the full-time labours of contingents whose primary purpose was to assist civilians — probably a first in UN peace-keeping history — and the part-time or spare-time assistance efforts of other units and individuals.

Also positive was the spirit of collaboration established over time between UN troops and aid groups. That would seem unremarkable were it not for serious problems which developed between soldiers of rescue in other peace-keeping missions and the agencies whose efforts they were supporting. For UN staff transferred to Rwanda from Somalia, the contrast could not have been more striking. While UNAMIR's "purely humanitarian mandate was negligible", observed one UN aid veteran of both theatres approvingly, the efforts of UN troops in Rwanda butressed and reinforced those of traditional humanitarian groups.

Looking back, UNAMIR's second Force Commander Major-General Toussignant saw "an evolving partnership" between military and humanitarian institutions. Despite occasional difficulties, he observed, UN troops and aid personnel as of October were working "hand in hand", evidencing "a complete meshing of talent, resources, and know-how". The greater presence of humanitarian organisations in areas where UNAMIR was also well-represented suggested a positive correlation.

Tousignant's experience contrasted rather sharply, however, with that of his predecessor. The first Force Commander had discovered UN organisations and NGOs to be "aggressive, strong, unilateral and autonomous", vastly complicating UNAMIR and UNREO efforts at collaboration. As a result, Major-General Dallaire observed, civilians in areas already under the control of the advancing insurgent army received more aid than those behind government lines, where most of the need was located but greater insecurity prevailed. (Aid agencies counter that had security been provided elsewhere, they were prepared to assist civilian populations there as well.)

The lack of proportionality of aid distribution created major political problems for UNAMIR. It "only heightened ... UNAMIR's difficulties in negotiating any truces or cease-fires between the belligerents", Dallaire concluded. "Indeed, at one point, UNAMIR was accused of supporting the [government's] war effort because of this undisciplined humanitarian effort". Dallaire also believed that "the lack of co-operation between humanitarian assistance organisations and the military precluded any co-ordinated plan to reintegrate Rwandan refugees, even when UNAMIR forces were becoming more available in late July and early August". (Dallaire, 1996). As a consequence of the lack of co-ordination, the positive synergy for which both military and humanitarian officials hoped was slow to materialise.

Weighing UNAMIR's accomplishments in humanitarian support and relief activities against its failure in protection and prevention, it is difficult to avoid the conclusion that what UNAMIR failed to achieve was more important that what it managed to accomplish. In circumstances of civil war deteriorating into organised genocide, fostering a secure environment for civilians and aid agencies was a political-military challenge clearly beyond the capacity of the aid groups on the scene. Given UNAMIR's inability to stop mass murders, the credibility of the entire peace-keeping operation, and those associated with it, suffered (Destexhe, 1994).

In the absence of a secure environment, effective aid activities by either military or civilian actors were difficult to sustain. While UN troops may have had a comparative advantage over aid agencies in carrying out relief activities in times of anarchy and insecurity, that was not, with the exception of the British contingent, the primary reason why they were on hand. With the return of greater normalcy and of the aid agencies to the scene, aid tasks could once again be assumed by civilians. In short, UNAMIR failed to do what it alone could do and helped do what the aid agencies themselves eventually were able to tackle.

Implicated in the paradox were problems in each of the sets of UN actors — military, political, and humanitarian — and at their interface. Among the most critical was the absence of experienced senior officials on the ground. The first Special Representative of the Secretary-General, Cameroonian diplomat Jacques-Roger Booh-Booh, was widely criticised for having sent biased and inaccurate information on developments to New York and for having compromised the UN in the eyes of the RPF by spending weekends in the Gisenyi residence of President Habyarimana (Braeckman, 1994; Des Forges, 1992).

The performance of the first UNAMIR Force Commander, won widespread praise in diplomatic and humanitarian circles. Yet General Dallaire was without previous African experience — his longtime duty station had been NATO headquarters in Brussels — and was dispatched without adequate briefing into a situation of great political sensitivity and potential danger. When he took up his post, a Canadian study concluded, he "had not been warned to expect anything out of the ordinary. He was led to believe that this, his first peace-keeping mission, was to have been a relatively tranquil affair" (LaRose-Edwards, 1995)[22].

UNAMIR also lacked adequate delegation of authority from New York. A generic problem in UN peace-keeping missions, the need for quick decisions, was underscored in the Rwanda crisis, where, as one observer noted, "the lightening speed of change could alter the situation in public health, security, and population movements almost overnight". "A week here is a long time", observed a UNAMIR veteran of six months in Kigali in October. The institutional wheels in New York and Geneva turn at a far more leisurely pace.

Serious problems existed at the military-humanitarian interface, despite the co-operation between UN troops and aid personnel cited earlier. UNAMIR's proposal of Operation Rondaval in November, resettling the internally displaced, illuminated a fundamental imbalance in the UN system. UNAMIR had played a major role in the humanitarian sphere early in the year and was regarded by the government as focal point for dealing with the internally displaced, a challenge with clear political and security dimensions. Yet as the year progressed, aid agencies resumed their more customary activities and the resources from the international community for resettlement, and the personnel with the mandate and expertise, were concentrated among them.

A more effective balance was eventually struck. Realising the importance of greater involvement by the humanitarian professionals, both sets of officials agreed in November to create an Integrated Operations Centre, which was launched in December 1994 and has improved co-ordination in the intervening months. The issues encountered there, however, are ultimately structural ones faced to one extent or another in most theatres where UN peace-keeping troops are present.

Effective policies — political, military, and humanitarian — are of the essence, each in their own right and at their interface. The interconnections in complex emergencies, however, make their formulation and management difficult.

"The Office of the SRSG is best suited to nurturing the political process, as generally defined by the Security Council", concluded a DHA evaluation of the Rwanda response, "and lacks the capacity and operational authority to identify and prioritise needs or to oversee the allocation of resources in spheres of activity beyond the immediate political arena" (Donini and Niland, 1994). Yet the converse is also true: that humanitarian policies and programmes need to be framed by an effective political framework.

Conclusion

UNAMIR failed to foster what Rwanda needed most, a secure environment for civilians and for those who sought to assist them, when it was needed most, during the genocide. At a time when it was imperative for the international community to halt the genocide, UNAMIR did not do so. Contributing to that failure was a lack of political analysis and preventive action by senior UN political and military personnel on the ground and at headquarters, a lack of political will on the part of the UN Security Council and member governments, and a lack of the necessary authority and resources vested in UNAMIR itself.

While failing in the task of providing security, UNAMIR succeeded in supporting the work of humanitarian organisations and made a major contribution through aid activities carried out by UN troops themselves.

UNAMIR may have even broken new ground by having national contingents specifically assigned aid-support and direct aid functions.

The UNAMIR experience highlights a number of missing institutional ingredients in an effective multilateral response mechanism for major crises such as Rwanda's. One was a capacity, perhaps along the lines of a standby military force, which could be activated quickly and take charge on the ground at once in order to head off a humanitarian disaster. Another was a clearer division of labour between the UN's military and humanitarian institutions in the form of a pre-agreed template reflecting the comparative advantage of each.

The overarching question thus emerging from the UNAMIR experience is not whether UN troops who came to the rescue were able to make a difference. The question is whether the policies they served and the tasks they tackled were the appropriate ones. In the final analysis, the response of the United Nations system to the Rwanda crisis lacked the balance and complementarity, military and humanitarian, which the circumstances required.

Notes

1. For a recap of UNAMIR's historical background, cf. UN Department of Public Information (1994).

2. Security Council resolution 872, Para. 3g. Excerpts from this and other relevant Security Council resolutions are included in Annex 2.

3. The ensuing discussion draws on United Nations documents, press reports, and a study commissioned by the Canadian government (LaRose-Edwards, 1994).

4. Special Report of the Secretary-General on the United Nations Assistance Mission for Rwanda, S/1994/470, April 20, 1994, Para. 7.

5. Security Council Resolution 918, Section A, Para. 3b.

6. MSF-France, Rwanda Communiqué, "Des équipes chirurgicales de Médecins sans frontières prêtes à partir pour Kigali, April 8, 1994.

7. *The [London] Times*, "Devastated Rwanda", [editorial], July 20, 1994.

8. *Médecins sans frontières*, "MSF Fears that UN Reinforcement may come too late", Press Release, May 17.

9. The observation is made by Dick A. Leurdijk in "A UN-Rapid Reaction Force", a paper prepared for a meeting on that subject held in March 1995 in the Hague under the joint sponsorship of the Dutch government and Institute Clingendael. The paper has subsequently been published as "Proposals for Increasing Rapid Deployment Capacity: A Survey", *International Peacekeeping*, Vol. 2, spring 1995, No. 1, pp. 1-10. The paper has now appeared in Dick A. Leurdijk, ed. (1995), "A UN Rapid Deployment Brigade: Strengthening the Capacity for Quick Response", Netherlands Institute of International Relations, Clingendael, The Hague.

10. Letter to the Editor, *New York Times*, Aug. 22, 1994, p. A.12.

11. In April 1995, UNAMIR was criticised for failing to intervene to prevent a massacre of Hutus by government troops at the Kibeho camp for internally displaced persons. The circumstances are described in Chapter 9.

12. UNICEF, "U.N. Opens New Relief Links to Rwanda", Joint UNICEF/WFP Press Release, PR/94/14, May 3, 1994.

13. UNICEF, Emergency Information Note 34/94, May 20, 1994.

14. Interview in Kigali, October 13, 1994.

15. Maggie Murray-Lee, "Rwanda's Lost Souls", UNICEF Emergency Information Note 94/49, August 22, 1994.

16. Army News Release, Ministry of Defence, "Fact and Activity Sheet: BritCon — Operation Gabriel — Rwanda, 17 August-17 November 1994".

17. Communication with the authors dated Jan. 26, 1995.

18. *Ibid*.

19. The British contingent, which identified three orphanages for special assistance by troops in their spare time, reported dramatic improvements in "the quality of life of the children in these homes". The homes received more than two tons of clothes and toys collected by the families and schools in the communities from which BRITCON units were drawn. One unit ran relay races in south-western Rwanda to raise funds. Cf. Army News Release, *op. cit*.

20. Annan is quoted to this effect by Dutch Foreign Minster Hans van Mierlo in a statement to the UN General Assembly on Sept. 27, 1994. The statement of the Foreign Minister is referenced in Leurdijk, *op. cit*.

21. As Belgian General Briquemont has observed, with special reference to his experience leading UN peace-keeping operations in the former Yugoslavia, "The international community is generous with its mandates but reluctant with its resources". Statement at a meeting in Brussels in October/November, referenced by Neill Wright, "The Hidden Costs of Better Co-ordination", in Whitman and Pocock (eds.), forthcoming.

22. Dallaire is reported to have warned that a programme of genocide was systematically planned. On November 9, 1995, he stated in an interview on *Radio Télévision Belge Francophone* that he had warned his superiors in New York to that effect several months in advance of the April 1994 events. The Belgian Defence Minister was quoted in *Le Monde* on November 11, 1995 as acknowledging that his Ministry had been informed in January 1994 of the plans for genocide. See also:*Early Warning and Conflict Managements*, Report of the Study Team II, Multidonor Evaluation of Emergency Assistance to Rwanda.

23. For a detailed review of military-civilian co-ordination problems and of the functioning of the Integrated Operations Centre, see Kent (1996).

Chapter 5

French Troops: *Opération Turquoise*

Opération Turquoise was a two-month intervention mounted by France and authorised June 22, 1994 by UN Security Council under Chapter VII of the UN Charter. Troops began arriving by airlift the next day from bases in Africa. Within a week, 2 500 personnel, 700 vehicles, and 8 000 tons of material had been sent to Goma, Zaire and south-western Rwanda. French troops were joined by soldiers from six African countries. Withdrawing from Rwanda August 22 — about 500 soldiers remained in Goma until September 3 — the French handed over activities to UNAMIR. French officials place the cost of the operation at FF 1 billion, or approximately $200 million.

Coming at a time when the UN peace-keeping troops were still overwhelmed by events, the initiative helped restore order and save lives in south-western Rwanda and in Goma. Termed a humanitarian intervention by the Security Council and the French government, a major actor in the Great Lakes region and a supporter of the ousted Hutu regime, the initiative had many political overtones and repercussions. Short-term benefits to the civilian population were offset by longer-term complications for UNAMIR and the new government.

Terms of Engagement

Proposed by President François Mitterrand and Foreign Minister Alain Juppé in mid-June, *Opération Turquoise* was the subject of great controversy in the UN Security Council. On the one hand, the situation on the ground was continuing to unravel. UN efforts to strengthen UNAMIR were proceeding extremely slowly. France, having announced plans to proceed within a week with or without UN blessing, was serious about acting. It had already completed *Opération Amaryllis* to rescue French and other expatriates and associates. The Secretary-General, rebuffed in attempts to accelerate contributions to the UN peace-keeping effort, welcomed the French initiative.

On the other hand, reservations abounded. Given France's historic and current ties with Hutu political and military leaders of the *ancien régime*, were the real purposes of the operation to slow the advancing Tutsi army and to retain French influence in the region? Rather than buying time for UNAMIR, would the operation detract attention from the need to enhance the UN force? Would French troops leave when promised? Harbouring such concerns, the OAU, key UN secretariat staff, and some member governments opposed the initiative.

The result was a compromise. *Turquoise* received the Security Council's blessing as "a multinational operation" of "strictly humanitarian character" which would be "conducted in an impartial and neutral fashion". Inasmuch as "the magnitude of the humanitarian crisis in Rwanda constitutes a threat to peace and security in the region", the Security Council, acting under Chapter VII of the UN Charter, authorised "all necessary means to achieve the humanitarian objectives". The undertaking was framed as a stop-gap measure until a strengthened UNAMIR could take over.

Even in compromise form, the resolution attracted only ten votes. Abstentions by Brazil, New Zealand, Nigeria, Pakistan, and the People's Republic of China reflected the prevailing disquiet. A negative vote by China would have denied *Turquoise* the UN's blessing. The US and Russia voted in favour of the undertaking, mindful of UN-blessed peace-keeping initiatives they themselves were undertaking in Haiti and Georgia.

Under the Council's mandate, *Turquoise* troops were to identify and protect threatened civilian populations on Rwandese soil and to assist the injured. They were not given authority to arrest criminals, nor was protection of property and neutralisation of *Radio mille collines* broadcasts included in the mandate as such. The Operation's commander General Jean-Claude Lafourcade later acknowledged that given the effect on the Rwandese population of such broadcasts, radio jamming should have been a priority (Déguine and Ménard, 1995; MSF, 1995)[1].

Ten days into the operation, France informed the Secretary-General of its intention to establish a humanitarian safe area (*Zone humanitaire sûre*, or ZHS) in south-western Rwanda. A departure from original plans, the creation of the ZHS represented a creative response to a deteriorating security situation. Quickly established, it extended from Cyangugu to Kibuyé and from Kibuyé to Gikongoro and on to the Burundese border. Acting under its interpretation of resolution 929, France informed the UN but did not to request formal approval for such a sanctuary[2].

The new Rwandese authorities, hostile to *Opération Turquoise*, also opposed the creation of a protected zone. They feared such a sanctuary would prevent their army from arresting perpetrators of genocide and delay establishing authority over a large portion of Rwandese territory. Reservations were expressed in France as well. President Giscard d'Estaing, who had signed a defence agreement with Rwanda in the 1970s, questioned the depth of penetration and scope of the duties to be assumed within Rwanda. French Foreign Minister Juppé countered that for the moment Rwanda was a country with a "limited sovereignty" (Braeckman, 1994). French troops proceeded as planned.

Although French in origin and character, *Turquoise* was not an exclusively French undertaking. Aware of criticisms of acting on political rather than humanitarian grounds, the French government from the start sought to give the undertaking a more international character. A Senegalese contingent took part from the outset and was soon joined by units from Chad, Congo, Guinea-Bissau, Mauritania, and Niger, also equipped by the French.

With the departure of French troops after two months, these contingents were gathered into UNAMIR's FRAFBATT — that is, the French (speaking) African Battalion, or, as it was called, the "inter-African battalion". Egypt also sent military observers who were integrated into *Turquoise*. While generally not carrying out specific humanitarian tasks as such, the non-French contingents were involved in providing security in the northern part of the zone, a task they accomplished, by most accounts, effectively.

Opération Turquoise was to execute its mission only in Rwanda, using Goma as a support base. With the influx of refugees into Zaire, however, French and associated troops also became heavily involved in the humanitarian effort there. In each theatre, they played the triad of functions noted in the previous chapter: fostering a protective environment, supporting the activities of humanitarian organisations, and carrying out relief activities themselves.

Activities

The initial emphasis of *Opération Turquoise* in south-western Rwanda was on re-establishing security. Security was "a prerequisite for humanitarian actions", French military officers explained, "because humanitarian missions are impossible to fulfill when people are wandering about in an insecure environment". Only later did French troops provide support to the activities of NGOs and UN agencies and carry out relief operations themselves.

The focus on security needs fuelled speculation about why the French had chosen to intervene and what they were really doing on the ground. The OAU, the new regime, and others held that the French intervention was designed to come to the rescue of former allies in their hour of need (*Le Nouvel Afrique-Asie*, 1994; *Socialisme International*, 1994; *Le Bolchévik*, 1994; *Le Prolétaire*, 1994; Leymarie, 1994; Bijard, 1994; Bolton, 1994; Smith and Guisnel, 1994, de Clerzac, 1994; *Rivarol*, 1994.) Some analysts and public opinion saw the operation as a cover for bringing back French military counselors and weapons (Braeckman, 1994). Some sensed a French desire to eradicate the "Fachoda complex": that is, to preserve the French-speaking character of Rwanda through preventing a military victory by English-speaking insurgents[3]. The activities of *Turquoise* troops were therefore closely watched in south-western Rwanda. Their performance reassured some but did not allay the fears of others.

Compared with the cloud of suspicion which accompanied the deployment of French troops in Rwanda and dogged their presence throughout the south-west, the situation in Zaire was much less highly charged. The law-and-order functions which preoccupied the French military in the ZHS were largely absent in Goma. Instead, the influx of a million persons in the short space of three days created a massive challenge. As a result, supporting the work of humanitarian organisations and doing direct relief work themselves became the principal preoccupation. In fact, the contribution of French troops in Zaire helped ease criticism of their presence in the region. Because of differences in Rwanda and Zaire, a review of the three sets of activities needs to differentiate in each instance between the two areas.

Fostering a Framework of Overall Stability

Approaching the task of re-establishing security in south-western Rwanda, French Special Operations forces began by forming patrols which quickly fanned out throughout the area. While troops succeeded in disarming "uncontrolled elements" in some areas, the zone was so large that disarmament was not particularly successful. Guns remained in the possession of some former Hutu army and militia, a number of whom had sought shelter in the camps for the internally displaced. The weapons made those camps the scene of unrest until they were closed by the government in April 1995.

To help maintain order throughout the zone, French troops organised and trained a 250-man Rwandan *gendarmerie* which they supervised as long as they were present. *Opération Turquoise* also reorganised the administrative authorities in the villages and towns to facilitate the prompt return to normalcy. Rwandans chosen for the tasks were selected from among people who were not politically active and were prepared to co-operate with the new government. In fact, hard-core Hutu leadership did not reassert itself in the zone until after the French had left.

Even with the help of newly trained locals, however, French forces did not succeed in preventing the destruction of property in certain areas. The looting and plundering of Cyangugu in August was particularly flagrant. In response to criticisms that French soldiers had stood by during the rampage, French officials pointed out that the protection of property was not in their mandate and that, in any event, there was little they could have done to prevent what happened. The French denied any complicity between soldiers and looters.

Soldiers of other nationalities also played a role in re-establishing security in the Zone. Once the initial deployment of French troops had taken place, French-speaking African troops arrived and familiarised themselves with the situation, took part in security functions, and were on hand to help ensure a smooth handover to UNAMIR. As noted above, they stayed on in the UNAMIR ranks. Their language skills proved an asset in a French-speaking country, an advantage not shared by the Ethiopian blue helmets, who replaced French and French-speaking troops in Cyangugu.

By and large, *Opération Turquoise* succeeded in creating a more secure environment throughout south-western Rwanda. In one of the few incidents in which French troops used their weapons, the French soldiers returned fire against RPF fighters who had challenged the convoy, which then proceeded without further incident. French troops also evacuated some 270 Rwandan civilians, including orphans and a dozen European clerics, from Butaré.

Another indicator of success was that upon the departure of French troops in late August, the massive exodus from the ZHS to Bukavu which had been feared did not materialise. In fact, some NGO personnel who had been most sharply critical of the operation when it was launched were among the most vocal proponents of extending its stay in order to avoid a second Goma (UNREO, 1994d; UNREO, 1994b). Their about-face suggested the extent of the contribution of French troops to re-establishing security throughout the south-west, as well as the value of concerted planning by international actors to ease the transition.

At the same time, French troops created expectations that those who would follow them — first UNAMIR and then the new government authorities — had difficulty fulfilling. The practice of paying wages to local officials and school teachers, for example, recognised their importance to the re-establishment of a sense of order and well-being and the impossibility that their needs would be met otherwise. Sustaining such payments, however, required expenditures beyond UNAMIR's resources or mandate and, as the situation evolved, resources which the new regime itself did not possess.

French troops also helped create and maintain a secure environment in Goma as well. While *Opération Turquoise* had established a base there initially to support activities within Rwanda, French military presence in Goma at the time of the mass exodus in mid-July positioned them strategically to assist. French troops provided a framework of security within which aid organisations assisted the refugees, in effect, assuming temporary responsibility for ensuring law and order in the camps. Unlike the security challenge in Rwanda itself, a nation then rent by civil war, the need at the time in Goma was rather for maintaining a kind of police presence and functions.

Aid personnel, reluctant to venture into volatile situations to distribute relief supplies, particularly appreciated crowd control activities by French troops. The service was especially indispensable in Goma, where Zairean soldiers, described by aid workers as "completely drunk after 5 p.m.", often behaved as laws unto themselves. In addition to tensions within refugee camps, there were frictions between refugees and the local Zairean population, and between the local population and Zairean authorities. French troops also helped avoid and resolve frictions between the authorities and humanitarian personnel. In Zaire as in Rwanda, UN agencies and NGOs spoke favourably of their contribution.

Supporting Humanitarian Activities

Having moved quickly to establish security in south-western Rwanda, French troops were in a position to facilitate the activities of humanitarian organisations. The first problem faced by humanitarian organisations was to reach south-western Rwanda with relief supplies. *Opération Turquoise* arranged and escorted barges across Lake Kivu and truck convoys overland into the zone. French troops also served as a channel for food and other relief material from the bilateral French government agency *Aide Humanitaire France*. Such assistance was particularly welcome early on, when NGOs, by their own account, had "almost nothing" in the way of supplies or transport.

French troops were also a regular source of information on the security situation, frequently alerting aid agencies to situations of extreme human need. Briefings were organised by French troops for humanitarian agencies at least twice a week, more frequently if required. In the zone, these briefings focused on security threats; in Goma, they were part of a larger agenda geared to enhance the co-ordination of humanitarian activities.

The contribution of *Turquoise* in supporting humanitarian efforts in the zone, however, was constrained by the reluctance of some agencies to take advantage of the assistance offered. At issue were reservations about the political nature of French presence and the extent to which collaboration would compromise the impartiality of aid work in the eyes of the new regime and the Rwandan population.

French NGOs such as MDM, MSF, and AICF initially chose not to work in the zone under the protection of French troops. The MDM chairman Alain Deloche expressed the view that "France's intervention would be impossible from a humanitarian standpoint and, from a military one, could end up only in supporting the assassins". By contrast, his MSF counterpart, Dr. Philippe Biberson, called for immediate military intervention a week before French troops arrived. Soon after the deployment of French troops, MSF Chairman Dr. Jean-Louis Machuron dissociated himself from the strategy being followed by the military. In his judgement, the creation of "great refugee parks" was not the best way to provide effective humanitarian assistance. Such a solution, in his judgement, could represent a cure worse than the ill (Broche, 1994).

Over time, however, many NGOs did mount activities in the zone and did co-operate with *Opération Turquoise*. Their changed stance reflected both the performance of the French troops and the evolving situation on the ground. It soon became apparent that French troops were not fighting alongside troops of the former Hutu army but were making a serious and generally successful attempt at neutrality between the contending sides. The troops protected Tutsi refugee encampments located in the vicinity of RwAF camps as well as members of the former Rwandan army. The latter were not considered refugees by UNHCR because they were not civilians, nor were they prisoners of war who fell within the mandate of the ICRC.

French NGOs which maintained their distance from the military at a time of such extreme human need were criticised by French public opinion. Only one French NGO, *Secours populaire français*, which had a four-person aid team in the country, continued throughout to refuse to operate alongside French troops. Non-French NGOs were less outspoken in their criticism. OXFAM, Trocaire, Concern, Goal, and Save the Children operated in the zone and established good working relationships with the French military.

Relationships between humanitarian personnel and *Turquoise* troops in Rwanda were not altogether harmonious, however. The military had difficulty understanding why NGOs sent their own assessment teams to survey the situation when French military intelligence had already gathered information about the displaced. NGOs were often viewed by the troops as "boy-scouts" and amateurs. Conversely, some NGO workers were not particularly keen on the approach to their tasks taken by the Foreign Legion or the French Marines. Nevertheless, mutual respect did evolve over time.

Relationships between UN agencies in the zone and the French military were generally good. However, some differences developed around particular issues. For example, the French for practical reasons would have liked WFP convoys to proceed into the Zone through Burundi. WFP insisted on entering from Rwanda, for reasons both logistical (the limited capacity of the Bujumburu airport) and substantive (the desire to be viewed as neutral by the new Kigali authorities)[4].

With respect to Zaire, the support of humanitarian activities by *Turquoise* troops had a somewhat different tempo and focus. The choice of Goma as logistical base reflected the lack of airport facilities in Rwanda at the time the French deployed. With RPF forces closing in on the capital, the Kigali airport was hardly suitable for supporting an intervention as major and as politically sensitive as the French had in mind.

The Goma airport itself, however, was anything but ideal. The runways and off-loading facilities were unsuited for the wide-bodied cargo aircraft that would become regular visitors and, indeed, the backbone of *Opération Turquoise*. To expand airport capacity, French Air Force engineers laboured nightly from 2 to 5 a.m. at the necessary repairs. Airport utilisation increased from a few medium-sized planes to about 25 flights per day.

In assuming air traffic control functions, French military personnel stepped in with technical expertise the NGOs did not have. Whereas French troops orchestrated shipments into Goma early on, that soon became the responsibility of an air operations cell located at UNHCR in Geneva, to which the French and other militaries seconded personnel.

Reflecting the organising efforts of the military, incoming aircraft were off-loaded as soon as they touched down. Newly repaired runways and aprons accelerated the task. French military planes carried NGO and UN personnel and material free of charge from Goma to Bukavu on a space-available basis. Military barges ferried items across Lake Kivu to Kibuyé, Cyangugu and other destinations in Rwanda.

The aid chain was organised from Paris, but to facilitate co-ordination a "humanitarian meeting point" was set up at *Turquoise* headquarters in Goma. A civilian affairs cell was in charge of managing aid, together with a French Inter-Ministries cell (Defence, Co-operation, Foreign Affairs, Humanitarian Action). The meeting point provided humanitarian agencies with the latest information on new and unattended needs. French bilateral aid from the Humanitarian Action Ministry channeled through *Opération Turquoise* and other resources were deployed accordingly. The personnel, material, and facilities provided by *Turquoise* were well regarded by aid groups. The organisation of French military-civilian co-operation is indicated on Figure 5.1.

The troops of *Turquoise* had already made considerable progress when on July 14 the first of hundreds of thousands Rwandese refugees crossed Zairean borders and arrived in Goma. With the influx of more than a million refugees into Zaire in the space of the next few days, the attention of *Turquoise* was directed on a urgent basis to the needs in Goma and environs. The situation was so dramatic and the needs so critical — particularly in the area of sanitation and health — that French troops provided extensive support to aid organisations overwhelmed by the emergency. Reflecting on the high degree of co-operation, one NGO official recalled with appreciation that "*Opération Turquoise* worked for us."

Figure 5.1. **French Government Organisation of Humanitarian Action in Rwanda under** *Opération Turquoise*

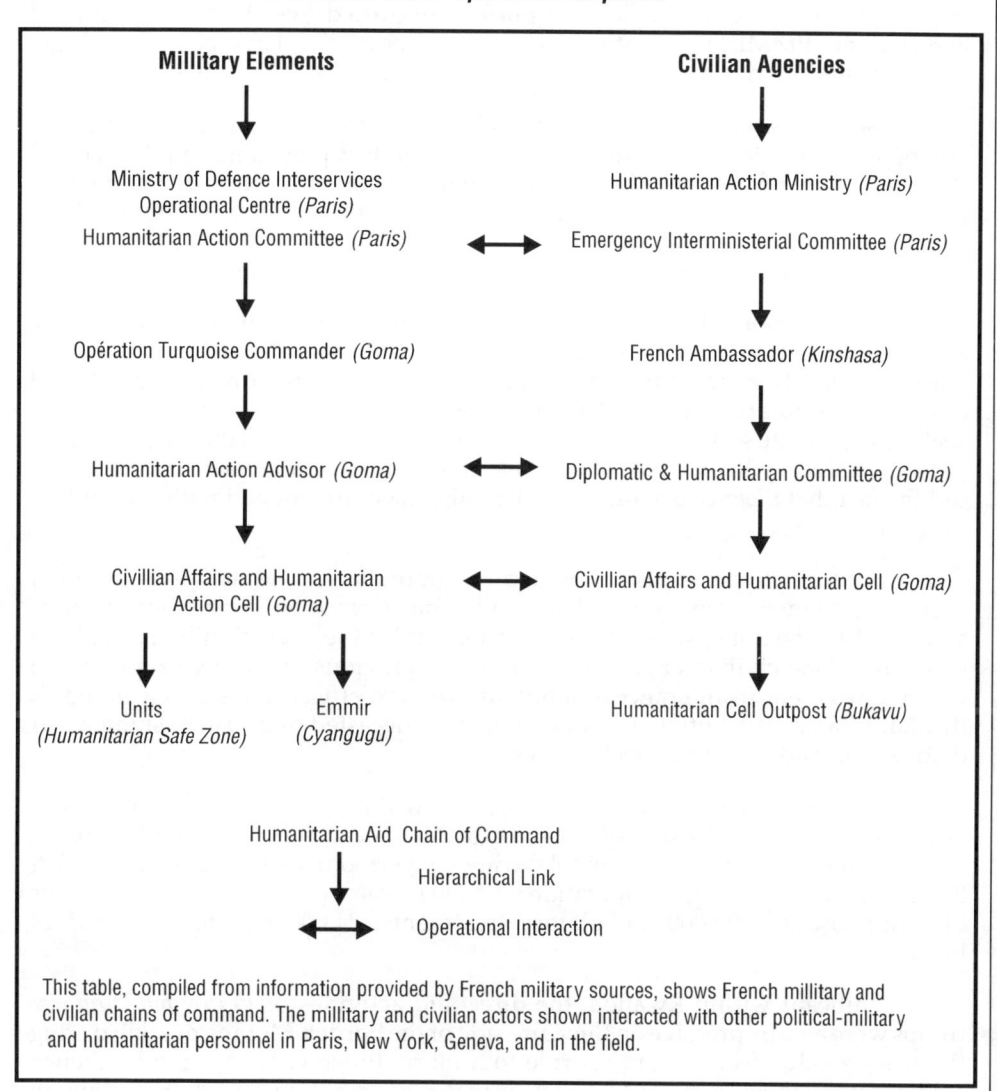

Military Elements	Civilian Agencies
Ministry of Defence Interservices Operational Centre *(Paris)*	Humanitarian Action Ministry *(Paris)*
Humanitarian Action Committee *(Paris)* ⟷	Emergency Interministerial Committee *(Paris)*
Opération Turquoise Commander *(Goma)*	French Ambassador *(Kinshasa)*
Humanitarian Action Advisor *(Goma)* ⟷	Diplomatic & Humanitarian Committee *(Goma)*
Civillian Affairs and Humanitarian Action Cell *(Goma)* ⟷	Civillian Affairs and Humanitarian Cell *(Goma)*
Units *(Humanitarian Safe Zone)* / Emmir *(Cyangugu)*	Humanitarian Cell Outpost *(Bukavu)*

Humanitarian Aid Chain of Command
↓ Hierarchical Link
⟷ Operational Interaction

This table, compiled from information provided by French military sources, shows French millitary and civilian chains of command. The millitary and civilian actors shown interacted with other political-military and humanitarian personnel in Paris, New York, Geneva, and in the field.

Carrying out Relief Activities

In Rwanda, the aid activities carried out by the *Turquoise* troops themselves were largely in the health and medical sector. In early July, with the situation critical in south-western Rwanda, the French Army dispatched to Cyangugu a medical unit, *Élément médical militaire d'intervention rapide* (EMMIR). A military hospital facility designed for use in natural disasters, EMMIR was used in Rwanda for the first time in a war setting. Staffed by 48 military medical and sanitary professionals, EMMIR included an operating theatre suite, two medical units, a 50-bed hospital, a laboratory-dispensary, and a radiological unit. The EMMIR hospital treated some 300 local persons per day.

EMMIR co-operated closely with NGOs to extend its own efforts and theirs. When French troops withdrew, EMMIR facilities were left to a French NGO, *Hôpital sans frontières*, while its medical supplies were turned over to NGOs and local associations. EMMIR's operating costs were reported to have been very high, although specific figures were not available from French government officials.

A second resource in the health sector was *Bioforce*, a French government emergency rescue team made up of medical and sanitary personnel with specialised disaster training from the ranks of the military. While only a few dozen, *Bioforce* personnel provided first aid, inoculated civilians, set up clinics, and trained local people. Its laboratories played a key role in diagnosing and confirming the diseases among refugees, benefiting affected populations and the wider aid effort.

Bioforce personnel worked with other epidemiologists on the ground in Goma and co-operated with NGOs even more closely than did EMMIR. Relationships were particularly good because *Bioforce* health services were provided in tents and other make-shift arrangements: that is, in settings where NGOs themselves were seeking to provide services and with a similar approach. The fact that NGO medical personnel already knew some of the *Bioforce* staff made for greater collegiality, as did the fact that *Bioforce* personnel, while uniformed, functioned without military protection.

Opération Turquoise also provided an umbrella for aid activities by other French personnel. Firemen from Paris and teams from French civil defence units were sent to the zone, where they operated under the French military chain of command. One civilian engineer, a veteran of previous work in Cyangugu and Gisenyi, was sent from France as a military reserve officer to restart Cyangugu's drinking water distribution network. Others also assisted by re-establishing water distribution and repairing electric lines.

The results of such direct aid activities within Rwanda were impressive. Grouping together EMMIR, *Bioforce* and other field health efforts, some 250 French military and civil-defence personnel during the period from June 22 to September 30 carried out 1 100 surgical operations, 17 000 medical consultations, 11 000 days of hospitalisation, 90 000 ambulatory treatments, 24 000 vaccinations, and 24 births[5].

Significant within Rwanda, the direct aid activities of *Opération Turquoise* troops were also impressive on the Zaire side of the border. Moving quickly during the mass exodus from a support role to a more direct assistance mode, French soldiers used their vehicles to assist in water distribution and helped Zairean humanitarian associations and NGOs organise nutrition centres, clinics, orphanages, and anti-cholera centres. A French military medical team, initially sent exclusively to treat French soldiers, pressed all of its own limited resources into service.

Working in liaison with the World Health Organisation, the French government sent *Bioforce* to analyse epidemic hazards and carry out a vaccination campaign. Medical clinics were opened to accommodate civilian needs after the field hospital operated by Israeli troops was closed. The French military sanitary service brought its own field hospital, complete with an operating theatre which it set up and managed. When *Opération Turquoise* withdrew, the facility, valued at nearly FF 3 million, was turned over by the French Defence Minister to a Zairean clinic. The French military used surgeons on duty at the time within the ranks, buttressed by reservists activated to provide additional back-up.

The most publicised achievement of French troops in Zaire was the burial of the bodies of cholera victims, a key task from the standpoint of public health and sanitation — and of psychology. Neither UN agencies nor NGOs were equipped to cope on their own with this urgent problem. The task required mechanical excavators to crack the hard terrain and quick lime to speed decomposition, neither available in adequate amounts in the area. French Air Force engineers — in fact, the night-time repair detail at the airport — took the lead in this unpleasant but necessary mission.

In mid-July, the situation was so desperate in Goma that military personnel and UN and NGO workers functioned virtually as a single team to cope with the humanitarian disaster. As with UNAMIR, some soldiers not directly involved in humanitarian activities spent off-duty time distributing food, water, and clothing. As the situation was brought under control and UN and NGO organisations were better able to cope, French troops reduced their own direct role. By the time *Opération Turquoise* completed work in Goma in late September — some 500 military personnel remained there after French troops had left Rwanda — the worst aspects of the situation had been addressed.

As for the cost of *Opération Turquoise*, Minister of Defence François Léotard on one occasion gave the figure of FF 5 billion (roughly $1 billion). The sum was later reduced to FF 1 billion (about $200 million) by General Lafourcade and Bernard Garancher of the Ministry of Foreign Affairs. The lower figure included rental of Russian military transport aircraft, the use of twelve jet fighters and of military bases in Cameroon, the Central African Republic, Chad, Djibouti, and Gabon, and the cost of French troops and the assistance they provided[6]. An additional $50 million was reported to have been spent by other ministries, including Foreign Affairs, Humanitarian Action, Health, and Co-operation.

There were indications in mid-1995 that reviews within the French ministry of defence had surprised officials at the size of actual expenditures, which may well have exceeded $200 million by a considerable amount. Whatever the actual figure, however, there is no doubt that *Opération Turquoise* was expensive, perhaps even to the point of discouraging replication. The undertaking "proved to be so costly", reported UNAMIR Force Commander Dallaire looking back, "that it is unlikely that [the French government] will embark on any similar venture in the near future". (Dallaire, 1996).

Assessment

Taken together, the triad of activities of *Opération Turquoise* in the areas of security, humanitarian operation support, and direct relief activities — made a strongly positive short-term contribution to the international relief effort, both in south-western Rwanda and in the Goma region of Zaire. The longer-term contribution was more mixed, with negative aspects offsetting positive features on both the humanitarian and the political fronts.

In the short term, the number of lives saved, Tutsis as well as Hutus, was impressive, perhaps ranging into the tens or even the hundreds of thousands. *Opération Turquoise* also reassured the 1.5 million displaced people living in the protected zone that it was safe to stay, thus discouraging a more massive exodus to Zaire (Vassall-Adams, 1994). The life-saving contribution of the French in Rwanda "should not be forgotten", observed an official from the new Kigali regime with evident gratitude. Given the initial opposition of the new authorities to French involvement, his comment deserves particular notice.

Acting as an interpositional force, *Turquoise* lent a calming presence to a highly volatile situation. To demonstrate its independence from the previous Hutu authorities, French troops entered Rwanda at Cyangugu and not Gisenyi, where the interim government was based. Relying on deterrence more than outright force, *Turquoise* succeeded in limiting challenges to its authority to a very few. In one situation, following the killing of some 50 Hutus in an RPF mortar shelling, French jet fighters flew immediately over the insurgents' stronghold, leading to a cessation of the attacks. In the rescue from Butaré noted above, the use of force was instrumental in ensuring the safe passage of the convoy.

The short-term results were equally positive in Zaire, where the activities of French troops became more widely known due to media focus on the Goma tragedy. The soldiers augmented the airport's capacity to meet the unusual demands of the situation, assisted relief agencies in coping with the influx, and buried the bodies of those unable to be saved from cholera. The contribution was indispensable, even though the troops themselves, like UN aid organisations and private relief groups, were initially overwhelmed by the challange.

Opération Turquoise deployment was positive both in Rwanda, where it helped prevent an even more massive exodus, and in Zaire, where it adapted its work to the humanitarian emergency. Such was the value of being in place to fill a vacuum into which no other government — or the United Nations itself — had moved with equal dispatch or equal numbers. Neither neighbouring countries, which appealed urgently for assistance only as corpses began to pollute their rivers and lakes, nor the international community itself, which had been unwilling to name and challenge the genocide, had acted. France thus deserves credit as the first nation, apart from those assisting in UNAMIR, to mount a major undertaking, saving countless lives and avoiding considerable fresh suffering.

Whatever the benefits of having *Opération Turquoise* troops at the right place at the right time, the soldiers who came to the rescue arrived, from another perspective, too late. Their mandate was to stop mass murders, yet they appeared only after the bloodletting had largely stopped. Taking up positions in the south-west, French soldiers remarked on how little killing was going on and how few Tutsis were visible, only to learn that most who were to lose their lives had already done so.

Characterising the French initiative as "brilliant but tardy", Bernard Kouchner, a French member of the European Parliament and long-time humanitarian activist, confirmed the prevailing view that earlier international action would have helped stop the genocide rather than simply protecting those who were lucky enough somehow to have survived it[7]. The accomplishment of *Opération Turquoise* in preventing further loss of life was thus undercut by the awesome numbers to whose rescue French troops came too late.

The contrast between the *Opération Turquoise* initiative and with the lightening-quick action by the French and other outside militaries after the April 6 events was striking. Within 48 hours, French paratroopers in *Opération Amaryllis* were on the scene evacuating expatriates and Rwandan *protégés*. It was fully 15 weeks before French troops returned, by which time the toll from the mayhem probably exceeded half a million. The world can only ponder whether French, Belgian, and other troops involved in the April rescues, had they also reinforced the UNAMIR contingent already in place, might not have stopped, or at least slowed, the slaughter by Hutu militias.

The longer-term impacts of *Opération Turquoise* were mixed in both humanitarian and political contexts. On the humanitarian front, the description of the initiative as "humanitarian" and its French origin and character created a number of problems for aid agencies, particularly in Rwanda itself.

Turquoise was first and foremost a security operation, its primary mission to restore order in south-western Rwanda. Its aid efforts in Zaire were an offshoot of its presence at its logistical base in Goma, not its principal reason for being on hand. Save for a handful of French and West African civilians, all its personnel in all locations were military, wearing military dress and carrying military weapons. Moreover, the prevailing perception of the undertaking — certainly by the new

Rwandan regime, which opposed it, but also by others in the region and beyond — was of a heavily political agenda, reflecting French history and current relationships in the region.

A more accurate description for the operation than the "humanitarian" nomenclature of French political leaders and the UN Security Council was provided by Admiral J. Lanxade, then French chief of staff, who spoke of the French undertaking as "a military intervention with a humanitarian purpose" (Lanxade, 1995). The configuration of French troops was itself more geared to establishing security, with specialised units such as EMMIR and *Bioforce* arriving later to carry out specific aid activities. A humanitarian operation would have required a different package of forces, one featuring more logistics battalions and civil-affairs personnel and fewer special forces and commandos.

Given the political lay of the land and of Rwandan perceptions of the French initiative, aid organisations working in Rwanda felt forced to choose between operating in RPF-controlled territory or in the French-protected zone. The issue was a pivotal one for humanitarian principle and practice. Not only did they wish to convey their commitment to assist people irrespective of ethnic background or political affiliation. They were also anxious to position themselves for the longer haul, when French troops would be gone and the new regime would be setting the terms for international activities within Rwandan borders. Thus even those who choose to work in the zone preferred not to co-operate too closely with French troops.

The new Rwandan authorities "would have liked humanitarian agencies to boycott the ZHS", explained Ms. Umutoni, Principal Private Secretary of the Minister of Rehabilitation and Social Integration in October 1994. Indeed, some NGOs mounted activities only in areas controlled by the new government, while others worked within the security framework provided by French troops. There is no evidence of government retaliation against those who exercised that right by denying them access elsewhere. "The Government took no measures against NGOs which have worked in ZHS", noted Ms. Umutoni. "It was their right".

Yet operating in the south-west did strain relationships with the authorities. According to the country director of a French NGO, relations between government officials and NGOs working in the ZHS were tense. One NGO interviewed did not feel that its personnel could readily enter or leave the zone or that its Kigali staff had the full co-operation of the Rwandese authorities. UN officials, too, feared that their activities in the south-west would complicate working relationships with the new regime. Nevertheless, most aid personnel in the zone indicated that after the withdrawal of the French, their relations with the new regime had proceeded on a businesslike basis.

The problem of aid politicisation, exacerbated by *Opération Turquoise*, existed independently of the French intervention. Rent by the genocide, Rwandans were divided between sympathisers with the *ancien régime* — largely internally displaced persons (IDPs) in the camps in the south-west and refugees in camps across the border — and supporters of the new authorities, largely people who had resumed their lives within Rwanda. In choosing where to work and how to allocate resources, aid agencies, too, seemed to be making a political statement. Thus, "in common with UN Agencies and UNAMIR, NGOs had to contend with the opprobrium associated with providing assistance to IDP camps in the former *Zone Turquoise*. And like UN Agencies, the work of the NGOs in the refugee camps outside Rwanda was regarded by many within the country with a degree of suspicion if not open hostility" (Kent, 1996).

Many of the aid organisations critical of a "humanitarian" undertaking which aggravated political tensions would have welcomed a straightforward security initiative, within whose parameters their work could proceed more effectively. The fact that the mission was carried out initially by a combination of troops from the French Foreign Legion, Marines, and Navy Commandos was viewed as evidence of political motives. Had *Opération Turquoise* been a bona fide humanitarian mission, some argued, EMMIR and *Bioforce*, along with the all-essential logistics and engineering units, would have been on the scene from the very beginning .

French officials countered that, with troops already committed to peace-keeping operations in other places such as Lebanon and the former Yugoslavia, the only soldiers available for quick deployment were those based nearby in the Central African Republic, Djibouti, and Gabon. Moreover, Special Forces units were best trained to operate in insecure areas, where re-establishing security was top priority. In fact, the situation provided an opportunity to implement a scenario in the Ministry of Defence's *White Book* which places humanitarian interventions among low-intensity operations "in support of peace and international law". It was precisely that blurring of the political and the humanitarian, however, to which aid groups objected[8].

On the political front, the longer-term impacts of *Opération Turquoise* were largely negative. The French initiative, as noted, accomplished its purpose of stabilizing the situation in the south-west. This it did by preventing the extension of effective control by the new regime over all of Rwandan territory. Given the prevailing fear that the Rwandan army, pursuing a routed Hutu military and civilian population, would carry out bloody retribution, international troops succeeded in interrupting the cycle of violence. While thus avoiding retribution, *Turquoise* also delayed the assumption of full authority over the country by the new leadership.

The "humanitarian safe zone" became, in effect, a safe haven for the very people suspected of perpetrating genocide. "The rump Hutu government responsible for the genocide took advantage of the haven", noted one reporter, "effectively putting itself under the protection of the French forces"[9]. While some from the discredited *ancien régime* fled abroad to escape judgement and retribution, many others remained in south-western Rwanda (or returned after the departure of the French) to cause problems later.

> France's early-on action was an example of admirable determination to do the right thing. Would that other European countries had felt the same. But France's action was condemned from the start to only partial success. That was determined by lack of means and by earlier involvement in Rwandan affairs..."
>
> *The Observer*, "Rwanda Shows Aid Is Not Enough," [editorial] July 24, 1994.

UNAMIR, which took over when the French departed in August, found it necessary to give top priority to the security situation. The Secretary-General reported in October 1994 that since "it has been necessary for UNAMIR to concentrate its efforts in this potentially volatile area ... the requirement to extend UNAMIR presence throughout Rwanda is yet to be fulfilled" (UN, 1994e). When the new regime took over from UNAMIR, it viewed the camp concentrations of internally displaced persons within the zone as "Rwandas within Rwanda", that is, as threats to its sovereignty. Eventual government moves in 1995 to relocate such persons to their home communes resulted in the violence described in Chapter 9. The negative humanitarian and political consequences of the transplantation intact of the Hutu power structure across the border into Rwanda are described elsewhere.

The interposition of French troops also confirmed the prevailing sense of persecution among Hutus. Welcomed upon their arrival in south-western Rwanda by Hutus demonstrating with banners and placards, *Opération Turquoise* was viewed as confirming the reality of a Tutsi threat. Paranoid feelings among displaced Hutus were reinforced by Hutu Power propaganda, which presented the RPF as devils bent upon perpetrating genocide against Hutus. Rumours also discouraged the return of people who feared that they would not get back their properties and could lose their lives. The perpetrators of genocide were thus able to use *Opération Turquoise* to shift the blame for the recent violence onto those who had borne the brunt of the brutality. This strengthened the "culture of impunity" and delayed serious reconciliation and reconstruction.

Finally, French policy after *Opération Turquoise* slowed the regime's progress in taking on those tasks. France took the lead among donor governments in discouraging aid flows for post-war reconstruction. The slow pace of rehabilitation of essential government infrastructure — police, prisons, and courts were particularly critical areas — contributed to widespread civil unrest and discouraged the return to their homes of refugees and the internally displaced. The exclusion of Rwanda from the Franco-African Summit in November 1994 reinforced the belief that French interests in the region were, after all, political and that *Turquoise* had been little more than a political intervention — or at best a brief humanitarian detour from an unchanged political trajectory[10].

Conclusion

Several conclusions emerge from the foregoing description and analysis. First, the French initiative resulted in positive contributions by the military on all three humanitarian fronts. The security umbrella provided *Opération Turquoise* was critically important, especially in Rwanda but also in Zaire. Troops facilitated the humanitarian activities of aid agencies and provided useful relief in their own right. In Rwanda, they made a major contribution to the health sector; in Zaire, they helped halt the cholera epidemic and dispose of the bodies of those who succumbed to it. In both locations, the level and effectiveness of co-operation and respect between the military and the aid agencies improved over time.

Coming after the negative experience of Somalia, *Opération Turquoise* demonstrated that military forces could indeed play useful roles in the humanitarian sphere. In Somalia, as senior French military officers pointed out in interviews as they reflected on the different experience in *Opération Turquoise*, military and humanitarian personnel tended to be competitors in aid efforts, neither understanding the other's limits nor appreciating the other's comparative advantages. In both Zaire and Rwanda, a more complementary approach was taken, with an emphasis on co-ordination and collaboration. "Military forces can be supportive of humanitarian action", French officials rightly concluded, although they cautioned at the same time that "NGOs and UN agencies should not be diverted from their own goals".

Opération Turquoise commander General Lafourcade offered a helpful overall assessment in which others concur[11]. The experience demonstrated, in his judgement, that combattant soldiers could play a useful role in humanitarian operations but should not become humanitarian actors. That is, their task should be to provide security and support for humanitarian activities but not to engage in direct relief tasks themselves. That conclusion is borne out by their experience in the Rwanda crisis, where their principal and unique contribution was to re-establish security within which civil society, including aid activities, could proceed. At the same time, the exceptional circumstances lent merit to direct relief activities by especially equipped contingents from the military on a stop-gap basis.

A second conclusion is that a clearer separation of political-security and humanitarian objectives would have increased the effectiveness of associated aid activities. To the credit of *Opération Turquoise*, widely expressed concerns about a lack of impartiality were generally not borne out by events. Overcoming suspicion and criticism in the early going, French soldiers established themselves as providing the population, regardless of ethnic origins, with effective protection. At the same time, the confusion of the political and humanitarian objectives of the undertaking complicated the work of aid organisations.

Labelling the undertaking a security intervention rather than a humanitarian action would probably have reduced confusion, although it would not have quieted all of the criticism or mooted all issues of aid politicisation. The Rwanda experience confirms that humanitarian organisations would prefer a more limited and transparent security contribution by the military, allowing aid groups themselves to implement humanitarian activities within the security framework provided. At the same time, direct relief activities by the military may be welcome when aid personnel themselves are overmatched by an emergency.

Third, a mandate and willingness to use force contributed to *Opération Turquoise* success. Many concur with General Lafourcade's view that such interventions should be grounded in Chapter VII of the UN Charter, allowing the use of force and providing the necessary deterrent means. *Opération Turquoise* contrasted sharply with UNAMIR, which, operating under Chapter VI, was able to use force only in self-defence.

While French troops, acting with discipline and restraint, applied such force sparingly for preventive and protective purposes, their willingness to do was an effective deterrent. Having skilled troops who are able to use proportionate force proved indispensable.

Finally, *Opération Turquoise* demonstrated what one nation, prepared to deploy military assets in a major international humanitarian crisis, can achieve. Coming at a time when UN peacekeeping in Rwanda and beyond was overextended, the short-term success of an undertaking contracted to a member government was widely viewed as a credit to the United Nations and the Security Council itself. At the same time, it illuminated the need to enhance the capacity and responsiveness of multilateral institutions so as to decrease trade-offs in the future between acting with dispatch and proceeding multilaterally.

The mixed record of *Opération Turquoise* is captured in the judgements of two persons involved in the events of the day. The first is a Rwandan official in the new regime who requested anonymity; the second, Chairwoman Nathalie Duhamel of the French NGO AICF. Taken together, their perspectives, however different, capture the essential reality. "Without *Opération Turquoise*", observes the government official, "the situation would have been five times worse. It would have been better, however, to expand *Turquoise* to other parts in Rwanda"[12]. "France did not bring a long-term solution", notes the NGO official. "We are facing again almost the same problem as the one which existed in Rwanda before the intervention" (Broche, 1994).

Notes

1. Interview in *Armées d'aujourd'hui* #194, October 1994. Eventually, the French did jam RTLM, although the date on which broadcasts ceased is a matter of some disagreement.

2. See "Chronique des faits internationaux", *Revue générale de droit international public*, vol. XCVVIII, 4, 1994.

3. On the "Fachoda complex", see Glaser and Smith, 1994; Verschave, 1994. Also (Brauman, 1994). In an interview with the authors, the French ambassador to Rwanda Jacques Cortin dismissed the Fachoda complex as a factor in the intervention, reasoning that Rwanda would be unable to afford reconstructing its existing educational system to replace the French language with English.

4. The illustrations were provided at a symposium organised by Centre d'études de recherches internationales communautaires (CERIC), 1994 Humanitarian Intervention in Rwanda, Université Aix-Marseille III, Aix-en-Provence, April 6, 1995.

5. Fédération nationale des anciens des missions extérieures *Infos Extérieures #6*, Dec. 1994.

6. Their comments were made at the CERIC symposium referenced in note 4. Defence and Foreign Ministry spokesmen now use the figure of FF 1 billion with regularity.

7. TV debate on "Le devoir d'ingérence", LCI, March 13, 1995. Kouchner's views on humanitarian intervention are mentioned in Chapter 1.

8. For an elaboration of French military policy, cf. *Livre Blanc sur la Défense*, 1994, Paris, rapports officiels, La Documentation française. For a discussion of the nature and earmarks of humanitarian action as distinct from political-security initiatives, see: Coq and Floquet, 1994; Tanca, 1993; Jonah, 1993; Gordon, 1994; Chopra and Weiss, 1992; Damrosch and Scheffer, 1991; Sicilianos, 1990; Rougier, 1910, Pease and Forsythe, 1993.

   In the view of M.-J. Domestici-Met, humanitarian interventions were more coercive (that is, intervening troops did fight). She views *Opération Turquoise* as a belated protective measure unfortunately linked with international peace and security and not an "autonomous humanitarian action". While acknowledging the positive aspects of *Turquoise*, she expressed the view at the aforementioned CERIC symposium that "international humanitarian law is increasingly manipulated by the UN". On the same occasion, an ICRC official expressed the view that *Turquoise* fit the definition of a legal occupation.

9. Paul Gillespie, *The Irish Times*, July 23, 1994.

10. During the Summit, a conference was organised by two French NGOs on French policy toward Africa in general and Rwanda in particular. Cf. Agir Ici & Survie, 1995.

11. The General's comments were made at the symposium referenced in note 4.

12. Interview with the authors, September 1994.

Chapter 6

US Troops: Operation Support Hope

US troops made a significant contribution to the relief of acute suffering in the Rwanda crisis. The US initiative, Operation Support Hope, was by design separate from UNAMIR (Chapter 4). It was distinct in nature from the French-led security undertaking which preceded it (Chapter 5) and in scale from the commitments of troops by other governments for UN-related humanitarian purposes (Chapter 7). The largest single humanitarian undertaking by any of the militaries in the Rwanda theatre, it requires review in its own right.

Deployed July 23, 1994 when UN peace-keeping presence was still struggling to establish itself, Operation Support Hope followed more than a week's dramatic coverage by the media of the plight of refugees in Goma. Arriving on the scene a month after French troops, Operation Support Hope was more explicitly humanitarian than *Opération Turquoise*. While stand-alone in concept, it assisted UN peacekeepers, UN and other humanitarian organisations, military contingents from other countries, and persons affected by the crisis.

Using a force of just over 3 000, Operation Support Hope achieved its basic objectives of halting deaths due to disease and starvation and lending support to humanitarian organisations. Estimates of its cost range from $123.9 million to more than $1 billion. Most US troops withdrew from Goma and Kigali after five weeks, leaving behind a more manageable situation for aid organisations.

Terms of Engagement and Activities

Authorised by President Clinton on July 22, Joint Task Force Support Hope was given the mission of providing "assistance to humanitarian agencies and third-nation forces conducting relief operations in theatre to alleviate the immediate suffering of Rwandan refugees". Activities were to include water purification and distribution in Goma, airfield services in Goma, Kigali and other locations, and airhead and cargo distribution at Entebbe.

Joint Task Force Operation Support Hope was co-ordinated by the European Command in Stuttgart, Germany and implemented through civil military operations centres (CMOCs) established in Goma, Kigali, and Entebbe. Joint Task Force Alpha operated out of Goma, Joint Task Force Bravo from Kigali. The CMOC in Entebbe co-ordinated incoming flights and the onward dispatch of relief supplies by air and ground. In Germany, Stuttgart provided back-up support while the Rhein-Main airforce base was a frequent point of departure.

Rules of engagement stressed the humanitarian nature of the mission and the peacetime circumstances involved. "Force will not be used unless necessary", official guidance said, "and then, only the minimum". Although "a military humanitarian assistance operation carried out under the overall co-ordination umbrella of the UN", the undertaking was under US command and control. "US military personnel are not part of a UN peace-keeping operation", Secretary of Defence William J. Perry told a congressional committee. "Our participation is strictly in the context of the humanitarian effort at the urgent request of the UNHCR"[1].

The Operation used regular armed forces personnel, supplemented by reserve and Air National Guard units. Troops were drawn from 118 locations in the US and around the world. Rather than deploying entire units (for example, an engineer company), the Pentagon called up smaller modules (a bulldozer section) to ensure appropriate skills. No special training in humanitarian support functions was provided. "[T]he forces that performed so well in Rwanda, Zaire and Uganda", observed their commander, Lieutenant-General Daniel R. Schroeder, "were standard military units executing their wartime skills in a disciplined manner" (Schroeder, 1994)[2].

The incremental cost of the Operation was placed by the Defence Department at $123.9 million. Because the operation in its entirety was by definition humanitarian, all costs associated with it (for example, of sending public affairs officers and photographers to the region and servicing them there) were included in the figure. Also included was an item for transportation assistance provided to humanitarian organisations in the form of moving personnel and material into the region. The entire cost was borne by the Defence Department, the bulk of it through specially appropriated funds[3].

The event which triggered the decision to deploy US troops was the massive exodus of refugees into Zaire on July 14. By July 17, some 1.2 million had sought shelter in the North Kivu region of Zaire around the city of Goma. A shortage of food, potable water, health care and shelter quickly began to take its toll. The first case of cholera was diagnosed July 20; within a month, some 58 000-80 000 cases had been reported (Goma Epidemiology Group, 1995). International relief personnel already on the scene and those who hurried to the area were overwhelmed by the scale and the fast-moving nature of the crisis.

Members of an assessment team from the Defence Department arrived from Stuttgart on July 21. The first US troops began deploying July 23, touching down in Goma July 25. On July 26 at 10:47 a.m., potable water began to flow from the US Army's Reverse Osmosis Water Purification Units (ROWPUs) in Lake Kivu. Activities by US troops concluded in Goma on August 25. Operations in Kigali, which commenced July 30, concluded August 27. Within a month, most Operation Support Hope personnel had left the region. The three focal points of US military attention were Goma, Kigali, and south-western Rwanda.

Operations around Goma

The ordeal of refugees in Zaire triggered Operation Support Hope and provided the "initial centre of gravity for US efforts" (Schroeder, 1994). A visit to Goma on July 19 by USAID Administrator Brian Atwood and Nan Borton, head of the Office of Foreign Disaster Assistance, had lent additional weight to calls for US military involvement. The objectives for US troops in Goma were to establish and operate water purification and distribution systems and to provide 24-hour airfield services there.

Water purification began at once and grew steadily in volume. Production finally overtook storage capacity on August 12. Storage was subsequently expanded until, after August 27, there were sufficient supplies on hand to meet the survival requirement of five litres per person per day. (A significant reduction in numbers of refugees during this period aided the per capita production figures.) After August 11, water purification efforts begun by the US military were taken over by the UN, to whom the US military donated its equipment.

The Goma airport was small and congested. In late July, refugees and townspeople crowded the runways and surrounded aircraft on the ground. Limited capacity restricted the number and size of US and other military air transport that could be accommodated. The airport was operating under the direction of the French military as a point of entry for activities of *Opération Turquoise* in southwestern Rwanda. The US military thus joined efforts already under way, concentrating on increasing the facility's "throughput". The US brought in air-traffic controllers and runway lighting to allow for round-the-clock operation and provided forklifts to shorten loading time.

Media attention to Goma refugees and the US soldiers coming to their rescue highlighted an airdrop of food on July 24. Designed to assist refugees in Camp Katalé near Goma who had, it turned out, received a WFP shipment the previous day, the airdrop was undertaken without adequate warning to the aid agencies, was well off the mark, and damaged a banana plantation in the process. An official on the ground publicly dissociated the United Nations from the airdrop operation. Other aid officials labelled it a "publicity stunt". The Defence Department explained that "the first drops were, in effect, a practice run, to train personnel on the ground"[4]. The drop zone had been selected by UNHCR and was hit precisely from the air, they said; reporters had simply not been positioned properly to observe.

Despite start-up difficulties, activities in Goma saw the US military adapt quickly to the needs and realities on the ground. Troops concentrated on water and sanitation rather than on airdrops, shifting air operations to Kigali and Entebbe, which, some in the military insisted, had been the intention all along. Responding to unmet needs in Goma, however, the Air Force activated four KC-10 fuel tankers which provided mid-air refuelling for aircraft waiting to land and delivered fuel to Entebbe for use throughout the theatre.

Operations around Kigali

The objectives for Kigali were to provide 24-hour airfield services and support the humanitarian activities of UN and NGO organisations. The airfield and terminal facilities were in use but in disrepair when the US military deployed July 29 to expedite activities and begin round-the-clock operations. The following day, the airport opened for 24-hour operations; within two months, the number of flights and the tonnage offloaded had increased substantially (Schroeder, 1994).

US troops repaired runway damage from the war, trained airport personnel, and reorganised airport services. Commercial traffic began again September 8. Kigali was thus able to serve as the nexus for expanded security and humanitarian activities throughout Rwanda. Withdrawing from Kigali in later August, US troops left behind a small contingent with ongoing responsibilities in co-ordinating air logistics support and civil-military humanitarian activities.

To support the work of aid organisations in Rwanda, the US on August 5 set up a civilian military operations cell in the UNDP compound in Kigali. Staffed by a US colonel and associated personnel, the cell was located in the building which also housed the UN Rwanda Emergency Operation (UNREO). Also on hand and a partner in co-ordination efforts was the US Government's Disaster Assistance Relief Team (DART), which during the period of May 1994 through February 1995 carried out a range of assessment, reporting, and liaison functions. While for security reasons US troops were not permitted to leave the Kigali airport, exceptions were made for the CMOC contingent and for officials participating in regular briefings at UNAMIR.

As in Goma, however, there were complications. At the time of the initial deployment of Operation Support Hope, the US government lacked a Status of Forces Agreement with the Rwandan authorities. An airborne contingent from the Joint Task Force en route to Kigali was therefore diverted to Entebbe until the United States had recognised the new Rwandan government and had made the necessary legal arrangements to protect US government personnel and property. (That US troops functioned in Zaire throughout Operation Support Hope without a Status of Forces Agreement was an item of major US concern.)

Arriving in Kigali, too, US troops found many activities already under way. Rather than moving overnight and single-handedly to render the airport more fully operational, they joined with UNAMIR and other UN efforts toward that end. Also a partner was the Canadian air force, which had been using the field on a regular basis since April, including during wartime conditions, to supply UNAMIR and humanitarian organisations. As with the Goma airport, the tasks in Kigali were less dramatic and the scene more crowded with other actors than anticipated.

Support for Operations in South-western Rwanda

The third focal point was more indirect. In relation to south-western Rwanda, the US mounted a number of activities, none requiring troops on the ground. These included overflights to monitor population movements throughout the south-west; transport from Addis Ababa of the Ethiopian battalion which, under UNAMIR auspices, would take over from the French; transport of some of the *Turquoise* troops back to France; and reinforcement of strategies by aid organisations to discourage panic-generated flight from the south-west into Zaire.

Such efforts proved successful. "By 22 August, the UNAMIR relief of the French was completed", reported Operation Support Hope. "With the exception of a comparatively minor surge of some thousand refugees, the combined efforts of the [Joint Task Force], UNAMIR, UNREO, the NGOs and the [Government of Rwanda] succeeded in persuading the majority of displaced persons in the south-west to stay put". (Schroeder, 1994). Maintaining a careful distinction between its own humanitarian mission and UNAMIR, the US had nevertheless backstopped the peace-keeping operation as well.

Activities in all three areas were supported by the Entebbe-based Joint Task Force. The airport there became the co-ordinating base for Operation Support Hope and the hub for transferring incoming cargoes from larger aircraft to smaller ones more suited to airports throughout the operating theatre. The largest single US military in-theatre presence was in Entebbe, with 980 of 2603 troops stationed there as of August 7. Smaller contingents were based in Mombassa, Harare, and Nairobi. The US military airlift itself will be assessed later.

The activities of Operation Support Hope differed from those of UNAMIR and *Opération Turquoise* in that fostering a climate of stability for civilians and aid workers was not a major objective. To be sure, US indirectly helped maintain stability in south-western Rwanda, and aid workers in Goma "breathed more easily when US troops were on hand" (Schroeder, 1994). Operation Support Hope concentrated instead on the other two functions of the military in the humanitarian sphere: support for the activities of humanitarian organisations and relief activities by the troops themselves.

Humanitarian Support and Direct Relief

Operation Support Hope lent formidable logistical capacity to humanitarian organisations involved in the Rwanda relief effort. The US military was the major architect, or, perhaps more precisely, the major contractor, for the international air bridge into and around the region. From its hub in Entebbe and working in concert with the UNHCR air operations cell in Geneva, Operation Support Hope received incoming aircraft and dispatched planes with relief cargo and aid personnel to airfields throughout the region and, as indicated, enhanced air operations in Goma and Kigali.

A fleet of some 50 aircraft were used, largely military aircraft but also some commercially leased planes. Initially, priority went to water purification equipment, medicine, food, and vehicles, with a particular eye to achieving a multiplier effect. For example, the airlifting of ten vehicles for the World Food Programme into Entebbe allowed overland transport by WFP of essential food throughout the region. Extensive US military sealift capacity was also used, with military supply ships offloading water purification equipment and WFP trucks in Mombassa.

During the period between July 22 and the end of August, US military flights into the region totalled 903, or 46 percent of all relief flights. Of these, 273 sorties were "strategic": that is, using large incoming C5A and C141 military transports. The remaining 630 sorties were "tactical": that is, using smaller aircraft such as C-130s used for "intra-theatre" transport — between Entebbe, for example, and Kigali or Goma. UN flights, 1050 in number, made up the remaining 54 percent of such flights.

Decisions about what would be shipped when and where were made by an air-operations cell at UNHCR headquarters in Geneva, to which the Defence Department seconded personnel. Despite problems described below among aid agencies in establishing priorities, the military sought to be accommodating. When UNHCR on August 13-14 shifted priority to medicines, blankets, plastic sheeting, and other non-food items — adequate quantities of food were on hand in Goma — the new priorities were reflected in the cargoes moved.

The benefits of US logistic support to UNAMIR were also sizeable. During the week of August 17, Operation Support Hope moved quickly to airlift the Ethiopian battalion from Addis Ababa to Kigali, positioning it to take over the duties from *Opération Turquoise* in the south-west sector. US military transport also airlifted UNAMIR's Bangladeshi battalion and the Australian army's field hospital. The US military had a comparative advantage in air logistics *vis-à-vis* not only humanitarian organisations but also other militaries.

US troops were not involved in hands-on relief efforts in Rwanda, although had events proceeded as planned they might have been. Operation Support Hope's plans specified that once the Kigali airport was handling relief cargo more efficiently, US troops would transport relief goods into the countryside and if necessary handle their distribution. Delays in the return of the refugees rendered those tasks unnecessary.

As a result, the only direct aid activities were in Zaire. Operation Support Hope gave top priority to potable-water production as key to its overall objective of stopping the dying. The US on-the-ground contingent in Goma included water specialists as well as tanker drivers, and security and administrative support staff. Although a high-visibility effort, the group involved in water sector involved only a small portion of the 337 troops in Goma in early August. The troops in Goma, in turn, were a fraction of those in Operation Support Hope as a whole.

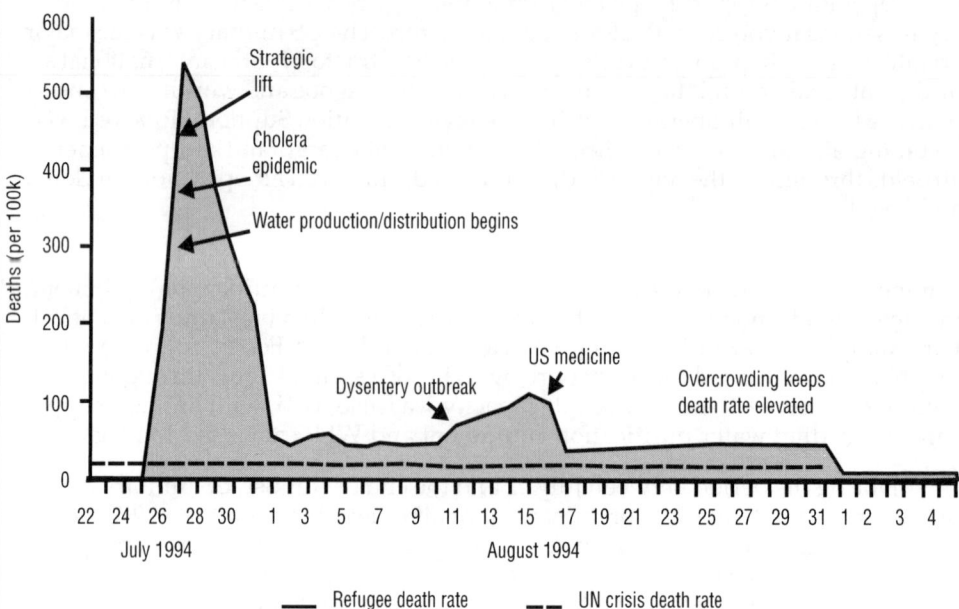

Figure 6.1. **Stopping the Dying**

[Chart showing deaths per 100k from 22 July 1994 to 4 August 1994, with annotations: "Strategic lift", "Cholera epidemic", "Water production/distribution begins", "Dysentery outbreak", "US medicine", "Overcrowding keeps death rate elevated". Legend: Refugee death rate, UN crisis death rate.]

Source: U.S. Department of Defense.

Death rates in Goma were quickly reduced once the US troops arrived, as iillustrated in dramatic fashion by Figure 6.1. The tally of bodies buried per day dropped from an high of 6 500 on July 27 to fewer than 500 on August 6 (Schroeder, 1994). In interpreting the startling results, however, US military officials themselves noted that "the mortality rate was dropping even as water systems came on line" (Schroeder, 1994). an observation confirmed by epidemological studies. "The [cholera] epidemic reached its peak during the third week of July, and by the middle of first week of August it was declining" (Siddique, Salam, Islam, Akram, Majumdar, Zaman, Fronczak, and Laston, 1995), observed one medical team from Bangladesh which set up a treatment centre in the Katindo camp. In other words, US troops were associated with a welcome result but were not themselves a decisive force in bringing it about.

The activities of US troops in both management of the airhead at Entebbe and water treatment and distribution in Zaire were part of service packages designed by UNHCR. Discussions of the services which the Defence Department agreed to provide had been under discussion at UNHCR's initiative even before US troops deployed; arrangements were finalised after they had arrived. UNHCR officials believe that preliminary discussions of the need for troops in humanitarian support roles may have encouraged the US to deploy military assets accordingly [5].

Assessment

The contribution of Operation Support Hope was generally positive in the view not only of the US officials who conducted it but also of humanitarian organisations who benefited from it. At the same time, its effectiveness was undercut by serious problems in planning, operational strategies, cost, and policy context. Both the positive and negative aspects require review.

The US military's assessment of Operation Support Hope was unabashedly positive. US armed forces, arriving when the crisis was out of control, performed a clearly delineated task well, took no casualties, and exited according to plan and on schedule. The attainment of all its objectives distinguished the Rwanda operation from the US experience in Somalia. Its timely wind-up set the Rwanda undertaking apart from its predecessor operation in northern Iraq which, while successful in rescuing the Kurds, continued more than three years later to absorb Pentagon resources.

Humanitarian organisations, too, gave the military generally high marks. Many, in fact, had encouraged their involvement. "To me it was clear when I landed that we needed military help", commented Filippo Grandi, one of the first UNHCR officials on the scene in Goma after the massive influx in July. "The mobilisation took longer than I would have liked, but once it arrived it solved many problems"[6]. UNHCR's spokesman Ray Wilkinson had called on the US military to impose "a military-style operation" at the Goma airport as the best way of accelerating the arrival, offloading, and departure of aircraft.

Many NGOs were highly positive. An official of the French NGO *Médecins du monde* found US troops "very efficient" and credited them with providing "invaluable help". Staff members of *Pharmaciens sans frontières* gave them high marks for assistance in unloading medicines from cargo planes at the Goma airport, often in the space of only 15-20 minutes. "They were really obliging", recalled logistics co-ordinator Michel Forget. "They put trucks at our disposal. They were always ready to help". Other NGOs mentioned with particular appreciation the use of army water tankers to supply the *Centre hospitalier* in Kigali.

Humanitarian organisations were particularly impresssed with the ability of the US military to implement the "support" approach conveyed in the Operation's name. A year later, General Schroeder himself remembered the humanitarian-support feature as the hallmark of the undertaking. "There are international agencies that can do humanitarian assistance much better than the military can. However, in very special circumstances the military can also play a role"[7]. Indeed, Schroeder's approach permeated the undertaking. "Our task was to help the aid organisations gain control of a very bad situation", recalled one of those involved. "The greatest thing we put down there was organisational structure".

Arriving with a clear humanitarian support mission, Operation Support Hope adapted its work to complement what other military and humanitarian personnel were already doing. This approach was facilitated by rules of engagement which gave the commander "considerable flexibility in determining his end state, and the manner in which he would accomplish his mission" (Schroeder, 1994). Despite massive assets in personnel, material, and lift capacity, Operation Support Hope consciously sought to avoid becoming "the supermarket of the [overall relief] operation". It was committed to "keeping the Joint Task Force footprint as small as possible". It withdrew at a time when "the UN and NGO community had recovered from the initial surge [of emergency needs] and were capable of maintaining the camps indefinitely" (Schroeder, 1994).

Planning

The first major area of criticism concerned planning. Effective collaboration between military and humanitarian organisations requires joint planning. In the rapidly deteriorating circumstances of Goma, however, planning was difficult. The assessment team from the Defence Department arrived in the region on the day before the president announced the operation, the first troops on the day after. "We simply had to jump into the thing", observed a Pentagon official. "Without having a clear picture of what was needed, our direction [from headquarters] was to lean forward and provide help". It is understandable, therefore, that serious consultations did not take place at the time in Washington, New York, or the region preceding deployment.

Yet the humanitarian crisis did not begin with the arrival of the first Rwandan refugees in Goma in mid-July. It had been evolving for months, preoccupying many of the same actors whose work the US troops would suddenly familiarise themselves with and seek to support. In this context, the misfired Goma airdrop was a telling symbol of a major player arriving late on the scene and looking for a constructive contribution to make — but without much awareness of what was already taking place.

Equally problematic was the short duration of the troops' presence. Some aid officials who acknowledged being so overwhelmed that they welcomed US military assistance were careful to balance appreciation for help received against disappointment that the troops were leaving — prematurely, in their view. NGOs who complimented the troops on assistance rendered also described them as slipping away "as thieves in the night". "They moved out with the same lightning speed they came in", noted one senior UN aid official, "leaving us all aghast".

The absence of planning made for initial problems of relationships with aid workers and other military personnel already on the ground. "A pre-planned deployment would probably admit to a more deliberate establishment of relationships between military and UN/NGO organisations", reported General Schroeder. "But in the case of Operation Support Hope, the US military and the UN/NGO community in theatre litreally 'met on the dance floor' "(Schroeder 1994). With working relationships and communications channels in place, embarrassing disconnects could have been avoided. The US military's contribution to disaster prevention and preparedness was necessarily even more limited.

Lack of co-ordination within the UN compounded the problem. At daily interagency meetings in Washington at which priorities were established, representatives from various US government offices would plead their cases for assisting either aid agencies or UNAMIR. The vetting included the State Department and AID as well as the Pentagon. Some officials wanted UNAMIR strengthened so that US troops might be withdrawn more quickly. Others held that Operation Support Hope's humanitarian-support mission was primary, arguing that "We had some important national interests to advance from a strictly humanitarian viewpoint".

Early on, US officials asked the United Nations in New York for UN-wide priorities, or a least a clear relative ranking of UNAMIR and UNHCR requirements. As in the US government, however, each of the various UN departments considered its own requirements pre-eminent. "The UN never came back to us with clear priorities, leaving us to fight it out among ourselves", observed one regular participant in the US interagency process. Had the UN provided the clarification requested, he said, "I'm not sure it would have saved more lives, but it would have created a more effective framework for decision making".

There were also co-ordination problems between and among humanitarian agencies. "Everything is a priority in an emergency", observed Peter MacDermott, a UNICEF emergencies officer. That being the case, concurred a US Army official,"The system works much better when you have an international organisation such as UNHCR or UNICEF in charge. Otherwise you can end up with too much water or too much food". Achieving co-ordination, however, proved difficult.

The UN Department of Humanitarian Affairs had a global mandate for co-ordinating relief efforts in complex emergencies. In the Rwanda crisis, it was represented in Kigali and around Rwanda by the UN Rwanda Emergency Office (UNREO), which had no mandate beyond Rwanda's borders. UNHCR headed the air operations cell in Geneva, having played a similar role in the Yugoslav crisis and being encouraged by the US and other militaries, who wanted a clear focal point. Yet UNHCR had no mandate for the internally displaced within Rwanda and experienced difficulty in conveying priorities that other UN organisations perceived as fair. The presence of scores of private relief groups added still other elements to the crowded dance floor.

Operational Strategies

Operation Support Hope's activities in the transport and water sectors came in for serious questioning, as did the military's preoccupation with security.

In the logistics area, there were disconnects — some minor, others major — as might be expected in any such massive operation mounted with such speed. A contingent of 600 British troops, promised US military air transport to the region, were kept waiting for more than a week. The US Secretary of Defence received an irate call from his Finnish counterpart who had been promised transport for four water tankers which, a week later, were still on the tarmac in Finland.

Conceding that more promises were made than could be honoured, Pentagon officials also stressed that tough choices were unavoidable. "Everybody wanted everything transported", they explained. "It came down to the number of airplanes the Operation had at its disposal". With some aircraft standing by for possible use in Haiti, where a military invasion by US troops to restore the elected president was planned, "The Air Force did a fine job within the constraints of availability. Sure, some of the shipments had to wait". Those deferred, the military indicated, were of lower priority than those which were transported. Moreover, they believed that humanitarian organisations had an unrealistic view of what the military could deliver on their behalf.

Illustrative of the problem was the experience of one NGO, Oxfam-United Kingdom and Ireland, in transporting equipment from England for its water project in Goma. Although Oxfam considered chartering commercial air transport with its own funds, military aircraft seemed ideal for the plastic piping needed to supply distribution points within refugee camps outside Goma with water drawn from Lake Kivu and tankered to storage vessels in the camps. The US Air Force, too, seemed ideal: it alone among the militaries involved had jumbo aircraft which could transport the necessary volume and payloads of plastic piping and associated equipment. The cargo was demonstrably humanitarian and the water sector was one for which the US military itself had assumed major responsibility. US troops worked closely with Oxfam on the ground in Goma.

On July 26, AID told Oxfam that US military transport would be provided, confirming three days later that two C-141 Starlifters (subsequently a single Galaxy C-5A) would do the transport. Departing Britain August 5 and after a stop in Germany, the C-5A was diverted to Italy for repairs. A subsequent diversion, again for mechanical reasons, rerouted the plane from Entebbe to Mombassa, where the cargo was unloaded. Half the shipment — as things turned out, the less essential half — was moved to Goma on August 11, where Oxfam supplies had run out August 3. The balance caught up several days later. The shipment arrived more than two weeks later than it might have had the NGO chartered two 707 aircraft, an expensive option discarded in favour of free air transport.

"The whole thing was a disaster", commented Marcus Thompson, Oxfam's Emergencies Director, looking back, more chastened than bitter. "We were ill-served by the American military, but the fault was also mine. I should never have put all my eggs in one basket. Accepting the offer of free air transport may be terribly tempting, but frankly I wouldn't do it again". There was, in fact, a better alternative: "Pay for the shipping yourself and you get what you want delivered when you want it". However, commercial charters themselves needed slots in the queue assigned in Geneva and might have faced even more difficulty in the vetting process without an interested inside advocate.

Serious problems also developed in the US military's own efforts in the water sector. The increase during a five-week period from no potable water to some 4 million litres a day was indeed impressive. However, the contribution of the US military to that overall result was relatively modest. Its Reverse Osmosis Water Purification Units (ROWPUs) were "designed to provide high-quality water for small numbers of people; whereas what was actually needed was safe water for hundreds of thousands of people" (Vassall-Adams, 1994). The army's two ROWPUs were able to produce 600 gallons of potable water per hour each.

Sizing up the situation on the ground, the US military rallied behind other efforts, particularly one by a small unit from the Mountain/Fire Rescue of Calaveras County, California. Its pumping equipment put 3 000 gallons of contaminated water from Lake Kivu per hour into tankers, where the cleansing action of chlorine as the vehicles were driven to distribution points rendered the water adequately potable. The water was then dumped into large tanks provided by Oxfam, allowing the tankers to return at once to the lake for more. Machinery and supplies had been ferried to the region by US Airforce C5-A transport in a quick mobilisation which involved interventions by a Californian senator and the White House.

Reflecting upon the experience, disease-control experts have questioned the approach taken by the US military and the aid agencies they were supporting. The Goma Epidemiology Group concluded that in future emergencies the kind of programme in the water and sanitation area which had in fact evolved by the second month of the crisis should be implemented at once. "In the emergency phase", the Group concluded, what should be used are "effective, low-technology measures [such as] bucket chlorination at untreated water sources, designated defecation areas, active case-finding through community outreach, and oral rehydration". (Goma Epidemiology Group, 1995). The US military itself conceded that had it had a better sense of what was needed, it would have dispensed with the ROWPUs, which were "over capable" for the circumstances, and concentrated instead on pumpers such as those of Mountain/Fire Rescue[8].

The military's preoccupation with security also affected its contribution. Aid agencies felt that having US water tankers in Goma move in pairs, each with a driver and companion, all four armed and flak-jacketed, was unwieldy and that restricting US troops to the Kigali airport reduced their utility. The military defended both procedures as necessary in the circumstances. "A uniformed person on the ground affects perceptions", noted General Schroeder, "and acts as a magnet". Moreover, the airport restriction kept the troops focused on their mission rather than having them drawn in to relief activities[9]. In short, normal military concerns for force protection limited the extent of support that even an exclusively humanitarian mission could provide.

Cost and Cost-effectiveness

A third problem area concerned cost and cost-effectiveness. The cost of Operation Support Hope is important in its own right and for its relevance to the use of US troops in future such emergencies.

Estimates of the cost of Operation Support Hope vary widely. The US Department of Defence uses the figure of $123.9 million for incremental costs, defined as "only those costs that would not have been incurred except for the operation". That figure excludes the US assessed share of peace keeping costs for UNAMIR of $72.6 million[10]. Also excluded are extensive expenditures on humanitarian assistance in the Rwanda emergency by the Department of State and USAID. Those latter expenditures as of September 30, 1994 totalled $155.4 million and by April 1995 had risen to $375 million (USAID, 1995).

Costs estimates significantly higher than $123.9 million have been mentioned in a number of quarters, however. As Operation Support Hope was proceeding, senior Defence Department officials used figures of "roughly $250 million"[11] and "approximately $270 million"[12]. Such estimates, the Department explained later, were made at a time when a more extended operation was anticipated. Mid-level officials associated with the operation place the figure higher still, perhaps as high as or in excess of $1 billion. Contacted in mid-1995, one official from a single element in the entire complex operation indicated that he himself had approved funds in excess of $123.9 million.

Pentagon officials acknowledge the difficulties in computing an accurate overall figure for such an operation. At issue is both a methodology for determining what items should and should not be included, and a system for tallying expenditures (and reimbursements). "There was no one single individual who was the resource manager or comptroller for the whole operation", explained one Europe-based US Defence Department official. Separate persons and units were in charge of expenditures on Operation Support in Europe and in the United States, and also for each of the services involved.

From a more detached vantage point, the US General Accounting Office has confirmed the problem. "[I]t should be recognised", observed one of its recent reviews of the roles of the Department of Defence (DOD) in peace operations, "that DOD's financial systems cannot reliably determine costs. The services [themselves] do not have the systems in place to capture actual incremental costs" (US GAO, 1995c). As a result, while it is highly likely that the incremental costs of the US military assets utilised in 1994 in the Rwanda crisis exceeded $123.9 million, the question remains whether that figure is low by a factor of two or three — or perhaps eight or ten.

Whatever the costs, US military outlays for the Rwanda operation pale by comparison with those of other major peace operations. GAO figures compiled for Fiscal Years 1992-1995 allow comparisons among expenditures for four major recent initiatives. Total US expenditures on Rwanda of $515.6 million are dwarfed by its expenditures on Haiti of $1.596 billion, Somalia $2.282 billion, and the former Yugoslavia $2.480 billion[13]. Even if estimates for Rwanda on the order of $1 billion are used, the undertaking ended up costing significantly less to the US than any of the other three major peace operations.

Figure 8.2 (in Chapter 8) provides an overview of the cost of Operation Support Hope in relation to other military assets utilised during the Rwanda crisis in 1994. Given the nature of UNAMIR/UNOMUR and *Opération Turquoise* as predominantly security undertakings, the US commited the largest amount of military assets of any nation to the Rwanda crisis for explicitly humanitarian purposes. US military assets probably exceeded the sum total of the UNHCR-associated troops described in the following chapter. More detailed comparisons would require firmer figures for both US and French military assets.

Such comparisons raise larger issues of cost-effectiveness, however difficult those issues may be in the absence of firmer cost figures. The Rwanda experience bears out the viewpoint expressed at the time by Members of the US Congress and senior Pentagon officials. They were in agreement that "The US military is the only organisation in the world that can bring to bear this kind of relief effort in a short time frame in an emergency situation"[14]. The data also suggest, however, the comparative advantage of the military may be narrower than generally assumed, and more costly. With respect to the airlift, probably the largest single cost element in Operation Support Hope, evidence suggests that while the US military was unrivalled in lift capacity, the costs of the services provided were far higher than those arranged privately.

Responding to the crisis in Goma, which began with the influx of refugees on Thursday, July 14, humanitarian organisations quickly put into place their own transport arrangements. "WFP was able to deliver food by air within 48 hours and establish a series of road convoys within ten days"[15]. The first aircraft chartered by the UN World Food Programme touched down at the Goma airport on Sunday, July 17. A commercially leased Ilyushin diverted from WFP's Sudan programme, the plane carried 40 tons of enriched food. On July 21, the first WFP convoy arrived overland from Uganda, with 11 trucks transporting 330 tons of food diverted from Sudan-bound stocks in Kampala. On July 22, a second convoy of 21 trucks transporting 572 tons arrived. WFP, which in 1994 managed almost 4 million tons of food aid worldwide, quickly brought to bear a network of relationships and resources to address the Goma challenge.

Experienced NGOs moved with equal dispatch. The first flight arranged by a consortium of religious organisations, Church World Action-Rwanda, arrived in the morning of Saturday, July 16. It carried the staff person who would head the relief operation in Goma and 14 tons of rice supplied by the ICRC. The consortium was able to respond within a day to a request because one member, the Lutheran World Federation, diverted a Hercules transport plane from an airlift operating in the southern Sudan. The flight was the first of 157, which by the end of September had moved hundreds of passengers and more than 2635 tons of relief supplies to Goma and south-western Rwanda[16].

With less experience but greater assets, the US military airlift took longer to be put into place. The first aircraft arrived on Monday, July 25, 11 days after the influx began and a week after the first relief flight, carrying some 20 tons of non-food and medical items for UNICEF. (The airdrop at the refugee camp described earlier had taken place the previous day.) While organisations such as WFP and Church World Action-Rwanda were able to respond more quickly, however, the scale of need overwhelmed their logistical capacity. The US military helped to provide desperately needed stopgap assistance.

The scale of need in Goma, however, was beyond what even the military, or the military and aid groups combined, could meet with air transport. Providing .5 kilograms of food per day to each of 800 000 refugees would require 400 tons per day. Given the cramped space at the Goma airport, receiving such tonnage by air would be difficult, even if air transport could be mobilised. The formidable strategic lift capacity of C5As and C-141s would require downsizing within the region to smaller payload aircraft.

Although air transport from a variety of sources provided critically needed assistance early on, US military officials realised from the start the limitations of air assets. Noting the difficulties of the Goma airport and the burgeoning needs of the refugee populations, one commented wryly, "Trucks is power". Overland supply of essential relief commodities would ultimately prove more critical than air transport.

As the Oxfam experience suggested, some UN and private agencies concluded from the Goma experience that while free military air transport has its advantages, they will seek to make their own arrangements with commercial carriers. Doing so provides greater control over what is moved and allows them to make decisions otherwise out of their hands. They believe that the commercial costs incurred are significantly below — by 40 percent in one estimate — the incremental costs of military air transport. Even though the freight bills of the military are not the responsibility of aid groups themselves, keeping costs to a minimum in a world of shrinking aid resources is an important consideration. In extreme circumstances, however, commercial arrangements may be difficult to negotiate and military assistance indispensable.

Cost factors thus make the comparative advantage of the military quite specific. "In most cases", commented Tun Myat, head of WFP's Transport Division, "we can probably arrange airlifts far quicker than the military can into places they wouldn't be prepared to go at a fraction of the cost"[17]. That is, the contribution of the military in air transport is likely to be greatest in the initial phase of major emergencies in areas served by secure and accessible airports when the amounts of relief materiel requiring transport exceed the ability or resources of aid agencies to provide or charter the necessary space.

Figure 6.2. **The Rwanda Crisis Before and After Operation Support Hope**

July 21, 94		September 28, 94
	Goma	
• Death rate: est. 3 000 +/day • Water distribution: nil • Airfield throughput: 15 flts		• Death rate: est. 250/day • Water distribution: over 3M ltrs/day • Airfield throughput: 30 flts
	Kigali	
• Airfield Service: Nil • Cargo Capacity: Nil • Throughput: Nil • NGO presence: 7 • NGO trucks: Nil		• Airfield service: day/night, all-weather certified • Cargo Capacity: 1000+ st/day • Throughput: 300-600 st/day • NGO presence: over 70 • NGO trucks: over 800
	Entebbe	
• Relief throughput: nil • CMOC: no co-ordination		• Relief throughput: 300 st/day • CMOC: co-ordinating relief
	The southwest	
• Massive displaced population • French withdrawal: 22 Aug. • UNAMIR forces: 350 (approx.)		• Refugee exodus *not* occurred • French out • UNAMIR forces: 3 500 (approx.)

Source: US Department of Defense.

The US Policy Context

The fourth problem area concerned the relationship between Operation Support Hope and US policy toward the Rwanda crisis. The main issues here were the timing of the US response and US policy toward the Rwanda crisis more broadly.

Judgements about the effectiveness of Operation Support Hope once deployed need to be viewed against the prior question of why it came late in the overall sequence of events in the crisis. US troops arriving in Goma July 25 were generally well received by humanitarian and military personnel, many of whom had been there since the influx began July 14, some of them considerably longer. The feeling among some, however, was articulated by a UN relief official who recalls telling the Americans, "If you had come ten days earlier, you'd have been welcome".

The larger question, however, concerned not a week lost here or there but a pattern of inaction by the US government dating back to April events and before. "The leaders of wealthy nations tend to wait until public opinion forces them to respond to disasters with enormous resource infusions", observed the Goma Epidemiology Group in its retrospective on the crisis. "Although this delayed response has included the deployment of military forces with their formidable logistic capability, the mobilisation of military resources is very expensive. Because military deployment depends on political decisions, it cannot always be integrated into disaster preparedness planning" (Goma Epidemiology Group, 1995).

Other disaster management specialists concur with the view that the massive nature of the Rwanda problem and the formidable scale of the response highlights the need for greater preparedness by governments and enhanced capacity among aid agencies. The conclusion drawn by the Goma group has considerable support in other quarters. "[W]hile continuing to explore ways of improving the efficiency and cost-effectiveness of the military role in emergency relief, donor nations would be wise to invest funds in strengthening the existing network of relief organisations" (Goma Epidemiology Group, 1995).

The policy context for Operation Support Hope was provided by Presidential Decision Directive 25 (PDD-25), approved in May 1994. Reflecting the experience of the United States in recent peace-keeping operations and heavily influenced by difficulties in Somalia, PDD-25 elaborated a checklist of detailed conditions which would govern US involvement in major future crises. "[T]he first full implementation of PDD-25 was in Rwanda", reported a study by the GAO. "Our evaluation of the [US] decision to participate in Rwanda indicated that the US agencies closely scrutinised operations against the factors outlined in PDD-25 before committing to support the mission" (US GAO, 1995c)[18].

US policy during the earlier phases of the crisis in the region cannot be examined here in detail. However, US efforts in the Security Council after the April events are viewed by some as having helped set the stage for the humanitarian tragedy to which the world was then forced to respond. "US success in reducing UNAMIR I and in delaying the deployment of UNAMIR II", concludes a Canadian review, "inadvertently but undeniably exacerbated the humanitarian crisis and made it necessary for the US itself to spend an estimated 50 times what an effective and preventive UN peace enforcement mission would have cost" (LaRose-Edwards, 1994)[19]. "It took the horrors of Goma", observed a *Guardian* editorial tartly, "to overcome Washington's reluctance to get involved"[20].

The success perceived by the military is also circumscribed by the continuation of the crisis in Rwanda long after the departure of US troops. The return of refugees to their homes was described by US Defence Secretary Perry in August 1994 as "the crucial end state we seek". The failure of repatriation and reconstruction is, not, of course, the responsibility of the US or other militaries. However, that the international community did not find the appropriate mix of policies to accomplish that stated objective dulls the luster of the troops' accomplishments. That troops were not available to provide security in the refugee camps in late 1994 and in 1995 represented a further complication.

Whatever the criticisms of US policy in the early phases of the crisis, the humanitarian nature of American involvement in Rwanda later in the year was clear. In fact, as early as April the US Office of Foreign Disaster Assistance had a relief-response mechanism in place, channelling generous US contributions and by May the US military itself was ferrying relief supplies into the region. The US government was the first to re-establish diplomatic presence in Kigali after the blood bath. The immediate impetus for doing so was to establish a political base which would facilitate, among other things, negotiation of a Status of Forces Agreement permitting the US military to mount major humanitarian activities.

In other situations, the presence of outside military forces has led to their involvement in aid tasks, or aid activities have been one of several tasks the military has taken on. In the Rwanda crisis, US interest in involving US troops in the relief effort accelerated diplomatic recognition of the new regime. "We're here because of the need for a humanitarian response", explained Ambassador David Rawson in October 1994. At the time, the US was one of several governments pressing donors to provide the Kigali authorities with resources to restart basic services and re-establish law and order. "We believe we ought to give this government a chance", he said. "A wait-and-see attitude is a recipe for becoming a spectator to another disaster"[21].

Conclusion

The balance sheet on Operation Support Hope is, within its own terms of reference, largely positive. It did the heavy lifting at a scale and pace well beyond the capabilities of civilian agencies at the time. Supporting UN and NGO aid organisations in Goma and Kigali and also UNAMIR, it made a significant difference in what they were able to accomplish. Its own direct relief activities in Goma were also important, helping to achieve the overall objective of stopping the dying which it shared with other actors.

The US military accepted a clearly delimited task and carried it out for the most part effectively and on schedule, helping persons both in Rwanda and outside without becoming identified with one side or the other. The military adapted its activities in response to evolving needs, taking care to support rather than pre-empt the work of humanitarian organisations. Pentagon officials view the initiative as "a model for mapping out future potential engagements".

There were serious problems, however, in planning, operational strategies, cost and cost-effectiveness, and broader US policy. The US initiative was launched without adequate consultation with UN and NGO officials on the ground, other military contingents, and the Zairean and Rwandan authorities. Responding in late July to a humanitarian crisis which had erupted in April, Operation Support Hope also adopted certain questionable operational strategies and proved a costly investment when more cost-effective and preventive approaches might have been found.

Nested in US policy toward Rwanda, toward Africa in general, and toward complex humanitarian emergencies as a whole, US soldiers sent to the rescue were ultimately only as effective as the broader US and international policies they served.

Notes

1. William I. Perry, "Rwanda: Challenge of Enormous Magnitude", A Statement before the Defence Subcommittee of the House Appropriations Committee, August 4, 1994.

2. The After Action Review is one of few published commentaries on Operation Support Hope as of this writing. While such reviews are carried out routinely by the US Armed Forces following major operations, this particular study represents the first-ever US after-action report to reflect consultation with UN and NGO personnel. The review contains a Commander's Introduction by Schroeder, an analysis of the operation, including lessons learned, and a series of detailed appendices.

3. By prearrangement, an additional $1.9 million, initially paid by the Defence Department, was later reimbursed by USAID. Shipments of DOD relief items (e.g. vehicles and medical supplies for the ICRC) which would not otherwise have been possible were thus able to go forward.

4. Voice of America dispatch, July 25, 1994.

5. The service packages entered into by other national troop contingents are discussed in Chapter 7.

6. Quoted in Jane Perlez, "Aid Agencies Are Grateful to Armies", *New York Times*, August 21, 1994 [dateline Goma].

7. Interview with the authors, June 8, 1995.

8. A second public health group concluded that the chances of surviving cholera in the Goma area were reduced by the strategies implemented, including "The slow rate of rehydration, inadequate use of oral rehydration therapy, [and] use of inappropriate intravenous fluids". Cf. (Siddique, Salam, Islam, Akram, Jajumdar, Zaman, Fronczak, Laston, 1995). The health officials are associated with the International Centre for Diarrhoeal Disease Research in Dhaka, Bangladesh.

9. Interview with the authors, June 8, 1995.

10. Data was provided by the Defence Department's Office of Humanitarian and Refugee Affairs and the US General Accounting Office. Expenditures for Fiscal Year 1994, the twelve-month period ending Sept. 30, 1994, are given as $106.7 million and for Fiscal Year 1995 as $17.2 million (USGAO, 1995b). Discussions with Defence Department officials confirm, however, that both sets of expenditures were made for activities carried out in Calendar Year 1994, thereby making the total of $123.9 comparable with other figures in the text and in Table 8.2. The largest single expenditures were $63.8 million by the Air Force and $58.9 million by the Army. The cost of transporting relief items into the theatre early in 1994 before the launching of Operation Support Hope are also included in the $123.9 figure.

11. Ron Davidson, Deputy Comptroller, Office of the Secretary of Defence, in testimony before the Senate Armed Services Committee July 25, 1994. Cf. Senate Armed Services Committee, *op. cit.*, p. 17.

12. Secretary of Defence William I. Perry used this figure in congressional testimony on August 4, 1994.

13. US General Accounting Office, 1995a.

14. The quotation is from a statement by Senator Sam Nunn of Georgia, Chairman of the Senate Committee on Armed Services. Lieutenant General John Sheehan, appearing before the Committee, responded that "There is not another organisation on the face of the Earth that can do this on this scale". Cf. Senate Armed Services Committee, *op. cit.*

15. Trevor Page, UN World Food Programme, Comments on the "Rwanda/Burundi Regional Operation" at the Launch Workshop for the Joint Evaluation of Emergency Assistance to Rwanda, Ferney-Voltaire, France, January 23, 1995.

16. Lutheran World Federation Emergency Operations, communication dated July 24, 1995.

17. Interview with the authors, October, 1994.

18. In 1995, a new Presidential Decision Directive (PDD-50) was being prepared which would provide policy parameters for US humanitarian relief efforts.

19. The factor of 50 mentioned is based on a calculation by Holly Burkhalter, Washington Director of Human Rights Watch. State Department officials dispute the proposition advanced by LaRose-Edwards.

20. *The Guardian*, "The Deadly Cost of Delay", August 22, 1994.

21. Interview with the authors, October, 1994.

Chapter 7

Other Troops

This chapter analyses the contributions of selected national military contingents to the international response to the Rwanda crisis. These troops are distinguished from those reviewed in earlier chapters because their point of entry was neither the peace-keeping of UNAMIR nor the more stand-alone undertakings of *Opération Turquoise* and Operation Support Hope.

Presented here are contingents from Canada, the Netherlands, Japan, Germany, New Zealand, Australia, Israel, and Ireland. Each of the eight had a distinctive character, reflecting qualities and interests of the nations which provided them. All became elements integrated into the broader international response by virtue of a connection with UNHCR, to whose request for services they responded. More modest in scale and cost than their counterparts in the other two frameworks described above, they nevertheless made significant and special contributions to the overall effort.

Taken together, they illustrate the rich variety of military involvement in the Rwanda response, the theme not only of this chapter but of the volume as a whole[1].

Canada

The contribution of Canadian troops to the UN peace-keeping force, reviewed in Chapter 4, included UNAMIR's two Force Commanders and support personnel at its headquarters in Kigali, military observers, and a contingent of some 400 troops who managed UNAMIR's communications and helped run the Kigali airport. The Canadian military airlift into Kigali, sustained from April 1994 onward, was also noted in Chapter 6. In addition to these UNAMIR connections, Canadian military personnel were also present as the result of a service package negotiated by the UN High Commissioner for Refugees with the Canadian Department of National Defence[2].

Responding to the rapidly deteriorating refugee emergency in Zaire in July, UNHCR approached Canada and other governments for assistance in eight specific sectors: airport services, logistics base services, road services and road security, site preparation, provision of domestic fuel, sanitation facilities, water management, and airhead management. For any given area, individual governments were invited to enter into a service agreement, under which they would provide equipment, supplies, personnel, and management support (UNHCR, 1995d). Contributions in the form of military as well as financial and other resources were solicited.

Figure 7.1. **International Troops Responding to Rwanda Crisis (1994)**

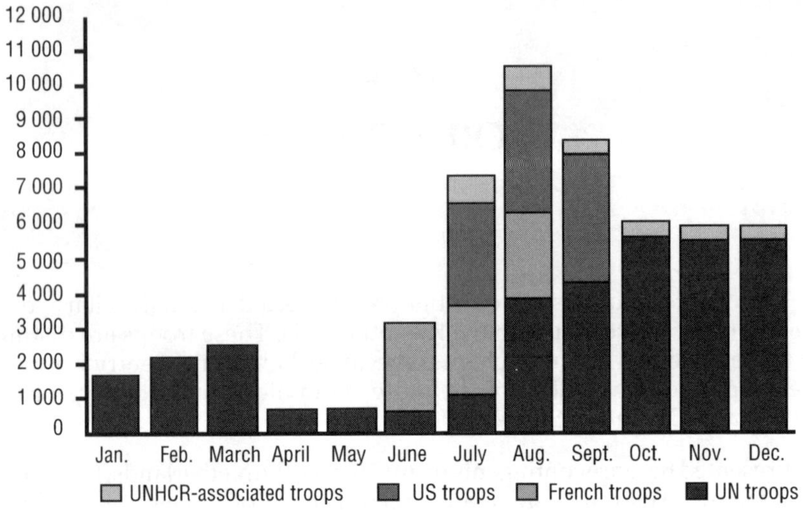

[Bar chart showing troop numbers from January to December 1994, with categories: UNHCR-associated troops, US troops, French troops, UN troops]

Note: The total figures shown on this table are approximations, based on available data. UNAMIR figures include military observers and civilian police as well as troops.

Figure 7.1 shows the numbers of international troops committed to the crisis during 1994; Figure 8.2 (in Chapter 8) indicates their costs. Each figure groups the military assets commited according to the three available frameworks—UNAMIR, the two stand-alone initiatives, and UNHCR-associated efforts.

Canada opted to provide assistance in the medical sector (activities were called Operation Passage) and in transport (Operation Scotch). Operation Passage made available a 200-person medical unit for the care of refugees and displaced persons. The contingent, drawn largely from Canadian bases at Petawawa and Valcartier, included 110 medical personnel, a platoon of some 20-30 security troops, a similar number of support staff, some 15-20 combat engineers, and a 15-member headquarters back team.

Anticipating the return of refugees from Zaire, Operation Passage established a health facility in north-western Rwanda, not far from Goma. When the return did not materialise, troops and facility were shifted farther south. During the three months between deployment July 25 and the departure October 21, Canadian troops did screenings of more than 22 000 patients, following up with in-hospital treatment of about one in every ten.

Operation Scotch was based in Nairobi and staffed by an Aircraft Logistic Control Element. Deployed April 8, Canadian troops and their Air Force Hercules transport evacuated European nationals, Belgian and Bangladeshi troops from Kigali, and moved in supplies for UNAMIR. A second C-130 aircraft was added in July to support the activities of UNHCR and other humanitarian organisations when the service package was put into place. Relief supplies from Canada, some of them purchased with funds from the Canadian International Development Agency (CIDA), were transported to the region for NGOs such as Canadian Lutheran World Relief, World Relief Canada, and *Collaboration santé internationale*.

Before Operation Scotch terminated at the end of August 1994, Canadian military air transport had moved more than 6 000 persons in and out of Kigali. Relief supplies totalling almost 2 600 metric tons had been delivered from Nairobi to Kigali, Goma, and Bujumbura as part of the airlift, which by then was co-ordinated by UNHCR. Offering the only air bridge into Rwanda early in the crisis, the Canadian operation was then broadened with the arrival of other military and eventually civilian aircraft.

Phasing out, Canadian troops handed over activities to the aid organisations staying on. "The work of the Field Ambulance unit has been outstanding", noted National Defence Minister David Collenette in announcing the transition, "but happily, the UN and non-governmental organisations like *Médecins sans frontières* and the Red Cross have stated that they are now able to handle the needs of the remaining refugees"[3]. To facilitate the handover, the troops left behind a basic stock of equipment and drugs. The Minister also praised the courage and professionalism of the pilots and crews who had flown the Operation Scotch missions.

From a command and control standpoint, it was anomalous to have two separate Canadian forces in Rwanda: one within UNAMIR reporting to the Force Commander, a Canadian, and another operating autonomously from UNAMIR under arrangements negotiated between the Department of National Defence and UNHCR. In actuality, the Force Commanders considered themselves to have broad authority over both sets of Canadian troops and kept themselves fully briefed on the work of those who did not, technically speaking, report to them[4].

In practical terms, the work of Canadian troops unrelated to UNAMIR was hard to distinguish from that of Canadian military personnel assigned to the UN peace-keeping operation. The medical platoon present in Rwanda to care for the needs of Canadian and other UNAMIR troops, as noted in Chapter 4, also treated Rwandan civilians. The main difference was that UNAMIR medics had other duties which came before assisting civilians. Yet they undertook on a time-available basis or in their off-hours the same kinds of assistance activities that their compatriots in the UNHCR-associated Operation Passage did full time.

Canadian military forces in Rwanda brought to bear expertise from decades of participation in UN peace-keeping efforts. Their sectors — primarily medicine, communications, and logistics — were ones which Canada had tackled in a variety of theatres. Earlier versions of the water purification technology they used in Rwanda had been employed by Canadian troops in Somalia and the former Yugoslavia.

In Rwanda, however, Canadian expertise found new applications. While Canadian troops had set up a field hospital in Saudi Arabia during the Gulf War, civilians had not been the primary beneficiaries. Operation Scotch evolved from the chance availability of a military transport plane in nearby Somalia, which was pressed into regular and then expanded service for Rwanda. As in other theatres, the involvement of Canadian military personnel gave the Canadian public at home a sense of participation in the broader humanitarian effort.

Another new element in the Rwanda crisis was the working relationships forged between Department of National Defence officials and UNHCR. UNHCR's normal interlocutors in Ottawa are at CIDA, which throughout the Rwanda crisis provided resources to UNHCR and other UN organisations, NGOs and the ICRC. Yet the fast-moving pace of events made it necesssary for UNHCR in this instance to deal directly with Canadian defence officials. "It's hard to rent airplanes on short notice", explained one CIDA official with understanding. "Either you do it through the military or you don't do it at all. Defence officials didn't need to go through us to get the job done".

But the Rwanda response also broadened the working relationships of CIDA officials, "changing the way we do business". As a result of the Rwanda experience, CIDA personnel now engage in what they call "rubbing brass" whenever needed. From its own budget CIDA paid incremental costs of $800 000 to the Department of National Defence for services rendered. With the phase-out of the Canadian airlift and reduction in non-UNAMIR related activities of the Canadian military, however, relationships among Canadian and UN officials have returned to a more normal pattern.

Despite their appreciation for the military assets provided, CIDA officials see the utilisation of Canadian and other troops for duties in the humanitarian sphere as truly exceptional, justifiable only as a stopgap measure in highly extreme circumstances where cost is not a primary concern. They counsel against making the provision of troops a regular feature of the world's humanitarian — or development — regime. "Situations such as Rwanda are so unusual that they break the mold", officials point out. "You cannot build global models based upon such exceptions".

Canadian military assets provided in the Rwanda emergency totalled C$ 103 million. Less than half was for UNHCR-associated military activities: C$ 23 million for Operation Passage (of which C$ 10 million were incremental to normal expenditures) and C$ 19 million for Operation Scotch (C$ 3 million incremental). The costs of Canadian participation in UNOMUR are calculated at C$ 7 million (C$ 1 million incremental) and in UNAMIR at C$ 59 million (C$ 26 million incremental), exclusive of assessed contributions. Canada anticipates eventual reimbursement from UNHCR for Operation Scotch and $19 million from the Department of Peace-keeping Operations for UNAMIR[5].

To achieve comparability with data from other nations, the costs of utilising Canadian troops shown on Figure 8.2 include only the incremental costs of C$ 40 million and only the costs of UNHCR, both expressed in US dollars. Humanitarian assets from CIDA for the year beginning April 1994 were $37.1 million, less than $1 million of which purchased services from the Defence Department (CIDA, 1995).

Reflecting their sense of the importance of the Rwandan crisis and response, Canadian officials launched a number of follow-on studies. One in late 1994 provided a sharply critical review, identifying several lessons to be learned (LaRose-Edwards, 1994). A second in April 1995 examined current constraints on rapid responses to such crises (LaRose-Edwards, 1995). A third proposed creating "a standing, operational-level, fully deployable integrated, multinational, military/civilian headquarters of approximately 30 to 50 personnel, to conduct contingency planning and rapid deployment as authorised by the Security Council". (Government of Canada, 1995). In a peace dividend of sorts, Canada in 1995 offered to provide financial and other support for such a headquarters at one of its own military bases.

The Netherlands

The Dutch military was involved throughout the genocide, mass exodus, and reconstruction phases of the crisis. In fact, its involvement preceded the April events. Beginning in June 1993, ten Dutch military observers had been provided to UNOMUR to assist in monitoring the Rwanda-Uganda border. Major participation on the humanitarian front was spurred by a personal fact-finding visit to the Goma region July 18-20, 1994 by Minister for Development Co-operation Jan P. Pronk. He described what he saw to Parliament as follows:

"Because of the unimaginable massiveness of the stream of refugees, the care providers are confronted by a task that surpasses [their] capacity by far ... The need is for the supply and distribution per day of about 600 tons of food and at least three million litres of purified water. In addition, medical care and construction of sanitary facilities (at least 60 000 latrines in the rock-hard volcanic soil), for at least 1 million exhausted people, among whom dehydration, diarrhoea, dysentery, and cholera create an increasing number of victims, with a measles epidemic feared". He reported that, "In my conversations with the aid organisations, a recurrent theme was that the management, logistical and technical support of aid supplies constitute the greatest problems, and that for this, a massive operation such as really can only be done by a military organisation ... is needed" (Pronk, 1994).

The Dutch military responded quickly. Reporting jointly to the Parliament two days later on actions taken and planned, Ministers of Defence A.L. ter Beek and Foreign Affairs W. Kok noted that, "In consultation with the Ministry of Development Co-operation, MSF-Holland, and the US European Command in Germany, we have reviewed ways in which additional aid might be provided", making use of a UNHCR list of the necessary aid supplies. "The Ministry of Defence is in a position to supply supplementary humanitarian aid in the shortest possible time" (ter Beek and Kok, 1994).

The Defence Ministry committed 50 trucks and more than 50 other vehicles to UNAMIR, along with 10 mobile kitchens and 15 electrical generators. The smaller vehicles included landrovers, ambulances, workshop vans, and trailers. The vehicle fleet represented something of a peace dividend, since the particular items had become, in the Minister's words, "redundant as a result of the reorganisation of the Ministry of Defence" (ter Beek and Kok, 1994). They helped equip UNAMIR's Zambian battalion, for whom 100 soldiers were also trained by Dutch troops.

During the period August 4 through September 4, the Dutch military provided 104 people to support the relief effort around Goma. Included were a medical contingent, transport and movement control personnel, and drivers, all chosen with humanitarian-support roles in mind. A handful of the troops remained at the Goma airport into October at the request of the aid agencies. The Dutch airforce also airlifted relief supplies to and around the region. Although a Dutch soldier served as an aide to Force Commander Romeo Dallaire in Kigali, the Dutch did not provide a contingent of their own forces to UNAMIR.

The contributions of vehicles and personnel formed the backbone of Operation Provide Care, an undertaking by Dutch troops to provide direct assistance to refugees in Zaire during August, September, and early October. The largest outlays were for the multi-million dollar costs of transporting relief materiel in Hercules and Boeing 707 Dutch military aircraft to Goma. Funds were also expended on meningitis vaccine and cold-chain equipment for use by Dutch medics. At the end of their stay, the Dutch military turned over remaining relief supplies in the health and water sectors to NGOs and UNHCR.

One innovative element was the close partnership between the military and Dutch NGOs. On July 18 a Dutch airforce flight into Goma airlifted Dutch troops and NGO personnel, along with relief supplies for both. Dutch troops worked closely with MSF-Holland in the Katalé camp and with Memisa, another Dutch NGO, in the Mugunga camp, each with some 200 000 inhabitants at the time. Dutch troops themselves provided assistance in the water and health sectors. A parallel Dutch grant to UNHCR enabled the purchase of medicines and vaccines, including 150 000 units against meningitis. Dutch troops transported some 870 tons of NGO supplies.

Despite close working relationships in northern Iraq and in natural disasters, this degree of planning and operational collaboration between Dutch military and civilian actors was unprecedented. While in general the collaboration went smoothly, NGOs were not unanimous in their enthusiasm. Deep differences of opinion emerged between agencies, and sometimes within the same agency, about the appropriateness of the involvement of the troops.

"The integration of military medical personnel into the MSF team led to quite some confusion among MSF personnel", reported MSF-Holland of its experience in the refugee camp at Katalé in Zaire, "particularly because the soldiers wore battle dress and carried arms on MSF premises. MSF personnel believed that the soldiers, as an extension of politics, jeopardized their organisation's neutrality" (Schenkenberg van Mierop, 1995). Some NGOs held that if the Dutch military were to be made available, they should be directed by NGOs themselves. Others took a more pragmatic approach: that given the dire extremity of the situation, military assets should be welcomed and utilised to the fullest on whatever terms possible.

Dutch and other aid groups that worked closely with the military are still assessing the experience. In MSF's case, the "unprecedented decision" to collaborate with the military was made quickly as the Goma situation deteriorated, without determining "where the military identity and mandate would stop and the humanitarian identity and mandate would start"[6]. As a result of the actual collaboration, however, "MSF no longer considers the integration of military medical personnel that are identifiable as such into its projects desirable for the future". The NGO will request "the deployment of national armies in humanitarian emergencies [only] in extreme situations", with the criteria for determining such situations yet to be hammered out (Schenkenberg van Mierop, 1995).

The contribution of the Dutch military was distinguished by its low-profile, gap-filling quality. Dutch troops provided services in the Israeli field hospital and transported people for treatment there. Under the direction of the British government aid agency and alongside US and French troops, Dutch military personnel assisted at the Goma airport. They took over water purification and distribution activities from French and American troops and upon departing, as noted, turned their tasks and resources over to other organisations. All in all, their work benefited many aid groups, including Dutch NGOs, non-Dutch NGOs such as Americares and the Adventist Development and Relief Agency, and international organisations such as UNHCR and UNICEF.

The Dutch contribution needs to be seen in the context of similar Dutch involvement in other UN peace-keeping operations. Characteristic has been a high level of co-operation and co-financing between the ministries of defence and foreign affairs and the personal interest taken by senior Dutch officials. Frequent trips to the region by senior officials reinforced a high degree of public and parliamentary engagement in the crisis.

As of mid-1995, the costs of the Dutch contribution in 1994 had not been fully tallied. The Dutch Ministry of Development Co-operation had transferred to the Ministry of Defence 3.6 million guilders ($2.25 million) for some of the costs incurred by the military, largely in the transport sector. The Ministry of Defence had assumed other costs, including those related to the secondment of ten people from the Ministry to assist UNHCR in the region. Since the items enumerated earlier as provided to UNAMIR were additional to the Netherlands' assessed contribution to the UN peace-keeping operation, the figure of $2.25 million on Figure 8.2 understates the scale of Dutch military assets provided.

Dutch government aid officials acknowledge the comparative advantage of the military during the initial ten days of such a major crisis, particularly in such matters as logistics and airport control. At the same time, they question whether expanding NGO transport capacity might not, in the long run, have been a better investment. The dramatic contributions of the military, they caution, should not obscure that some of the tasks can be performed more cheaply and effectively by civilian agencies, particularly as the situation is brought under control. For their part, some NGOs speculate that "the medical activities could have been done better by ourselves as an association of medical professionals with a long history and great experience".

Also noteworthy is Dutch government attention to building on the 1994 experience to strengthen humanitarian and peacekeeeping policy and practice. In mid-September 1994, the Foreign Affairs Ministry hosted a high-level conference, sponsored by the North-South Centre of the Council of Europe and the Dutch Committee for Education on Development. The meeting, attended by Rwandan and other government officials and the OAU, launched an urgent appeal for protection, reconstruction, and reconciliation in Rwanda (*L'Interdépendant*, 1994). The following March, the Dutch government sponsored the consultation noted earlier to review the lessons from the Rwanda experience regarding the need for international military standby capacity for use in humanitarian emergencies[7].

Japan

In early-October 1994, the newly arrived Japanese battalion in Goma was unpacking boxes, erecting tents, establishing a defence perimeter, and test-driving jeeps and armoured personnel carriers. The initial deployment October 2 involved a force of one hundred. Another complement of 120 arrived on October 12. By October 27, the battalion was at full strength of 260. It remained in Goma until year's end, backed throughout by a Japanese airforce unit based in Nairobi which forwarded relief material from overseas. The operation cost Y 6 billion (about $59 million), paid from the operating budget of the Ministry of Defence and from a special ministry reserve fund.

The Japanese contingent was made up almost exclusively of military personnel. Only three were civilians: one from the Ministry of Foreign Affairs, the other two from Defence. Carrying weapons for self-defence, the troops moved quickly to establish security, beginning patrols around the camp and the perimeter of the adjoining airport. All told, some 400 military personnel served at one time or another in the operation.

The troops' purpose was to provide sanitation, medical assistance, and water purification for the refugees, with 16, 70, and 43 specialists in those three fields respectively. The initial operations plan called for setting up health facilities in refugee camps around Goma and taking over a water distribution programme operated by a Swedish NGO. Even before deploying, however, the Japanese made major adjustments.

Several days before the troops arrived, the camps had been the scene of several serious incidents. Elements from the former Rwandan Hutu military and militia moved to consolidate their hold over camp populations and relief distributions. Intimidation and harassment led to the evacuation of the 90 expatriate aid personnel from the camp at Katalé. Reflecting the danger, Japanese plans were altered so that medical services would be provided in the Goma hospital rather than in the camps. Troops might be withdrawn altogether, Japanese officials cautioned, if the security situation deteriorated further.

"The Japanese are prohibited from entering Katalé, Mugunga, or camps north of Katalé because of the security problems there", explained Col. Makoto Nasu, commander of the advance team on the eve of the initial contingent's arrival[8]. Once the troops had deployed at the edge of the Goma airport, a battalion officer confirmed the change. "We don't like to fight with civilians", he stated. "This would be bad for future operations". While the change did not rule out involvement at a later date in some of the calmer camps, the Goma hospital remained the focus of the Japanese contingent's work.

From the outset, the Japanese emphasized the exclusively humanitarian terms of their engagement. Officers stressed that the troops' presence in Goma was a direct response to the invitation of the UN High Commissioner for Refugees, differentiating carefully from the UN peace-keeping operation in neighbouring Rwanda. "We just conduct humanitarian operations in Goma", explained Colonel Mitsunobu Kamimoto, Commander of Japan's Rwanda Refugee Relief Task Force. "We do not participate in UNAMIR"[9]. The Japanese did, however, receive briefings from the UN peace-keeping operation.

Asked whether Japanese troops would be prepared to evacuate UN and other aid personnel should the need arise, battalion officials demurred. "We can guard them if they come to us", an officer commented. However, there were limits to such assistance even though, in a crisis situation, the ranking officer might exercise his own judgment.

Participating in a peace-keeping operation *per se* would not have broken new ground. In recent years, Japanese defence forces had provided election supervisors to the UN Transition Assistance Group in Namibia (UNTAG) and in El Salvador (ONUSAL), logistics and engineering support to the UN Transitional Authority in Cambodia (UNTAC), and movement control services to the UN Operation in Mozambique (ONUMOZ). Five of the contingent in Goma had served in Cambodia.

Deployment of Japanese troops in such capacities had been authorised by the International Peace Co-operation Law of June 1992, which established "a domestic framework to provide manpower contributions to United Nations Peacekeeping Operations and humanitarian international relief operations on a full-fledged scale". Among the conditions established in the law were the existence of a cease-fire, the consent of the belligerents, and the impartiality of peace-keeping activities (Japanese Ministry of Foreign Affairs, 1994; Otani, 1993; Meyer, 1995). The commitment of Japanese Self-Defence Force personnel to the Rwanda relief effort proved less controversial in Japan than its participation in UNTAC. The constraints imposed by the 1992 law help explain the cautious approach taken by the troops to their tasks.

What made the Rwanda undertaking a "watershed mission" for Japan was its exclusively humanitarian terms of reference. "This is our first humanitarian deployment ever", explained Colonel Kamimoto. "It is important that we behave ourselves in a manner that will inspire the world"[10]. Thus while Japanese medical personnel had been deployed in UN undertakings overseas before, their task had always been to treat Japanese troops. In Goma, their chief purpose was to assist local civilian populations. The framing of the mission in humanitarian-only terms doubtless reflected a concern to avoid the loss of life and the controversy of the Cambodian experience.

Japanese officials were pleased with the outcomes. "This is a good experience for Japan and for me", observed Colonel Kamimoto in October. While any decision to participate in future humanitarian activities would rest with Japan's political authorities, he surmised that if the Rwanda experience continued to be positive, Japan would be inclined to offer such services elsewhere.

"Japan intends to continue to co-operate actively in ... UN peace-keeping operations", confirmed Mr. Yohei Kono, Deputy Prime Minister and Minister for Foreign Affairs in a policy statement to UN General Assembly just before the contingent deployed. He placed particular emphasis on peace-keeping and humanitarian activities as elements in what his government viewed as a comprehensive approach to conflict resolution, which also included "assistance for building social institutions, and aid for peace building, such as rehabilitation and reconstruction assistance"[11].

The first-ever deployment of Japanese military assets in the humanitarian sphere thus served the country's international political interests as well. According to one analysis from Japan, the goals were "to obtain permanent membership [in] the UN Security Council as well as an overseas deployment capability" for the Self Defence Force. By the same account, the decision to participate in the Rwanda effort "was made ostensibly at the request of UNHCR but was more a product of bureaucratic and political zeal". While collaboration between Japanese forces and NGOs at the field level had broken "new ground", such co-operation had proved "divisive" for the NGO community and "it remains to be seen how the relationship will evolve" (Randel and German 1995)[12].

Germany

The contribution of the German military to the Rwandan relief effort centred around the work of air transport planes, which ferried relief supplies to and around the region. In committing those assets, the government was responding to a request from UNHCR. Its decision was accompanied by more than a little speculation, with a positive response expected. "No decision on the request has been made", reported one account several days before the first military relief shipment became airborne. "But the Government of Chancellor Helmut Kohl is keen to show that Germany is willing to assume greater responsibilities in world affairs"[13].

The airlifting of relief supplies to Rwanda, reported the media, opened a new chapter in post-war German history. The take-off of a German airforce plane from the military airport at Cologne for Goma July 18, 1994 was heralded as the first involvement of the German military outside of NATO territory since the end of the 1939-45 war. In point of fact, the German military had been involved in earlier UN peace-keeping operations in Cambodia, providing a medical unit in support of UNTAC forces, and in Somalia, a logistical battalion in support of an Indian infantry brigade. Implicated in the confusion was a German Supreme Court decision only a few days earlier upholding the constitutionality of committing military assets to UN peace-keeping[14].

In announcing their decision, government officials made clear that Germany's point of contact was UNHCR. Direct participation in UNAMIR, and particularly the stationing of German troops in Rwanda, was not contemplated (Bundesministerium der Verteidigung, 1995). "The German Defence Ministry has offered support with planes and equipment", reported the media, " but has ruled out sending German troops to the region"[15]. Of course, pilots and an infrastructure to suppport aid flights would require on-the-ground military presence.

Germany stationed 35 troops in Nairobi and 12 in Johannesburg to expedite relief flights. During the three months beginning July 18, Germany flew 175 sorties, carrying some 2 500 tons of relief supplies, including 17 water-purification plants and a 500-bed field hospital. One 707 and two C-160 aircraft based in Nairobi made daily flights to Rwanda, Zaire, and Burundi. Cargo was also ferried from South Africa. To co-ordinate the effort, a German military officer was stationed in Goma through December 31, when German military involvement came to an end. Troops were rotated every three weeks. As of mid-1995, the cost of the operation was not available; discussions were proceeding between defence and foreign ministries regarding the accounts to be tapped.

The German government has drawn positive implications for the future from its experience in Rwanda and in other recent such undertakings. Like the Japanese government, Germany has concluded that participation in UN peace-keeping activities is a matter of "great importance, reflecting the foreign policy interests of Germany and serving to improve its international standing"[16]. Given Germany's membership on the UN Security Council in 1995-96, the world has great expectations of it, noted Bernd Wilz, Parliamentary Under-Secretary of Defence[17]. "Germany has shown itself a reliable partner in the international community", the authorities have concluded. "In the future, the German armed forces will be in a position even more fully than previously to take on complex international operations jointly with its allies and other partners"[18].

New Zealand

Like Germany, New Zealand lent substantial air assets to the relief cause. Under an agreement between the New Zealand Defence Force and UNHCR, its Air Force contributed a Hercules C130 transport plane for four weeks, initiating operations from Entebbe, Uganda into Goma, Kigali, and Bukavu on August 3, 1994 and extending them for an additional two weeks thereafter. The aircraft flew daily missions to Bukavu — the only such aircraft to do so — and made occasional runs to Goma and Kigali as well. It lifted 1 750 tons of relief supplies, largely food, shelter, utensils, and equipment, and more than 250 passengers. "Ours was a purely humanitarian contribution", explained one official in describing what was called Operation Reforge, "short, sharp, and to the point". New Zealand's activities are described elsewhere in this chapter.

Operation Reforge involved 36 military personnel, for whom UNHCR made the necessary legal arrangements with the local authorities. The cost to New Zealand was $1.4 million, paid largely from emergency resources within the New Zealand Overseas Development Programme. The disaster contingency fund of the New Zealand Defence Force also contributed. "We paid our own way", recounted one official, "... and did not look for reimbursement of costs from others."

The New Zealand contribution was well received by the UN, which praised it as prompt, efficient, and effective. New Zealand officials were equally pleased. "The operation gave New Zealand a high profile, enhancing our international standing, within the UNHCR both locally at Entebbe and Geneva", they said. "The media also showed considerable interest in the crisis and the excellent work of [our troops] in assisting the relief effort attracted good media coverage". Defence officials credit the efficiency of the operation to "the simple, direct command and control arrangements. The detachment commander had the authority to undertake the mission without an intervening national or joint headquarters between himself and the UNHCR"[19].

The contributions of the military were but one aspect of New Zealand's total involvement in the Rwandan crisis. Presiding over the Security Council during the first six months of the year, New Zealand's ambassador played a pivotal role in discussions of the crisis. From the outset he pressed the Council to strengthen UNAMIR and to condemn and prosecute genocide. As noted in Chapter 4, New Zealand was one of five absentions in the Security Council on extending the UN's blessing over *Opération Turquoise*, its ambassador strongly favouring a more multilateral approach.

On the relief side, New Zealand's Overseas Development Assistance Programme contributed more than $2 million to humanitarian agencies, including four NGOs. A grant of $50 000 in response to a special appeal by the UN Commissioner for Human Rights underwrote the deployment of additional human rights monitors in Rwanda. "New Zealand's was one of the first governments to provide resources to deal with longer-term needs arising out of the process of restoring stability there" (Randel and German, 1995). New Zealand NGOs themselves raised more than $7 million, an "unprecedented" amount[20].

In short, the country's involvement — military and civilian, diplomatic and operational, governmental and private — became a major national preoccupation during 1994. For a country of 3.5 million persons, the scale of its efforts was noteworthy.

Australia

Like Germany and New Zealand, the Australian airforce also lent assets to the heavy lifting challenge of the Rwanda relief operation. On August 1, 1994 two Hercules C-130s arrived in Kigali with water-purification equipment and supplies. The mobile water purification unit had been arranged by the Australian International Development Assistance Bureau (AIDAB), to be managed by a technician provided by the Australian Committee for UNICEF. Also included in the shipment were water-purification chemicals and water bladder tanks[21].

The initial flights also carried medical supplies, including anti-malarial tablets and vitamin A capsules, as well as other relief materials such as high-protein biscuits and plastic sheeting. The aircraft also had consignments destined for a number of Australian NGOs, including the Adventists' Relief Association, CARE, and World Vision. The cost of the flights was paid by AIDAB, which had never before collaborated with the Australian Committee for UNICEF on an undertaking of these proportions. The contribution of the Australian Medical Support Force attached to UNAMIR, which provided direct medical services to Rwandan civilians, was noted in Chapter 4.

Australian emergency relief assistance to Rwanda — military and humanitarian, public and private combined — totalled A$ 65 million. On a per capita basis, this represented one of the highest Australian responses to any such emergency. "The goverment contributed A$ 35 million through aid and defence packages — A$ 10 million in direct humanitarian aid and A$ 25 million for an Australian Defence Forces medical support unit which treated UN forces, NGO personnel and the local population". The remaining A$ 30 million was comprised of public donations in response to NGO appeals (Randel and German, 1995).

As in other countries, the involvement of national troops in the Rwanda response built upon, and stimulated, discussions about peace-keeping and humanitarian need, multilateral and national action. Solid support existed for strengthening the United Nations so that, in the words of Australian Foreign Minister Gareth Evans, it might complete a "successful transition from the Cold War wings to the post-Cold War centre stage"[22]. Australian contributions to both UNAMIR and UNHCR did indeed strengthen the UN response. At the same time, NGOs, who strongly supported higher levels of development assistance, expressed concerns that the costs of deploying military assets in such capacities not be included in ODA calculations[23].

Israel

Operation Interns for Hope was launched July 22, 1994 by a decision by the Israeli government to dispatch a contingent from the Israeli Defence Forces on a two-week assignment, subject to extension as needed. The first of eight Hercules military transport planes touched down in Goma early on July 25.

Headed by Environment Minister Yossi Sarid, the contingent was comprised of 50 medical staff and 30 support personnel. The initial unit was replaced by a second team of 86 persons which arrived August 3. The operation ended August 31 with the return of the last personnel to Israel. Explaining the wind-up after six weeks, Brig. Gen. Michael Wiener, Surgeon General of the army medical corps, noted that worst of the health problems among Rwandan refugees were past. "Also", he said, "Monday is Jewish New Year's Eve and Israelis like to be with their families at this time"[24].

Working with UNHCR, Israeli troops quickly set up a 100-bed field hospital on the outskirts of Goma. The first patients were treated on the day after the troops touched down. During the first twelve days, 1 215 patients visited the emergency room, 723 of which required hospitalisation. During the five weeks of Interns for Hope, some 3 000 refugees were treated. The costs of $7 million were borne by the Israeli Defence Ministry.

The Israeli contribution consisted of a package of services along lines requested by UNHCR, which made many of the necessary arrangements. At the same time through its embassies in Kenya, Ethiopia, Eritrea, and Egypt, the government obtained landing and transit permissions for its military aircraft. The Israeli ambassador in Kinshasa negotiated an agreement for the undertaking in Zaire, including the presence of military personnel, weapons, and aircraft.

Interns for Hope, whose name itself conveyed a non-military flavour, sought to work closely with existing humanitarian organisations. These included UNICEF, which referred patients from a nearby camp to the Israeli hospital, and MSF, which had its own activities in the area. Some of the Dutch troops involved in medical work assisted at the hospital, as noted earlier. The Israelis themselves opened an ambulatory centre at the Katindo camp, where two doctors and two medics saw patients.

Israeli military medical personnel were overwhelmed by what they encountered. Visiting an orphanage near Goma, they were welcomed by a local doctor, Dr. Nimet Lallani, who had single-handedly been treating children during the initial two weeks of the crisis. Death rates had ranged from 10 to 30 per day. At her urging, IDF troops took away ten children — several they hoped to assist had died before they were able to leave — for treatment. A grateful Dr. Lallani nevertheless lamented the dearth of trained medical personnel earlier on. "What we needed was hands. I was the only one doctor for 3 500 kids", she told a reporter. "Why? Why did they come so late?"[25].

The Interns for Hope initiative marked the largest-ever Israeli military-medical undertaking in Africa or elsewhere. Earlier medical missions by the Israeli Defence Forces had visited Cambodia (1979), Cameroon (1986), Armenia (1988), and Moscow (1989). Medical aid unaccompanied by Israeli military personnel had been sent to the Kurds in northern Iraq (1991) and to Bosnia-Herzegovina (1992). On the military side, the Israeli Defence Forces had had considerable experience in Africa, which included training of the Congolese National Army in the 1960s.

The Rwanda effort coincided with a decision by the cabinet to send a cadre of 30 police officers to participate in the peace-keeping effort in Haiti. At about the same time, a rescue team was dispatched to Argentina, where a bomb blast had levelled a Jewish community centre. The government presented its Rwanda undertaking as "part of its [broader] efforts to participate in international humanitarian activities".

The initiative was applauded by Israeli public opinion. "The apathy being displayed by the world in the face of this genocide", commented an editorial in *Hatzofeh*, "stirs up sad memories especially among those people who saw a world indifferent to the destruction of the Jewish people during the Holocaust". In announcing its action, the Cabinet noted that, "The Jewish people, who endured the most bitter experience of the Nazi holocaust, and their country — the State of Israel — cannot stand idly by in the face of the horror in Rwanda"[26].

Private Israeli citizens also responded. Magen David Adom, a national NGO, launched a major appeal, as did the UNICEF national committee. The government received a number of inquiries about the adoption of Rwandese children.

Ireland

Among the many national military contingents involved in the Rwanda relief effort — the plethora of contingents was not generally known outside individual countries which focused on their own troops — the involvement of Irish soldiers was perhaps the best-kept secret. Even getting information on the nature and extent of the involvement proved difficult. "Because the Irish army was not involved on an official basis", explained a government spokesman apologetically — speaking, of course, off the record — "no information is officially available".

The government of Ireland provided some 60 military personnel on a voluntary secondment basis to 3 humanitarian organisations. Beginning in late July, UNHCR received the services of 37 persons; 2 Irish NGOs, GOAL and Irish Concern, were assisted by another 24. The initial duration of the assignments was for three months, often extended once or twice. Salary and transport costs were met by the Ministry of Defence. Local expenses and support costs were contributed by the receiving agencies.

Irish military personnel resurfaced in the humanitarian organisations as regular staff members, functioning without uniforms or weapons and otherwise indistinguishable from regular staff. They were, they said, simply aid personnel who happened to be provided by the Ministry of Defence. Their assignments were tailored to their backgrounds, from engineering, medicine, and logistics to administration, communications, and security.

Paralleling these military personnel was a second group, also made available to the same humanitarian organisations by the Irish government. It consisted of some 10-20 civil servants provided, again at no expense to the receiving agencies, by their respective government ministries such as education, health, and social services. "The secondment procedure was found to operate satisfactorily", observed a government spokesman describing the contributions of military and civilian personnel alike. "The individuals, aid agencies, and government ministries were positive about the results".

Both sets of secondments followed a major public debate in Ireland about the nature and terms of engagement of the Irish government and troops in the Rwandan crisis. As the humanitarian situation deteriorated in July, Concern and GOAL launched a campaign to persuade the government of Prime Minister Albert Reynolds to commit Irish troops to the crisis. GOAL's director John O'Shea also made a personal appeal to South African President Nelson Mandela in early August to mobilise faster-paced international action.

In August, GOAL requested a UN force to provide enhanced security in the refugee camps, where some 58 GOAL volunteers were working at the time. In the absence of an effective UN force, GOAL told a parliamentary committee, Irish troops should be sent to protect the aid staffs of Irish NGOs. Speaking before the same committee, however, the NGOs Concern and Trocaire took a different approach. They supported deploying a multilateral security force but discouraged a separate Irish initiative, concerned about whether protection by the Irish military might provoke rather than quell violence and about the appropriateness of Irish troops protecting Irish NGOs.

The secondment arrangement gave the Irish government the best of several worlds. It responded to public entreaties from those who were horrified by the suffering in Rwanda and wanted Irish troops to intervene. Yet it also reflected the concerns of the Irish military that dispatching troops to Rwanda would overextend financial and personnel resources and might involve them in an internal armed conflict, possibly in a peace-enforcement mode. The course selected was also something of a middle option between more major involvement in the form of committing Irish troops to UNAMIR and a still lower profile such as the transfer to Rwanda of equipment no longer needed by the Irish military serving with the UN in Somalia.

"In the absence of a formal military contingent", observed a government spokesman, "the secondment of military personnel and public servants provided the means for the Irish government to be involved, if only indirectly, in providing assistance to the disaster area". The secondment responded to an upsurge in public concern in late July, when Irish NGOs received more than £1 million in donations. Reflecting the political importance of being involved, the Irish Minister of Foreign Affairs Dick Spring himself announced a contribution to private agencies of £2 million.

As in Canada, the Netherlands, Australia and elsewhere, the debate also highlighted the need for a more rapid UN response capacity to future Rwandas. "The mobilisation of Irish soldiers is a difficult and complicated exercise", noted the *Sunday Press* in an editorial in late July. "Ireland is a small country with limited resources and we can't operate in trouble spots around the world in isolation. The United Nations should, however, be in a position, after all the experience it has gained, to react speedily to a crisis"[27].

Conclusion

The experience of national troop contingents provided to the United Nations for tasks in the humanitarian sphere was rich and multifaceted. Summarised here, that experience is compared in Chapter 8 to the experience of troops in the other two major frameworks and brought to bear on the broader issue of military-humanitarian co-operation.

> Relief officials are taking a lesson from the tragedy of the Hutu and Tutsi refugees. What the world's relief agencies need, they now believe, is more logistical support from the world's armies. Relief experts have in mind not so much the high-profile, and risky French military presence in Rwanda ... Rather, the experts are more encouraged by the success of the discreet non-combat support provided here by the Americans, Irish, Israelis and Dutch.
>
> Jane Perlez, "Aid Agencies Are Grateful to Armies", *New York Times*, August 21, 1994 [dateline Goma, Zaire]

The major contribution of the national troop contingents reviewed in this chapter was in supporting the work of humanitarian organisations, especially in logistics and health, water treatment and sanitation. The troops also carried out major relief activities themselves, particularly in the mass exodus phase and among Rwandan refugees in neighbouring countries. The contingents generally did not have mandates to provide security to civilians or relief agencies, although in some circumstances their presence had that effect and intent.

The humanitarian nature of their assignments was underscored because their point of contact with the UN system was UNHCR rather than UNAMIR. Through service-package agreements, UNHCR offered governments a vehicle for matching their resources with specific assignments within the overall relief effort. As a result,

UNHCR mobilised assets that otherwise might not have become available or been utilised as effectively. Most of the service packages took effect some time after mid-July 1994; all of the troops involved had left the theatre by the end of the year.

In addition to the eight contingents whose work is reviewed in this chapter, another eleven governments — Austria, Belgium, Denmark, Finland, Italy, Luxembourg, Norway, Spain, Sweden, Switzerland, and Turkey — and the European Union entered into service packages, providing civilian rather than military assets. As indicated in the previous chapter, activities by US troops in water treatment and distribution in Goma and airhead services in Entebbe were part of the UNHCR framework. French troops in *Opération Turquoise* assisted the UNHCR effort, although a separate service package involving France included only civilian assets. The United Kingdom also provided civilian assets to UNHCR in addition to its UNAMIR unit which performed humanitarian tasks. Taken together, 22 nations and the European Union thus provided military and/or civilian assets under the service-package rubric.

Within that common framework of association with UNHCR, there were significant differences in the participation of the various national contingents. Variables included the timing and duration of their presence in the crisis area, the cost and how it was met, the degree of experience in complex emergencies, the relationships established with humanitarian agencies, and the links between troops and their governments' other humanitarian and policy interests. There were also differences in the degrees to which military personnel, uniformed and weapons-bearing or otherwise, were integrated into humanitarian organisations and welcomed by them.

Generally speaking, the experiences of the national contingents were strongly positive. That was the view of the troops themselves, the governments providing them, the UNHCR which orchestrated their work, most of the humanitarian organisations with whom they collaborated, and Rwandans themselves. Policy makers, parliaments, and publics in the sending countries evidenced a sense that important national and international interests were well served. National troops also provided a point of entry and sense of involvement for the countries participating, some of them with smaller populations and fewer resources to contribute, in the world's response to the crisis[28].

The humanitarian focus of the work of the national troop contingents had an unexpected negative consequence, however. Because governments exercised the option provided to pick and choose among elements of the United Nations to support in this particular crisis, it became arguably more difficult for the world body to attract the full range of assistance needed. Weighing peace-keeping functions in volatile settings against humanitarian support roles, governments in all likelihood committed fewer troops to the tougher security assignments, opting instead for the lower-risk, higher-visibility, and undiluted command and control arrangements the service packages afforded.

A strongly positive experience regarding the significant contributions that troops may make in the humanitarian sphere, the overarching lesson was nevertheless therefore also a sobering one. At the end of the day, the sum total of the efforts of these national contingents, highly beneficial in their own terms, were no substitute for an effective multifaceted international strategy to address the Rwandan crisis in its many aspects and at its roots.

Notes

1. Data for this chapter was compiled through interviews in the Great Lakes region, information supplied by the governments involved, and discussions with military and humanitarian personnel in the relief effort. The resulting material is somewhat uneven and incomplete. Most officials interviewed insisted on speaking off the record. Documents cited have been translated by the authors where necessary.

2. In an arrangement separate from the service package, Canadian General Ian Douglas served as Commander of the Civilian Security Liaison Group, an initiative by UNHCR in 1995 to provide security in the refugee camps in Zaire described in Chapter 9.

3. Canadian Ministry of National Defence, "Canada Scales Down Rwanda Commitment", News Release, Sept. 22, 1994.

4. There was considerable debate between the Ministries of Foreign Affairs and Defence in the immediate aftermath of the April 1994 events about whether Canada should quickly provide additional support for UNAMIR.

5. Correspondence from Lt.-Col. G.C. Szczerbaniwicz, Department of National Defence, July 26, 1995.

6. Joelle Tanguy, Executive Director, MSF-USA, interviewed by the authors in July 1995.

7. A number of earlier policy studies by the Dutch government are mentioned in Chapter 1.

8. "Japan's Force to Avoid Peril in Zaire Sites for Rwandans [Reuters], *New York Times*, October 2, 1994.

9. Interview with the authors.

10. "Japanese Troops in Zaire to Aid Rwandans", a Reuter dispatch from Goma, Zaire dated October 2, 1994.

11. Statement at the 49th Session of the United Nations General Assembly, September 27, 1994.

12. The comments cited are from the country profile of Japan, contributed by Tatsuya Watanabe of the Japanese NGO Centre for International Co-operation.

13. Evan Hays, Voice of America broadcast from Bonn, July 16, 1994.

14. The air transport subsequently provided, like the other support functions carried out earlier, could have proceeded without the court's ruling. Cf. also Tomuschat, 1993.

15. Evan Hays, Voice of America broadcast from Bonn, July 29, 1995.

16. "Informationen", *op. cit.*

17. Bernd Wilz, Parlamentarischer Staatsekretar, in *ibid*.

18. "Informationen", *op. cit.*

19. Government of New Zealand, "Rwanda-Humanitarian Assistance by New Zealand", communiqué from the New Zealand Permanent Mission to the United Nations, May 2, 1995.

20. The $7 million figure is from "Rwanda-Humanitarian Assistance by New Zealand", *op. cit.* The description of the sum as "unprecedented" is from *The Reality of Aid — 1995, op. cit.*

21. Since March 29, 1995 AIDAB has been called the Australian Agency for International Development (AusAID).

22. Gareth Evans (1993), *Co-operating for Peace: The Global Agenda for the 1990s and Beyond*, Allen and Unwin, St. Leonards; Australia, p. 170. The Evans volume was undertaken as a contribution by Australia to the international debate on the issues framed by the Secretary-General's *An Agenda for Peace*.

23. Randel and German 1994, *op. cit.*, p. 37.

24. "Israeli Doctors Quit Goma for Jewish New Year", Reuters, August 31 [dateline Goma].

25. Larry James, Rwanda Orphans, Voice of America broadcast, July 26, 1994.

26. Government of Israel, Cabinet Communiqué, May 22, 1994.

27. *The Sunday Press*, "UN Must Set Up a Quick Reaction Force for Future Rwandas", July 31, 1994.

28. Building on the experience in Rwanda, UNHCR, in consultation with donor governments and humanitarian organisations, has subsequently expanded the number of service packages and refined their provisions for use in future emergencies.

Chapter 8

Conclusions and Implications

A half-decade into the post-Cold War period, the international community is establishing the place of the military and of military force in the humanitarian economy of the future. As the discussion proceeds, the experience of the Rwandan crisis is important both in its own right and for its wider meaning. The experience in 1994, reviewed here, sheds light on the policy issues identified in Chapter 2 and summarised in Figure 8.1. Follow-on events in 1995 form the subject of Chapter 9 which follows.

Terms of Engagement

The first policy issue concerns the appropriateness of enlisting international military assets in humanitarian tasks during complex emergencies. The guidance afforded by the experience of utilising the military in the Rwanda crisis is helpful although far from unambiguous.

International military assets were involved in each of the three phases of the Rwanda crisis during 1994 — genocide, the mass exodus, and reconstruction. They were present in three separate frameworks: the multilateral peace-keeping forces of UNAMIR, stand-alone operations by the French and US with security and humanitarian objectives respectively, and national contingents carrying out humanitarian activities within the multilateral rubric provided by UNHCR. Troops performed each of the three generic functions in the humanitarian sphere — fostering a secure environment, supporting the work of humanitarian organisations, and carrying out relief activities themselves.

The appropriateness of involving international military forces was less of an issue in Rwanda than in other recent crises such as Somalia or Bosnia. During Phase I, the egregious nature of the genocide lent special justification and urgency to UNAMIR presence, although concern about the safety of the troops and about what they could realistically accomplish led to lengthy and divisive debates in the Security Council about appropriate forms and levels of international presence. The case for having augmented rather than reduced UNAMIR's mission and strength in April 1994 is now more widely accepted than it was at the time.

During Phase II, the massive scale of the dislocation into neighbouring countries and the challenge of relieving the suffering of those affected elicited widespread commitments of massive military assets, mooting discussion of whether soldiers should be involved. At the time of the mass exodus, the prevalent criticism of governments was not for mobilising their troops but rather for not moving even more quickly to assist the suffering refugees. Nor was the appropriateness of continued military presence a major issue during Phase III, though with humanitarian programmes resumed by aid agencies, the assistance profile — but not the number — of UNAMIR troops and other national contingents was reduced.

> Figure 8.1. **Policy Issues Related to the Use of Military Assets in the Humanitarian Sphere**
>
> 1. Terms of engagement: determining the appropriateness of enlisting international military assets in the humanitarian sphere in complex emergencies.
>
> 2. Comparative advantage: identifying the specific tasks and circumstances in which military assets enjoy a comparative advantage and matching these with the needs of humanitarian organisations.
>
> 3. Costs: assessing the costs, financial and otherwise, to the military and to humanitarian interests of the utilising military assets in operations other than war.
>
> 4. Cultural differences: coming to terms with the differences between military and humanitarian institutions.
>
> 5. Damage limitation: minimising the often negative impacts of military assets on countries and societies in crisis.
>
> 6. Effectiveness: establishing benchmarks for evaluating the performance of military assets.
>
> 7. Stewardship: using military assets creatively to address human suffering.

As soldiers came to the rescue, they collaborated closely with humanitarian agencies on the ground. UN organisations, NGOs, and the ICRC — all of them overwhelmed during the genocide and the mass exodus and some of them having requested the deployment of the military — welcomed such assistance. Subsequently, however, many of those involved have examined the collaboration, negative and positive aspects alike, in more detail.

Initial reservations were directed most toward *Opération Turquoise* and Support Hope. French NGOs in particular viewed collaboration with troops from France, a country with a history of support for the Hutu regime in Kigali and strong ongoing political interests in the region, as undermining their ability to deal with all victims of the conflict and with the new authorities. Some NGO and UN personnel at the outset viewed the US effort as more slapdash than serious. However, over time the professionalism of both operations reassured humanitarian organisations, who came to co-operate closely with them.

The results-oriented approach of the military combined with the extraordinary nature of the circumstances to facilitate effective working partnerships. A good example of necessity as the mother of collaboration emerged from the human rights sphere. Noted earlier were the reservations of some staff of the UN Centre for Human Rights Rwanda in Kigali about co-operating with international military personnel, given the poor reputation of African militaries on human-rights matters. Hard pressed to deliver on the UN's commitment to field human rights monitors throughout Rwanda, however, the Centre welcomed the logistic, telecommunications, and security support provided by UNAMIR. Misgivings of other humanitarian personnel about collaborating with the military also moderated over time.

With more and more humanitarian personnel entering the scene, relationships between military and humanitarian organisations became less ad hoc and more structured. As the humanitarian emergency was stabilized, thanks in part to indispensable assistance from the military, and as attention shifted to reconstruction needs, emergency relief personnel were rotated out and troops wound down their operations. The passing of the emergency allowed for greater thought about the terms of the engagement, a process that has continued down to the present.

The experience of Dutch NGOs was, in effect, a microcosm of the process of reflection in the wider community. Having initially welcomed the involvement of the military and having arrived in Goma aboard Dutch military transport aircraft,

MSF-Holland came to question the appropropriateness of working hand-in-glove with Dutch troops. While the urgency of expanding assistance otherwise available was not disputed, the integration of uniformed and weapons-bearing soldiers into humanitarian teams on humanitarian premises was viewed as compromising the humanitarian mandate[1]. Upon reflection, therefore, the Rwanda experience has narrowed rather than broadened MSF-Holland's willingness to collaborate with the military in the future along lines noted in Chapter 7.

Some other humanitarian organisations perceived the interaction in less negative terms and regarded the space for collaboration with the military as greater. Many organisations gratefully accepted military air transport for aid vehicles, material, and personnel. For most, the services of troops in civilian clothes and without weapons raised few problems. In a broader sense, however, the humanitarian community as a whole is, like Dutch, Japanese, Australian, and other NGOs in their own national settings, now facing the challenge of articulating in greater detail how military and humanitarian mandates and identities interrelate and what should be the ground rules within which collaboration should proceed.

On the application of force in situations such as Rwanda, there is now broader consensus on the indispensability of having military personnel on the scene, authorised and prepared to use force to prevent bloodshed and protect civilian life. The Rwanda experience provides both negative and positive illustrations of this point, as the earlier comparison between the terms of engagement of UNAMIR and *Opération Turquoise* suggested. The ability and willingness of French troops to use force made the French undertaking far more effective than UNAMIR in providing security. The key issue for the future is not whether force should be applied in such circumstances but whether multilateral mechanisms can be fashioned which combine the quick-reaction capacity represented by French troops with fuller multilateral character, mandate, and accountability of a UN operation.

Comparative Advantage

The second policy issue facing the international community concerns identifying the specific tasks in which military assets enjoy a comparative advantage and matching these with the needs of humanitarian organisations. The three broad tasks of the military are, as indicated, fostering a secure environment, supporting the work of humanitarian groups, and carrying out direct assistance to civilian populations. The Rwanda experience suggests that while the troops which came to the rescue performed all three functions, they were least successful at what aid organisations most needed: providing a protective environment for civilians and for humanitarian activities.

The importance of fostering a protective climate was demonstrated with stunning clarity by both its absence and its presence. UNAMIR lacked the forces and mandate to protect those endangered in Kigali and beyond. With more troops at his disposal in early April and able to exercise preventing and protecting roles, UNAMIR's first Force Commander believes in retrospect, genocide might have been nipped in the bud. Behind the UNAMIR failure to prevent and protect was the failure of the Security Council to authorise and of member UN governments to provide. By contrast, *Opération Turquoise* succeeded in affording protection within the safe-zone established in the south-west of Rwanda. Despite incidents of property destruction, the French managed to create and maintain space within which civilians were secure and aid programmes could proceed. Evacuations of personnel followed a similar pattern: UNAMIR had difficulty where French and Belgian efforts succeeded.

Although fostering security is an area in which armed forces may make an indispensable contribution — certainly humanitarian organisations have no comparative advantage in the matter — the Rwanda experience illustrated the general reluctance of most military forces to take on security chores. For the United States, Rwanda was the first occasion for implementing Presidential Decision Directive 25, which specified the US military assets would be deployed only in situations which required the "unique military capabilities" of US troops and which involved "minimum risk" to them. The reluctance of governments to tackle security issues also contributed to the attractiveness of the UNHCR service packages. Those participating — the Japanese, the Germans, and the United States are examples — stressed the humanitarian-only nature of their duties and distinguished their involvement carefully from UNAMIR and its security rubric.

In the second major task area, Rwanda demonstrated the comparative advantage of the military in supporting the activities of humanitarian organisations. Chapters 4 through 7 provide countless examples of such support. They include UNAMIR's assistance to the ICRC and other aid organisations in the chaotic April days and, in the ensuing months, its support of the activities of a host of UN agencies and NGOs. Operation Support Hope put massive air assets at the disposal of the international relief effort. Individual military contingents associated with UNHCR provided sizeable and focused support to UN organisations, NGOs, and the ICRC.

Yet the actual comparative advantage in this regard was narrower than many assumed. In Goma, aid organisations arranged commercial air charters for relief supplies more quickly than the military, although the magnitude of initial needs was such that a boost from the military was essential to provide stopgap coverage during the peak of the emergency. In fact, the scale of the need was such that aid agencies had no alternative to overland transport, a task which itself received a boost from the military, which moved essential vehicles into the theatre by air. Thus in the heavy lifting, the comparative advantage of the military was keyed to the scale of the need, the rapid onset of this particular crisis, and the particular period until aid agencies could regain control of the situation. The Rwanda airlift also proved unresponsive to the needs of some agencies, as the Oxfam experience in Chapter 6 illustrated. To the extent that cost considerations are a factor, the comparative advantages of the military are narrowed further.

As for the third role, the many examples of soldiers in the direct provision of relief cited in the preceding four chapters require careful interpretation. UNAMIR assumed a variety of direct relief activities in April after many humanitarian personnel had been evacuated and, in the ensuing months, utilised its British, Canadian, and Australian contingents for an array of medical, engineering, sanitation, and communications tasks. The efforts by French and Israeli military doctors to analyse diseases in their medical laboratories in Goma and the labours of French troops in their off-hours collecting and disposing of bodies in Goma were also noteworthy. Activities by troops from the US, the Netherlands, Japan, and other countries also made a significant difference. One novel element was that unlike other emergencies in which outside military assets helped civilian populations because the troops happened to be there, many of the soldiers in Rwanda, whatever the military configuration, had that specific mission as their primary one.

However helpful the direct relief work of the military, troops by their own admission enjoyed no particular edge in many of the tasks requiring attention. While working energetically with humanitarian agencies to augment what was accomplished, most of the troops themselves, while skilled in their own areas, had no unique competence in such matters as refugee camp construction, community health and disease control, or shelter management. Moreover, their security preoccupations — for example, the prohibition against most US forces from leaving the Kigali airport, the reluctance of the Japanese to work in refugee camps — also circumscribed what the troops themselves were able to achieve.

The reading of military officials themselves of the Rwanda experience in direct relief tended to be restrictive rather than expansive. French General Lafourcade, as noted in Chapter 5, held that combattant troops could and should provide security and support for humanitarian operations but should not themselves become dispensers of relief. General Schroeder, too, sought to keep Operation Support Hope activities in Kigali focused on supporting the organisations that "can do humanitarian assistance much better than the military can". Such comments recall the view of US Secretary of Defence William I. Perry, quoted in Chapter 2, that "Generally the military is not the right tool to meet humanitarian concerns".

In all three functions — and the comparative advantage of the military narrows progressively from each to the next — the vaunted quick-response of the military was not borne out by events. It was not until May 17 that the initial reduction-in-force of UNAMIR was reversed, and not until five months later that UNAMIR reached the approved strength of 5 500. Even the French, who acted with more dispatch, arrived in south-western Rwanda after much of the bloodletting had run its course. The comment cited earlier by the local Goma physician, the only doctor for some 3 500 children, about the Israeli military medics, could be writ large over the entire international Rwanda response, humanitarian and military alike: "Why did they come so late?"

Paradoxically, troops were least available when most needed. Figure 7.1 provides an indication of the numbers available at different points during the year. In the wake of the outbreak of violence April 6, UNAMIR forces were reduced when presence in greater numbers might have exercised a deterrent effect, reducing the scale of the humanitarian crisis and the ostensible need for additional troops later in the year. More numerous military presence in the final three months of the year, when security in the camps became an increasing problem, was also sought after by many humanitarian organisations. Peak availability of the troops was reached during July, August, and September, when the need was great, but primarily for humanitarian support and direct relief.

The experience suggests not that the military cannot move quickly, but that the decision-making processes that activate them may reduce their respective advantage. Disagreements within the Security Council and a lack of responsiveness on the part of governments undercut UNAMIR's ability to function. While the French and US undertakings moved with greater dispatch, both were activated well into the crisis and Operation Support Hope encountered serious institutional problems in gearing up the military to play its prescribed roles. In short, when serving as a humanitarian resource, the military are not free agents but an instrument responsive to political decisions, priorities, and timetables. Comparative advantages otherwise enjoyed by military assets may thus be constrained by political disadvantages inherent in their utilisation.

The Rwanda response illustrated not only respective comparative advantages of the military and humanitarian organisations but also comparative advantages within the humanitarian sphere among different militaries. Each military framework and contingent had its special strengths. Thus US military air transport did the major lifting not only for humanitarian organisations but also for other militaries as well. Regarding global military assets, the best of all possible worlds would combine the broad-based international support embodied in a UN peace-keeping force, the dispatch with which the French acted, the lift capability of the US, and the specialised competence of the various national contingents that answered UNHCR's call.

In sum, the Rwanda experience underscored the importance of identifying and maintaining comparative advantage. The issue is not the value of the military but the value added by the military to the existing humanitarian effort. Troops need to be a single element in a multifaceted international response to humanitarian emergencies, not a substitute for a balanced approach that includes political, diplomatic, and security as well as humanitarian elements.

Cost

If the militaries in the Rwanda crisis did not maximise their comparative advantages, neither did the soldiers who came to the rescue proceed more cheaply than humanitarian organisations. The cost of utilising international military forces, a factor likely to play a role in determining the utility of the military in the humanitarian regime of the future, was a sizeable one, if difficult to quantify. In fact, the absence of accurate and comparable cost figures is itself a major agenda item for the future.

The cost of utilising military assets in the Rwanda crisis during 1994 totalled more than $600 million. If higher (and probably more realistic) figures are used for the French and US undertakings, the total could be increased by a factor of two or three. Figure 8.2 provides a recap of the data presented earlier in the volume. The figure seeks to place the costs of the various militaries involved on a comparable and consistent basis, although the number of explanatory notes suggests the difficulties of doing so.

Table 8.2. **Costs of Utilising Selected Military Contingents in the Rwanda Crisis (1994)**

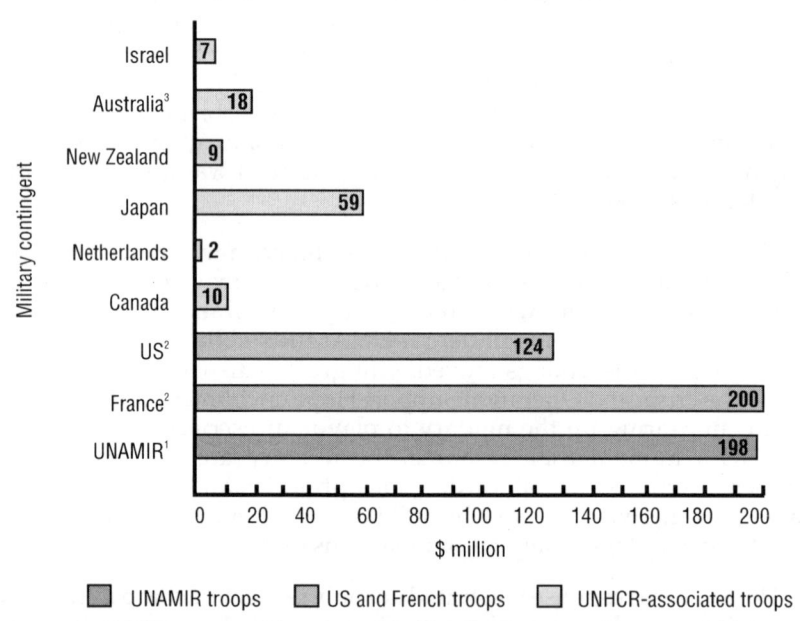

Military contingent	$ million
Israel	7
Australia[3]	18
New Zealand	9
Japan	59
Netherlands	2
Canada	10
US[2]	124
France[2]	200
UNAMIR[1]	198

■ UNAMIR troops   ▨ US and French troops   □ UNHCR-associated troops

Notes: 1. The UNAMIR figure includes 1994 cost of UNOMUR as well. Payments to UNAMIR by governments which also provided troops associated with UNHCR are not included within the individual entries under UNHCR-associated troops.
2. Some estimates place the costs considerably higher.
3. While this figure reflects principally the costs of Australian troops serving in UNAMIR, it also includes costs of Australian troops associated with UNHCR.
Costs shown are "incremental": that is, additional to normal operating costs in the absence of Rwanda activities.

The major budgetary components of the Rwanda response were four in number, corresponding to the troops reviewed in Chapters 4, 5, 6, and 7 respectively. The cost of UNAMIR (including UNOMUR) in 1994 was $197.5 million. Costs for

Opération Turquoise and Operation Support Hope are given as $200 million and $123.9 million, even though actual costs, particularly for the latter, may have been significantly higher. The costs of UNHCR-associated military assets appear to have been on the order of $100-$150 million. Military assets utilised in the 1994 response thus exceeded $600 million.

These need to be set against the resources available through humanitarian organisations reviewed in Chapter 3. DHA figures place the totals of such assets at $562.7 million for activities within the UN InterAgency Consolidated Appeal. An additional $646.9 million was reported to DHA for activities outside that framework. However, since that figure includes some funds military assets such as those provided under Operation Support Hope, comparisons become difficult. As a generalisation, it appears safe to conclude that military and humanitarian assets of at least $600 million each were utilised in the Rwanda crisis during 1994. Actual expenditures were higher by an unknown factor on both sides. The difficulties of getting to the two bottom lines and of comparing the two demonstrate major problems of comprehensiveness, consistency, and comparability.

Evidence suggests that using the military was a costly option, confirming afresh through the Rwanda experience the issue framed in Chapter 2. True at the aggregate level, the high cost is also applicable to individual sectors. In the case of the airlift provided by Operation Support Hope, commercially contracted air transport was less expensive, although not available in the necessary amounts. The relatively large number of back-up personnel for each soldier engaged in aid tasks also made using the military expensive. Moreover, solutions employed by the military are often technology- and maintenance-intensive, adding further to the cost.

Factors other than purely economic ones, however, need to be taken into consideration in establishing a comprehensive balance sheet. For one, the necessity of saving lives may be viewed as outweighing the actual costs of doing so, however great. For another, the political advantages of employing a nation's armed forces may offset the simple cost calculation of doing so. The Royal Air Force was used to transport British relief supplies in the Rwanda crisis when commercial charters were known to have been available at substantial savings. France chose to launch its own operation rather than investing in UNAMIR.

In the absence of reliable and consistent data about costs, cost-effectiveness calculations regarding the utilisation of the various configurations of military assets are also difficult. Neither data nor methodology exists for reaching judgements about the relative value of UNAMIR troops costing $197.5 million for a year as against French troops at $200 million or US troops at $123.9 million for almost two months. Whether the investment of C$ 106 million over more than a year for Canadian troops with peace-keeping, peace-keeping-cum-humanitarian, and humanitarian mandates represented one of the better bargains will remain conjectural, as will whether the Israeli cost of $7 million for the medical treatment of 5 000 refugees was as high as it appears. The state of the data also makes it impossible to test the hypothesis that a single dollar spent on prevention may be worth dozens spent on cures.

The Rwanda experience dramatised that there was no single pot of resources, co-ordinating mechanism, or point of accountability for the entire emergency response — military or civilian, international or even, in some instances, national. In some countries, the costs of the military were borne by government aid ministries and humanitarian organisations. The UNHCR in its service packages, the Canadian International Development Association, the Netherlands Ministry of Development Co-operation, and the New Zealand Overseas Development Programme are examples. In such instances, aid agencies had a direct interest in assuring that they were getting their money's worth.

In most other instances, defence ministries themselves absorbed the costs, as in the cases of France and Japan. In such instances, military assets represent clear additionality over what would otherwise have been available for aid efforts. However, the question remains whether those assets were utilised by the military in ways that increased the outreach and effectiveness of humanitarian organisations. Aid agencies themselves also indicated that when services were available at no cost from the military, they were sometimes less disciplined than they would have been had they been paying the full cost themselves.

In addition to what militaries contributed at their own expense, the balance sheet should also reflect the heightened public awareness of the issues and augmented public contributions to private agencies associated with the involvement of national troops. Ireland and New Zealand are cases in point. Additionality may also have been involved when governments — Germany and Israel are examples — provided cash in support of aid activities in which their troops were engaged. The secondment of military personnel to humanitarian organisations at no cost to government aid agencies or receiving organisations also needs to be taken into account.

Attempts to calculate the cost of using the military in Rwanda also expose methodological problems within the existing system of accounting. Different militaries use different approaches to calculating what they consider the "incremental" costs of their military assets. In the case of the US, the goverment's own accounting office confirmed that the US military had no way of disaggregating or even of totalling all its expenditures on Rwanda. Some governments provided no data at all on the costs of their involvement, whether because they did not exist or because their nature was somehow sensitive.

Institutional glitches within the UN also became apparent. DHA, responsible for co-ordinating aid efforts in complex emergencies, did not figure in negotiations between the UN Department of Peace-keeping Operations (DPKO) and national defence ministries such as the British which were providing troops to UNAMIR for specific humanitarian tasks. Nor did DHA play a role in follow-on arrangements made between the UN and commercial contractors who would continue such services after the departure of the troops. An effective mechanism also did not exist linking UNHCR, which negotiated service packages with national defence departments, and DPKO, the normal UN interlocutor with those ministries.

In sum, the Rwanda experience demonstrated that the cost of utilising military assets is high but also that governments under certain circumstances are willing to pay that cost. It also dramatised that a system more attuned to an era of limited resources and to tough issues of comparative cost-effectiveness will require greater attention to the costs of all available options — military and humanitarian, preventive and curative, security and assistential — and to establishing methodologies for determining them.

Institutional Cultures

The fourth policy issue concerns coming to terms with the acknowledged cultural differences between military and humanitarian institutions. Given the scale, prominence, and variety of the military assets committed to the Rwanda crisis, the experience was instructive. The interactions between humanitarian and military personnel were numerous and intensive, multidimensional and ongoing. In the light of the serious and high-visibility problems which had accompanied such interaction in other recent major crises, the fact that in this instance cultural differences did not undermine effective collaboration is noteworthy.

The viewpoint expressed in Chapter 2 of an institutional culture clash rooted in "a lack of familiarity" of military and humanitarian personnel and characterised by an "attitudinal abyss" between them was not a major problem in the Rwanda crisis. "We liked and respected the military people — US, French, Dutch, Israelis, and others — that we dealt with in Goma", commented one public-health professional of his experience in late July. "What we struggled with were not personality or even operational problems but rather structural ones".

That the expected differences did not loom larger was a reflection of the professionalism on both sides in responding to the extremity of the crisis. Troops in each of the four frameworks did their best to minimise frictions. UNAMIR was eminently approachable by, and responsive to, aid workers. *Opération Turquoise* was businesslike and non-political in going about its tasks. Operation Support Hope enhanced rather than upstaged the work of humanitarian organisations. UNHCR-related national contingents had supportive humanitarian terms of reference. In each instance, the presence among the troops of personnel with competence in the humanitarian sphere exercised a bridging influence across cultural divides.

Collegiality notwithstanding, there were three areas in which structural differences were particularly difficult to resolve: planning and co-ordination, continuity of presence, and approach to security concerns.

Good-faith efforts were made by military actors to co-ordinate their activities with those of humanitarian organisations. The UNAMIR humanitarian cell, *Opération Turquoise* civilian and humanitarian cell, UNREO, the UN's Integrated Operations Centre, the Civilian Military Operations Centre of Operation Support Hope, and UNHCR service packages and Geneva air operations cell were all mechanisms for orchestrating common action across military/humanitarian lines. However, many of the military and humanitarian actors were, in General Schroeder's words, "meeting on the dance floor" for the first time.

The crisis did not begin on April 6 in Kigali or on July 14 in Goma, however. In the latter instance, the abrupt arrival of US military forces a week later underscored their absence from earlier collaborative planning. While the arrival in June of French troops in Rwanda had not been well co-ordinated with UNAMIR, concerted planning by military and humanitarian organisations for their departure in August 1994 helped avoid panic flight from the south-west ("a second Goma"). In the case of other national contingents, problems of planning and co-ordination were eased, although not altogether avoided, by the service-package approach.

Such disconnects are difficult to resolve, especially where stand-alone interventions are concerned. The military approach to the planning task — bureaucratic, top-down, personnel-intensive — was foreign to humanitarians and minimised possible contributions in the area of disaster prevention and preparedness. Problems were compounded by the lack of co-ordination among humanitarian organisations and between the UN's humanitarian and military arms. While improvements can and should be made based on the Rwanda experience, the difficulties encountered involve fundamental differences in institutional culture.

A second area of difficulty involved continuity of presence. Canadian troops were involved beginning with UNOMUR in mid-1993 and were expected to stay on through the end of the UNAMIR mandate in late 1995. Personnel seconded by the Irish military were on hand for an initial three months, with many extending the stay for an additional rotation or two. French and US troops were on the scene for about two months. Israeli troops touched down on July 25, 1994 and had left by the end of August after three two-week rotations. German troops were rotated every three weeks.

Humanitarian organisations, by contrast, stressed continuity and follow-through. Many doubted the utility of contributions by soldiers who came and went quickly. They generally preferred more extended troop rotations, which provided greater payback for the time necessarily invested in establishing effective working relationships with the military. Problems for the humanitarian effort of the late arrival and early departure of the troops are reviewed in a later section.

As for security concerns, force protection matters loomed large for many of the militaries involved. Humanitarian personnel, themselves often more willing than the military to take risks, believed that the utility to the aid effort of US troops was reduced in both Goma and Kigali by the preoccupation for their safety. Aid activities by the Japanese contingent in Goma were constrained by their own legal requirements that conflict should be avoided. Other militaries such as the Dutch were less preoccupied with the security and health of the troops, even though Dutch soldiers retained their weapons in assisting NGOs. Irish troops shed their uniforms and reported directly to aid organisations.

The conclusion from the experience was not that military officials should not be concerned about protecting their troops but that risk avoidance may limit their utility to the humanitarian effort. Military assets are part and parcel of the culture of military institutions. The illustrations also suggest the existence of differences within the military culture as well as on the humanitarian side.

In the Rwanda crisis, the world's response will be remembered not only for the dedication of humanitarian workers, who are expected to perform however difficult and risky the circumstances. Also a matter of record are the bravery of individual UNAMIR officers and rank-and-file soldiers during the April days in Kigali, the energy of French troops in helping on the "body detail" in Goma in July, the collaboration between military and humanitarian personnel in the UNHCR air cell in Geneva, the personnel support and security counsel provided to aid agencies by Irish and other militaries, and the off-hours activities of Canadian and other troops. The Rwanda experience expanded the circle of humanitarian contributions to include the full array of military personnel, multilateral and bilateral, peace-keeping and humanitarian alike.

The Rwanda experience demonstrated that practical ways and means can be found for overcoming some of the cultural differences between military and humanitarian institutions. Military forces can work collegially with humanitarian organisations and enhance their effectiveness. Since fundamental differences are likely to persist, however, the broader question arises of whether the limited resources and energies of the international community should go into improving the cost-effectiveness and humanitarian-friendly aspects of the military, or into enhancing the capacity and responsiveness of humanitarian organisations themselves.

In this context, the suggestion of the Goma Epidemiology Group noted in Chapter 6 merits consideration: that rather than seeking to narrow ongoing differences between military and humanitarian institutions, priority be given instead to strengthening the capacities of aid agencies themselves.

Damage Limitation

The problem of minimising the often negative impacts of military assets was identified in Chapter 2 as one of the more troublesome among the seven policy issues for the military. In a broad sense, the Rwanda experience corroborated those difficulties. The absence of adequate awareness by the military of the complexities of the crisis is a case in point.

The Rwanda crisis involved deeply rooted historical tensions which played themselves out in civil war-cum-genocide, rending the nation's social fabric and destroying its people and its infrastructure. As with other complex emergencies in such places as the former Yugoslavia, Somalia, Angola, Mozambique, and Cambodia, meeting urgent human need necessarily had political ramifications. Those attempting to assist might become caught up in the war; even the successful alleviation of emergency need might worsen longer-term prospects for a more secure future.

In responding to the complexities of this particular emergency, military forces had difficulty charting their course. On some occasions, they would forge ahead, apparently irrespective of — or undeterred by — longer-term consequences. Thus *Opération Turquoise* succeeded in providing security in south-western Rwanda but created problems for UNAMIR and Rwandan authorities who took over thereafter. While French troops were highly professional in how they approached their task, their presence confirmed a sense of persecution among Hutus, thereby setting back prospects for critically needed reconstruction and reconciliation.

UNAMIR in November 1994 made detailed plans for transporting the internally displaced from camps back to their communes, a job of enormous political sensitivity. Approaching the task as primarily a logistical challenge, UNAMIR proceeded without the essential consultation with humanitarian organisations who had expertise in resettlement and human rights protection, although eventually a collaborative approach was found. In both the *Opération Turquoise* and UNAMIR examples, the activities of the military responded to political agendas.

On other occasions, the military seemed to defer too completely to humanitarian organisations. Was it ill-advised, one senior UNAMIR military officer with humanitarian responsibilities was asked, for the military to concentrate on immediate problems at the expense of reconstruction priorities? The issue was "irrelevant" to the work of the military, the UNAMIR official countered. "We are simply providing a humanitarian service". On the contrary, there were serious policy issues involved in the balance struck between relief and reconstruction. Providing relief itself involved complex choices of policy and strategy.

At some points, both military and humanitarian actors seemed, in retrospect, to have pursued dubious policies. In the choice of water-purification strategies in Goma, for example, the high-tech approach selected by the military has subsequently been questioned, but health experts have also faulted the strategy taken by humanitarian organisations on the scene as well. Or again, to the extent that the international relief effort outside of Zaire played into the hands of Hutus committed to retake power in Rwanda, humanitarian as well as military actors were implicated, however difficult it was, even in retrospect, to frame preferable alternatives.

The timetable of the military was also a problem, as noted above. From the start, military forces — or, more precisely, the national governments which made them available — were preoccupied with a prompt exit from the scene. In fact, entrances were deferred until exits were ensured. Chastened by recent experience in Somalia and Bosnia, most military assets were committed to the Rwanda crisis for carefully delimited purposes within a tightly compressed time frame.

From an emergency and longer-term standpoint, however, the timing of the troops' presence raised many questions. Their "late" arrival limited their prevention and protection capacity. Their "early" departure raised questions about the unfinished business they left behind and, in a broader sense, about the commitment of the international community to reconstruction. It was telling that most were not on hand late in 1994 when security problems in the camps brought humanitarian activities to a halt.

Moreover, at a variety of points during the crisis, it was apparent that despite the presence of many troops — perhaps even because of their presence — an appropriate balance of policies was lacking. To be sure, the commitment in Rwanda during 1994 of about equal portions of military and humanitarian assets avoided the ten-to-one imbalance in favour of the military which had prevailed in Somalia. However, committing military assets is no substitute for effective longer-term policies to address underlying problems. As noted throughout, the contributions of troops are only as valuable as the policies they serve are effective. The danger that humanitarian organisations will be used as substitutes for political and diplomatic policies is equally great for the military, whose very presence and activities may conceal the lack of effective longer-term strategies.

If the soldiers who came to the rescue sometimes seemed unaware of complex historical and societal processes, the conclusion is not that they should have taken their cues from humanitarian organisations. Aid groups had their own difficulties in understanding the dynamics of the situation and in formulating effective strategies. Clearly the challenges of prevention and nation building are no easier for them than for military actors. The conclusion is rather that all who engage in such crises need to be prepared to struggle with the complexities. In fact, given the particular nature, scale, and timing of military interventions, the military need to be particularly astute in their interventions.

On a more positive note, several factors worked to limit the counterproductive effects accompanying military involvement in the Rwanda theatre. For one, the scale of military presence and the approach taken by the troops was calibrated to leave the smallest possible "footprint" on the local scene. Articulated by Operation Support Hope but embraced by other militaries as well, this approach counteracted what one analyst has called "the tendency for military-security issues to eclipse political and social issues when military actors arrive on the scene" (Bush, 1995).

For another, the generic problem of the scale of military intervention overwhelming local structures and decision making turned out not to be an issue in this instance. With many indigenous local institutions in disarray and/or weakened by their involvement in the genocide, the danger of displacing local leadership was reduced, although still real. Since the new Rwandan civilian and military leaders were initially anxious to prove their bona fides, the risk that foreign military personnel and resources would reinforce retrograde social policies, a problem in other crises, was also reduced. In fact, in the case of Rwanda's refugees, the international aid effort is criticized for having been too deferential to Hutu leadership in the camps.

Even having avoided some of the typical negative impacts in some areas of military involvement however, the Rwanda experience is still troubling because of the unresolved nature of the underlying problems. If with the passage of time Rwanda experiences a major new humanitarian crisis, a critical reappraisal of the resources invested and strategies pursued during 1994 — military as well as humanitarian — may be launched. Even by late 1994, there were signs that the massive military assets committed had not helped secure Rwanda's future. Those assets may also have made a balanced set of international policy responses — political and diplomatic, humanitarian and military — more difficult to achieve, both in the immediate crisis and beyond.

> The humanitarian community felt itself increasingly burdened by the genocide. The standard rules of protection and assistance seemed to lack a certain relevance when faced with a reality that in the course of three months, from April to June 1994, a plan of the previous government, almost incomprehensible in terms of its cruelty, cold-bloodedness and efficiency, had been implemented, resulting in the torture and murder of between 500 000 and 1 000 000 supposedly ethnic Rwandan Tutsis. The humanitarian situation was further compounded by the fact that after July 1994 the new Government of Rwanda never failed to remind the humanitarian community that in refugee camps along the nation's borders perpetrators of the genocide were being fed and maintained by UN Agencies and NGOs alike.
>
> Randolph Kent, "The Integrated Operations Centre in Rwanda: Coping with Complexity," in Whitman and Pocock, 1996.

Effectiveness

The sixth policy issue concerns establishing agreed-upon benchmarks of effectiveness for evaluating the contributions of military assets to the humanitarian enterprise. In this regard, the Rwanda experience illuminated the urgency for such benchmarks but did not itself produce them.

As noted in Chapter 1, the early post-Cold War period has witnessed the growing utilisation of the military in major humanitarian crises. These have included northern Iraq, Cambodia, Somalia, Bosnia, and now Rwanda. In each, the challenges faced by the military have been different; in each, the response has been informed by previous experience. Five years after the rescue by US troops of Iraqi Kurds from the mountains along the Turkish border, the military has become a more common instrument — but not yet the instrument of choice — for responding to such emergencies.

The Rwanda chapter in this progression shows both the strengths and the weaknesses of international military assets as an effective tool of humanitarian policy and operations. In the genocide period of the crisis, outside military forces were largely ineffective in preventing violence and in assisting the victims of it. During the mass exodus, they played a generally positive role. During the reconstruction period, they were conspicuous by their relative absence, particularly as problems of a security nature materialised wherein they might have made a contribution.

There was an apparent correlation between the presence of significant numbers of troops and their effectiveness. While it seems axiomatic that if military personnel are not present they cannot make a positive contribution, it does not necessarily follow that their presence will assure positive results. The data and analysis in Chapters 4-7 have amply demonstrated various militaries at their effective best — and at their ineffective worst.

Given the panoply of troops involved, conclusions about the relative effectiveness of military and humanitarian activities in the humanitarian sphere should be possible. What emerges from the present study and from other research to date, however, are largely hypotheses in need of further testing and refinement. One hypothesis, suggested by the data on UNAMIR and *Opération Turquoise* in Chapters 4 and 5 and the discussion in the Terms of Engagement section in the present chapter, might be that in the area of prevention and protection, action led by a single country was more effective than a broader UN effort. Troops in the French undertaking played a positive role whereas their UNAMIR counterparts for the most part did not.

In the area of military support for humanitarian organisations, a second hypothesis, based on data in Chapters 6 and 7, is that some of the more focused, smaller scale projects of national contingents within UNHCR's multilateral framework represented a better investment than the larger-scale activities of Operation Support Hope. This thesis, too, requires additional study, not the least because the US undertaking evolved from a stand-alone initiative to one eventually more integrated into the UNHCR service-package framework. In the area of the direct conduct of relief activities, the hypothesis that humanitarian organisations do things more cheaply and better than the military is, for the moment, conjectural though plausible based on available evidence.

The balance sheet from the Rwanda experience has both positives and negatives. Recapping these from earlier chapters and earlier portions of the present chapter, the positives include: the financial, technical, and logistical capacity that the military are able to bring to bear on a crisis; the problem-solving and can-do approach of the troops; the collaborative approach taken to their tasks; the ability of the military to attract media attention and to mobilise public interest and support; and the military's demonstrated interest in assessing performance and drawing lessons for the future. Taken together, the positives suggest that military assets represent a resource which, at a time when humanitarian resources are seriously overextended, need to be harnessed to serve otherwise unmet needs.

The negative side of the ledger includes formidable problems encountered by humanitarian organisations in receiving the kind of support needed when needed and in usable forms; the predisposition of the military toward state-of-the-art solutions to basic problems when simpler approaches may be more effective; an understandable preoccupation with security to the detriment of humanitarian support functions; the absence of serious joint planning until intervention in a given crisis has become likely; and an agenda and timetable driven by considerations external to the dynamics of the humanitarian crisis itself. Taken together, these negatives suggest a significant unwieldiness in the military as a humanitarian instrument. While some aspects of the instrument may be made more responsive, as in the case of Rwanda, structural problems are likely to remain.

Reviewing positives and negatives, the international community has yet to reach consensus on the relative weighting of each. Some new policy directions are emerging: the commitment of various militaries to extensive orientations for their troops regarding tasks in the humanitarian sphere; the reluctance of some humanitarian organisations to rely in the future on military air transport and the decision of other aid groups to collaborate only in the most exceptional circumstances; and the concern about the pre-emption of funds for crises of the scale of Rwanda's from resources otherwise available for crisis prevention and economic development elsewhere.

Underscoring the pivotal nature of the Rwanda crisis in the sequence of major emergencies, the experience is the subject of active review by humanitarian and military institutions alike. From the military side, the reflection process is characterised by a widely shared sense of satisfaction in jobs well done. Many militaries are actively engaged in "humanitarian exercises" designed to avoid the problems encountered in recent crises and build effective structures for future collaboration. The irony, of course, is that while all troops except those associated with UNAMIR have now finished their Rwanda assignments, the success of the various military contingents in 1994 is not reflected in the current situation on the ground.

In contrast to the general optimism permeating effectiveness reviews by the military, the reflection process on the humanitarian side is far more somber, concentrating on unfinished business rather than limited success. The Federation of Red Cross and Red Crescent Societies held a major consultation in December 1994 to analyse the Rwanda experience and to identify priorities for action during the post-emergency phase (IFRC, 1995)[2]. Already in 1994 Oxfam (UK and Ireland) published a comprehensive report reviewing the underlying issues, the emergency response, and the lessons to be learned for the future (Vassall-Adams, 1994). UNDHA has completed its own in-house evaluation of the Rwanda effort (Donini and Niland, 1994). The Rwanda experience is also the subject of the multi-donor evaluation referenced in the Preface and due for publication in early 1996. Each such review identifies serious problem areas in military-humanitarian co-operation.

In sum, the effectiveness of the contribution of international military forces to the world's response to the Rwanda crisis, like the other elements of the response as well, is a matter of ongoing study. Reflecting increased constraints on resources and a more tough-minded approach to matters of cost-effectiveness, increasing attention is being given to establishing criteria for effectiveness and measuring performance. However, whether the result will be to strengthen humanitarian assets, enhance military capacities, or to improve collaboration between the two is not yet clear.

As indicated in Chapter 1, powerful geo-strategic developments have contributed to the availability of international military forces for use in humanitarian crises. Their deployment in a given crisis may reflect quite obvious, or more hidden, political interests and objectives. Whether the openness of the military to such involvement is a passing infatuation or an enduring reality remains to be seen. In any event, effective humanitarian action requires the development of safeguards so that the effectiveness of humanitarian programmes is enhanced and their integrity protected.

The Rwanda experience suggests that however well or poorly international troops and humanitarian organisations performed, the desideratum is neither to turn the military into a humanitarian organisation nor to refashion aid institutions in a military mold. The hallmarks of effective interventions are common, however, whether the actors are military or humanitarian. Successful efforts are generally carried out by dedicated and energetic professionals who are well-informed about the complexities of a given situation and well-trained in their respective specialties, pragmatic rather than ideological in approach, and able draw on institutional experience to adapt strategies and resources to circumstances.

Stewardship

The final policy issue concerns the extent to which providing troops for duties in the humanitarian sphere has come to represent a key dimension in the exercise of global responsibility by national governments. On this point, the impact of the Rwanda experience is clear: the commitment of troops was undertaken by many as an exercise in global responsibility. There is reason to believe that, in one form or another, that pattern may characterise the future as well.

The sheer number of nations contributing military assets in the Rwanda crisis, perhaps an all-time high, suggests the importance attached to doing so. The composite figure would include 26 nations providing UNAMIR with troops, military observers, or civilian police, the French and the US initiatives, and the score of UNHCR-related contingents. While the actual numbers of military personnel was exceeded by those in Bosnia and Somalia, the number committed to explicitly humanitarian tasks and the diversity of those tasks makes the Rwanda experience distinctive.

The element of perceived global responsibility was routinely stressed by governments in interpreting their actions. Explaining the presence of British troops carrying out humanitarian tasks within UNAMIR, Major M.W. Hiskett noted that "The government wishes to demonstrate the United Kingdom's ability to perform this type of operation to meet a crisis quickly". He saw the work of BRITCON as "a demonstration of our political willingness to be involved in this type of operation in the future"[3]. The commitment of troops by New Zealand reinforced concerns expressed by its ambassador, who chaired the Security Council at the time of the April events, that the international community should not remain sidelined during the crisis.

The commitment of troops by Germany as part of a UNHCR service package was an expression of its desire "to assume greater responsibilities in world affairs"[4]. Indeed, German presence on the Security Council during 1995-96 was seen as requiring such action. As a result of Rwanda and other recent experiences, "the German armed forces will be empowered even more strongly than in the past to undertake complex international initiatives with its allies and other partners". (Bundesministerium der Verteidigung, 1995). Japan, a contender for a permanent seat on the Security Council in any future reorganisation, also framed its participation as an exercise in global responsibility. As with Germany, the positive nature of the experience contributed to an expressed Japanese willingness to accept other humanitarian operations in the future.

Governments which were not Security Council members at the time or had no expressed hopes of becoming such also attached great importance to involvement in the Rwanda effort. The Irish, whose military resources were already committed at the time, found a way of participating through the secondment of a small number of military personnel to aid agencies. As in other countries, the debate about national responsibilities engaged the public and policy-makers in formulating a course of action.

While many governments were anxious to play a contributing role to an effective international response, however, the existing international system did not facilitate that outcome. A report in late 1994 for the Canadian government chronicled the grueling debates in the Security Council in the wake of the April events, puzzling over the success of key nations in blocking action. "It appears curious", the study noted, "that the handful of 14 middle-power Western nations who at a conservative estimate have a total annual military budget of $70 billion and a total of 1 100 000 troops, are not capable of making common cause with like-minded developing countries. Those [latter] countries may lack peace-keeping skills and equipment but give every indication of being prepared to take their place on the world stage if only given a hand [by the middle powers]" (LaRose-Edwards, 1994)[5]. Delays in international action also drew critical comment from the media at the time. Reflecting on the welcome, if belated, decision by the Clinton administration to harness the US military for Rwanda duties, one commentator noted the growing reluctance to bless UN peace-keeping and humanitarian interventions. "But surely", he mused, "permanent membership of the Security Council carries just such responsibilities, if not for unilateral intervention then for overseeing a more effective UN facility to do so"[6]?

"Many people remain suspicious", observed an editorial in an Irish newspaper, "that the large powers inevitably turn [major humanitarian catastrophes] to their own advantage and interests — a fact that helps to explain some of the disenchantment within their own populations about getting involved. There is room for smaller states, Ireland included, to take the initiative within the UN and the European Union on longer-term ways of developing appropriate means to respond to such disasters"[7].

In short, many of the smaller and mid-sized nations seemed to have developed a clearer sense of how their own national interests are served by effective international humanitarian action than have several of the larger and more powerful countries. The assumption among many US politicians that no one was willing to die, or to have others die, while serving in the US military on foreign soil, denigrated the public's capacity to distinguish between just and unjust causes. The uncertainty about the extent to which US national interests were served by an effective package of international policies, including the use of military force, recalled the discussion in Chapter 2 of distinctions between "vital" interests and humanitarian imperatives.

By and large, however, the Rwanda response demonstrated the interest of governments in making positive contributions, military and humanitarian, to a major crisis, particularly when it reaches massive dimensions. Looking back, they view their involvement as overwhelmingly positive. They now envision commiting military assets in another emergency, though leaving their options open in terms of the particular situations which might produce their involvement. Yet they acknowledge that the Rwanda crisis demonstrated the need to strengthen international machinery so that the authorisation and provision of troops could proceed with greater expeditiousness. The objective is not only a quicker response mechanism but also "a system of permanent international co-operation that can foresee and act to forestall such crises"[8].

Governments are stewards of not only humanitarian and military resources, of course, but also of political and diplomatic ones. What is needed, the Rwanda crisis demonstrated, is a more balanced response. "'Sending in the troops can be regarded as a government's highest expression of political commitment", observes analyst James Whitman, "but all too frequently in humanitarian peace support operations, the deployment of military forces is in some measure a substitute for commitment" (Whitman, 1996). In this sense, the commitment of troops, while perhaps a necessary condition in a given set of circumstances, is probably never a sufficient condition for effective humanitarian action.

In any event, an ethos is evolving in which the contribution of military resources to major humanitarian crises is coming to represent a key element in the exercise of global stewardship. The commitment of troops is becoming a new "coin of the realm". That is, providing troops is, as it were, an agreed-upon currency that may be lawfully tendered in payment of debts[9]. Governments who in earlier years provided humanitarian assistance now offer military assets, in addition to — or on occasion instead of — more traditional aid. Governments that had previously welcomed the established aid agencies now receive foreign troops as well.

The Rwanda experience suggests that of the three frameworks of military involvement in the Rwanda crisis, the one most likely to be replicated is that involving troops in a multilateral humanitarian rubric. That approach has the advantage of utilising the specific scale and configurations of troops available from a variety of countries. UN peace-keeping operations, while they may be strengthened in the future as a result of current discussions, seem unlikely soon to attract a wider range of major power contributions than at present. As for the stand-alone frameworks of Operations *Turquoise* and Support Hope, the larger-scale commitments of troops seem less likely to be replicated, with cost and domestic political reluctance the major deterrent factors.

That prognosis is a sobering one. If borne out, military forces will not then be provided in future complex emergencies such as Rwanda's in keeping with their respective comparative advantages or with the pressing needs of existing humanitarian institutions as highlighted in this most recent crisis. That would leave important lessons from 1994 unlearned.

Conclusion

The Rwanda experience demonstrated that major complex emergencies are no place for doctrinaire rejection of any constructive roles whatsoever for international military assets. Neither should they be occasions, however, for random deployment of troops without careful attention to their strengths and weaknesses, their tasks and impacts. While the military have been regular features of the world's recent responses to major humanitarian emergencies, it is not a foregone conclusion that they have earned a place in the humanitarian regime of the future. Neither is it be assumed, however, that they should be excluded from the humanitarian family.

As a single element in a multifaceted international response, they have indispensable contributions to make in fostering a secure environment for civilians and for humanitarian activities, preventing bloodshed and protecting human life. After all is said and done, their comparative advantage may be precisely in what they know best: war and security. They may also play an important role in supporting the work of humanitarian organisations and even, in extreme circumstances, in carrying out relief activities themselves.

One element in a wider institutional universe, military forces are no substitute for effective policies geared toward conflict prevention and conflict resolution, development and peace. In that respect, they are like humanitarian action itself, which has an indispensable but at best partial contribution to make to a more just and secure world.

Notes

1. The more fulsome co-operation of aid organisations with *Bioforce* than with EMMIR in *Opération Turquoise* illustrates a similar tension.

2. The report, *Under the Volcanoes: Rwanda's Refugee Crisis* (IFRC 1995), which focuses on the dilemmas of humanitarian action, includes comments on the role of the military.

3. Interview by the authors in Kigali, October, 1994.

4. Evan Hays, Voice of America Broadcast, Bonn, July 16, 1994.

5. The eleven countries are Austria, Australia, Canada, Belgium, Denmark, Finland, Ireland, Italy, the Netherlands, New Zealand, Norway, Portugal, Spain, and Sweden. LaRose-Edwards concluded, "It seems a little simplistic for middle powers as well as the UN membership at large to ascribe UN gridlock to the [Permanent Five members of the Security Council] and others. All should look to themselves for solutions as the UN moves into its 50th year amid cries for reform from the governed".

6. Paul Gillespie, *Irish Times*, July 23, 1994.

7. *Irish Times*, editorial, July 30, 1994.

8. *The Observer*, "Rwanda shows aid is not enough", [editorial] July 24, 1994.

9. This definition is adapted from one provided in *Webster's Encyclopedic Unabridged Dictionary of the English Language* (1989), Garmency Books, New York/Avenel, NJ.

Chapter 9

Epilogue

The end of 1994 did not draw down the curtain on the Rwanda crisis, or on the world's response to it, or on the dispatching of soldiers to the rescue in the area. Concluding the primary analysis of events as of the end of calendar year 1994, as this book does, may be necessary for analytical purposes. However, it does not correspond to the nature and dynamics of the events and actors involved.

The crisis continued into 1995, along lines already well established in 1994. While significant progress had been achieved in the new year, the negative spiral of violence and counterviolence continued. As of mid-year, the future remained perilous, the possibility ever present of a military challenge to the regime from organised Hutu opposition in neighbouring countries and of new eruptions of accumulating discontents within Rwanda's borders.

In 1995, international military personnel were conspicuous by their relative absence. As was the case during the first three months of the previous year, the only outside military presence within Rwanda was comprised of UNAMIR troops. At full strength of 5 500 during the first half of 1995, UNAMIR made a solid contribution to the humanitarian effort. However, at the insistence this time of the Rwandese authorities, UNAMIR tasks were narrowed by Security Council Resolution 997, approved June 9. With an upper limit of 1 800 troops specified for October, the peace-keeping operation was expected to terminate altogether with the expiration of its mandate December 8, 1995.

No stand-alone initiatives such as those of the French and US described in Chapter 5 and 6 were underway. All the services described in Chapter 7 and contracted for by UNHCR had been concluded. In a new UNHCR initiative, a limited number of international security personnel, however, were supervising a cadre of Zairean troops working to achieve greater security in the Zaire camps.

International concern since the end of 1994 has focused on three areas: the need to attain greater security in the camps and the countryside, to accelerate action on reconstruction, and to address instability elsewhere in the region. Each requires brief review, again with special attention to the roles of outside military forces.

Achieving Security in the Camps and Beyond

During the first half of 1995, problems which had plagued the encampments of refugees abroad and of the internally displaced within Rwanda showed some promise of resolution. With regard to the refugee camps, the new element was not a greater disposition by governments to commit troops but rather a long-standing initiative by UNHCR which bore fruit.

UNHCR had been pressing for action on the problem of camp insecurity since September 1994. On October 24, 1994 at Kinshasa a Tripartite Agreement was signed between the UN refugee organisation and the governments of Zaire and Rwanda on the repatriation of Rwandese refugees from Zaire. The agreement set up a 16-member unit to monitor "the implementation of measures to facilitate the voluntary return of Rwandese refugees and the integration of the returnees in their communities of origin". (UN, 1994b). Zaire rejected as an infringement on its sovereignty the creation of a Chapter VII peace-keeping force. The proposed 12 000-member UN force would have separated former political and military leaders from rank-and-file refugees in the camps (UN, 1994d).

In January 1995, it was agreed that UNHCR, acting under its mandate to protect and assist refugees, would undertake an initiative to improve law and order in the camps and facilitate aid activities and repatriation. In February, a Zairean Camp Security Contingent (ZCSC) comprised of 1 513 Zairean military personnel was trained and deployed throughout the camps. Its work was monitored by a Civilian Security Liaison Group (CSLG), made up of some 60 international personnel with military or police background, functioning without military uniforms or weapons. Serving under retired Canadian General Iain Douglas, a veteran of UN peacekeeping in Liberia, CSLG personnel were provided by the governments of Benin, Burkina Faso, Cameroon, Guinea, the Netherlands, and Switzerland. All participants received advance training.

By mid-April, the new arrangements and personnel were in place. In early June, UNHCR reported that, "The deployment of the ZCSC has had a marked positive impact on the security within the camps in the North Kivu region". Relief distributions within the camps and repatriation to Rwanda were proceeding without major incident. In UNHCR's view, it was unlikely that "military training of any significant nature continues within refugee camp limits" (UNHCR, 1995c). Security outside of the camps, along with border control, remained the responsibility of Zairean military and police authorities.

UNHCR reported the following month that the ZCSC had been able to increase its surveillance within the camps but also that, on the negative side, some who lived in the Goma camps were apparently involved in armed infiltrations into Rwanda, using weapons stored outside the camps. While certain problems thus remained, UNHCR offered its judgement that "the experiment of a national military security force, working in collaboration with an international military/police liaison group, can be characterised as a success" (UNHCR, 1995b).

The fact that the international community had reclaimed control of the camps was a development of major significance. As a result, refugees would be more able to decide, free of intimidation, whether and when to return to Rwanda; aid personnel would be better able to assist them. However, the fact that the achievement had taken more than six months was, like other aspects of the international Rwanda response, a commentary on the inadequacy of existing institutions. That the solution took relatively few expatriate military personnel compared with the thousands involved at the time of the 1994 exodus was also noteworthy. The fact that the notoriously ineffective Zairean military had, under careful international supervision, made a major difference confirmed a positive prevention and protection role for soldiers.

Moreover, given confusions in the division of labour which had arisen between military and humanitarian elements during 1994, it was especially striking that the missing security feature was conceived and implemented by the humanitarian rather than peace-keeping side of the UN. "It marks the first time the UN High Commission for Refugees has ever hired soldiers of a national army to undertake a humanitarian mission in their own country", observed one reporter. "The United Nations adopted the unusual plan after failing to enlist support for more ambitious schemes that would have required foreign troops"[1].

Since refugee camp security is a recurring feature of humanitarian emergencies, the solution devised in the Rwanda crisis may hold promise for replication elsewhere. At the same time, questions were raised about where responsibility for such an initiative should properly be lodged. Widespread satisfaction that improvements had been made in the situation on the ground was balanced by questions concerning whether the role played by UNHCR was diversionary to its principal mission and damaging to perceptions of its impartiality[2].

The situation took a turn for the worse in August 1995 when the Zaire authorities began a campaign to force repatriation of people from the camps back into Rwanda. Initiated August 19, the campaign within the first week had returned an estimated 20 000 refugees to Rwanda. However, another 100 000 were reported to have fled the camps but to have remained within Zaire. The needs of those who had returned as well as those who had fled were viewed as creating a new crisis of still unknown dimensions. Noting the presence of some 1.8 million Rwandans within its borders, the government of Zaire justified its action on the grounds that the population presented a security threat and an economic burden[3].

Attempts to deal with insecurity in the camps within Rwanda were more contentious. In an effort to encourage people to return to their communes, the government moved rather abruptly on April 18 to close the eight camps in the south-west. Several hundred thousand Hutus had been encamped there since availing themselves of the protection of *Opération Turquoise* in mid-1994. The closing of seven camps was largely uneventful, although not without hardship for those forced to move. Violence erupted at Kibeho, however, with some 80 000 residents the largest of all the camps. After Rwandan troops had cordoned off the area, "A large number of deaths occurred from firing by government forces, trampling and crushing during the stampede and machete attacks by hard-liners in the camp, who assaulted and intimidated those who wished to leave" (UN, 1995b, Para. 10).

The camp closings and associated violence had serious humanitarian and political consequences. Aid agencies that had been planning to assist in the phased return of the displaced to their home communes were confronted with a sudden emergency. The International Organisation for Migration, NGOs, and UNAMIR itself provided transportation for over 70 000 persons and set up emergency medical facilities and feeding stations for people en route to their homes. UNAMIR's Australian peace-keepers provided emergency assistance, mobilising their own communications and engineering resources to co-ordinate convoy movements. UNAMIR provided security, supporting humanitarian organisations, and carried out relief activities.

As in April 1994, however, UNAMIR performance was criticized not for assistance rendered after the bloodshed but rather for failing to prevent or contain the mayhem. A contingent of 168 Zambians was on hand but did not intervene, nor were reinforcements sought from Ghanaian peace-keepers in an adjoining area. "One year after its troops did little to stop the genocide in Rwanda, the United Nations is under fire for the failure of its troops to try to stop Tutsi government soldiers slaughtering thousands of Hutus", observed a Reuter account. "The UN excused its inertia by saying the Zambians were outgunned by the 2 000 Rwandan government troops"[4].

UN officials explained that the suffering could have been worse had UNAMIR troops sought to interpose themselves between the Rwandan army and civilians in the camp. Other observers on the scene were sharply critical of UNAMIR's performance, however. Aid workers faulted the Secretary-General's Special Representative and the UNAMIR Force Commander for not having done more to prevent the disaster and the Ghanaian batallion for not having negotiated access for them to the camp's civilians. Some aid agencies felt that UNAMIR had not challenged the Rwandan undertaking more strongly because of a desire to see its mandate extended[5].

The political fallout from the "Kibeho massacre" was also serious. The event led to contentious disputes about the numbers actually killed (estimates ranged from 250 to 8 000) and the responsibility of government troops for the bloodshed. "Rwanda's latest bloodletting has strengthened the hand of extremists who want to topple its government and set back for years efforts to rebuild the shattered country", reported the Associated Press. "The slaughter also damaged moves toward national reconciliation after last year's genocide and sent a chilling message to more than 2 million refugees still outside the country that it may not be safe to return yet"[6]. UN military and aid officials were outspokenly critical of the tactics followed by the government and of the longer term repercussions of its action. The modest figures of returnees the following months seemed to confirm that effect (Kent, 1996).

Moving quickly to head off adverse reaction, the government set up an Independent International Commission of Inquiry on the Events in Kibeho to inquire into the event[7]. However, Belgium, the Netherlands, and the European Union announced reductions or suspensions of aid in protest. Meanwhile, condemnation by the UN and aid agencies of the incident led to demonstrations against them. Signs carried at a May Day rally said "UNAMIR go home" and accused UNHCR and UNICEF of colluding with Hutus in the camps abroad. Australian peace-keepers who had criticized the authorities for their handling of the Kibeho situation were vilified. The backlash contributed to government insistence on a reduced peace-keeping mandate during the second half of the year.

Accelerating the Pace of Reconstruction

The second focal point of international concern in 1995 was the need for more progress on reconstruction and reconciliation. An incipient theme in the waning months of 1994, the urgency of bringing about visible changes in the lives of ordinary Rwandans gathered force the following year.

The concern was reflected in, and spurred by, a Roundtable sponsored by the UN Development Programme and held in Geneva January 18-19. The occasion, originally planned for November 1994, was viewed as an opportunity for Rwandan government authorities to present reconstruction plans, improve communication and trust with the donor community, and mobilise resources for the longer haul. Envisioned was "the complete rehabilitation of social and economic structures of the country". The Rwanda Emergency Normalisation Plan (RENP), prepared by the SRSG and noted earlier, was tabled at the meeting.

Pledges made in Geneva in January 1995 totalled $634 million in relation to requirements estimated at $764 million. However, by mid-year only $69 million had been disbursed, of which more than a third was for debt repayment rather than for new projects. At a mid-term review held July 6-7, 1995 in Kigali, an additional $200 million was pledged. Meanwhile, a United Nations Trust Fund for Rwanda, established in the latter part of 1994 and administered by UNDP, by late July 1995 had received pledges of $22 million and contributions of $13 million and had made disbursements of $7.5 million (UNDHA 1995a; UN 1995a).

With an eye to the needs for emergency assistance and first-stage recovery, a United Nations Consolidated Appeal for persons affected by the crisis in Rwanda initially requested some $219.5 million for 1995. That amount was later revised downward to $159.8 million. As of August 7, pledges and contributions of $91.5 million had been tallied, or 56.7 per cent of the revised appeal figure. As in 1994, funds contributed for activities outside the appeal framework would expand the total resource availability[8].

The 56.7 per cent response figure for the first seven months of 1995 contrasted sharply with the appeal response in 1994, when, as noted in Chapter 3, 95.3 per cent of the requested funds were forthcoming, The decrease confirms "a definite downward swing in donor interest in the Rwanda crisis", say UN officials, reflecting reduced media coverage as well. Also a factor is waning international confidence in the Rwanda authorities following the Kibeho event. Should a new humanitarian emergency develop in the form of the forced repatriation of refugees to Rwanda, the mobilisation of the necessary additional funds might encounter serious difficulty.

Indicators of reconstruction progress other than finacial contributions also suggested mixed results, leading the UN Secretary-General in mid-July 1995 to describe Rwanda as "at the start of a very long journey"[9]. Efforts to distribute food among needy people in the countryside were being pressed by UN organisations, the ICRC, and NGOs; seeds, tools, and household items were also distributed, particularly among recent returnees. In the health sector, facilities were being rehabilitated, health workers trained, and health- and AIDS-education carried out. Foster care arrangements had been made for some 28 000 of the roughly 45 000 children who had lost or become separated from their parents.

Also on the positive side, UNAMIR's civilian police had helped design and implement a training course for Rwanda's new police force. A group of 300 trainees completed their work in late April; another four-month course was to begin in June. However, governments had provided only 64 of the 120 trainers requested by UNAMIR, and the entire programme was to be phased down in the more circumscribed UNAMIR mandate for the final six months of the year.

In the human rights area, 118 of the promised 147 UN monitors were in place as of August 1. Many of them were dispersed throughout the country in 11 field offices, monitoring developments in the areas to which people were returning and gathering information on earlier incidents of genocide for the International Tribunal. In addition, the Tribunal had its own investigators on the spot. The General Assembly on July 20, 1995 had authorised $13.5 million for the Tribunal's work. Contributions were languishing, however, at $6.3 million as of early August.

> "The Australian defence force contingent to Rwanda has added another honourable page to the proud narrative of the country's overseas operations with the United Nations. Though only 300 in number the contingent has performed extraordinary feats of medical and social assistance in a bewildering arena of hatred, violence, illness and pain. They will leave in August secure in the knowledge that their contribution has been all that could have been expected; but unfortunately it is insufficient to have made a difference to the larger struggle. The causes of the horror which have seen up to one million people killed, most in hand-to-hand butchery, have not been addressed by the international community. Nor, its seems, are they likely to be".
>
> "A Wilderness of Pain", editorial, *The Canberra Times*, May 25, 1995.

Of particular concern in mid-1995 was the deteriorating situation in the country's prisons. DHA in August described conditions as "a humanitarian nightmare and a glimpse of hell", with death rates exceeding 200 per week. Reflecting a weekly arrest rate of more than 1 000 in the early part of the year, 12 prisons with a capacity of 12 250 contained in excess of 38 000 persons, with predictions of a population of 50 000 by the end of 1995.

The judicial process itself was moving at snail's pace, reflecting a shortage of judges and other delays in the machinery of justice. A UNDP-administered programme to bring magistrates into the country had encountered delays. "You try to resolve the humanitarian problem by strengthening the justice system", mused one UN official involved in reconstruction efforts. "Soon, however, there is standing room only in the jails and you have a humanitarian problem there as well".

Following a visit to a Kigali prison which had left German Foreign Minister Klaus Kinkel appalled, the German government pressed for action. High-level officials from the Netherlands and the United Kingdom also expressed concern and made contributions. In August, DHA accelerated its own ongoing efforts to help ease the overcrowding and to speed lagging improvements in the justice system (UNDHA, 1995c).

Overall, negative developments on the reconstruction front overshadowed positive ones. The lack of progress in long-identified problems — prison overcrowding and deaths had been flagged as a serious issue as early as October 1994 — contributed to a general sense of disillusionment. As the year 1995 progressed, what many had concluded in the early months was increasingly clear: despite massive assistance, humanitarian and military alike, the international community had failed to help the new regime to its feet. From their side, the Kigali authorities had themselves on occasion made the task more difficult.

Frictions between the government and international organisations also boded ill for the future. In a visit to Kigali July 13-14, 1995 the Secretary-General conveyed a pointed challenge directly to the Rwandan parliament. Drawing a connection between the treatment of the country's Hutu majority and the broader task of reconstruction and reconciliation, he noted, "Unless you find a way to integrate the refugees and have them return, you will not have any real reconstruction". Pleading that the entire Rwandan nation be allowed "to participate fully and democratically in the management of the country's affairs", the Secretary-General encouraged the authorities to "engage a dialogue with the great mass of refugees". He concluded that "policies of exclusion would make it exceedingly difficult for the international community to assist, co-operate, and collaborate with your country"[10].

As a result of the absence of needed improvements within Rwanda, the desired increase in the return of Rwandans from abroad had yet to materialise. Few would dispute the Secretary-General's observation that "the earliest safe return of refugees would diminish the threat of infiltration" (UN, 1995a, para. 29). However, as of August there remained an estimated 1.86 million refugees. During the month of June, the number of those returning from Zaire, where more than one million were in residence, totalled only 2 727 (UNHCR, 1995a; UN, 1995a, para. 29). While the closure of the camps within Rwanda, however heavy-handed a tactic, had increased the numbers who returned to their communes, their presence added to pressures on the authorities to improve the quality of life, address competing land and property claims, protect human rights, and adopt a more inclusive polity.

Tensions with the United Nations on the military, political, and reconstruction fronts led to a hardening of the attitudes of the authorities toward UNAMIR. Reporting to the Security Council in June, the Secretary-General observed that the army "has continued to deny UNAMIR access to parts of the country, has searched and seized UNAMIR vehicles and other equipment and has participated in anti-UNAMIR demonstrations" (UN, 1995b, para. 8).

Nettled by UN criticism of its policies and anxious for domestic political reasons to assert its authority as sovereign government in its own right, the regime sought a marked reduction in UNAMIR presence. In its view, with the civil war over, the rationale for UNAMIR had been overtaken by events. In any case, its continuation would require the consent of the authorities. In June 1995, Vice-President Paul Kagame indicated that only a small UN "observation force" would be allowed to remain in Rwanda, which, he observed, had become a functioning society once again. The bulk of the UN troops should be sent to eastern Zaire, where security issues remained so serious that they constituted an ongoing threat Rwanda (*Libération*, 1995).

The Kigali authorities proposed paring UNAMIR from 5 500 to about 1 800 troops. The Secretary-General sought an ongoing presence of 2 300 troops, shifting from peacekeeping to confidence building but with a continuing mandate to support humanitarian operations. Security Resolution 997, approved June 9, 1995, reflected a compromise, approving a reduction of troops within the first three months to 2 330 followed by a subsequent cut to 1 800 within a month thereafter. The numbers of military observers and civilian police would remain without reduction throughout at 325 and 65 respectively. Extended through December 9, UNAMIR's mandate seemed unlikely to be extended further.

Thus just a year after contentious Security Council debates concerning the mission and size of UNAMIR, the tables had turned. Protection of humane values in Rwanda, many on the outside believed, required a broad mandate and considerable international personnel; the Rwandan authorities sought narrower terms of reference and fewer outsiders. The outcome made it unlikely that the United Nations would be given an opportunity to put flesh on the Secretary-General's proposal that "UNAMIR, in co-operation with UNDP, United Nations agencies and NGOs, assist in the implementation of an integrated multifunctional plan of action in the field of rehabilitation, resettlement, repair of infrastructure and the revival of justice" (UN 1995a, para. 59).

As UNAMIR personnel and resources were cut back, co-operation between UN troops and humanitarian organisations was affected. On the positive side, there were few signs that UNAMIR's growing unpopularity with the government and the public had undercut the credibility of the UN's humanitarian organisations. Avoiding a problem in other major emergencies such as Somalia and Bosnia, the work of relief, reconstruction, and human rights by the UN and associated agencies proceeding without substantial interference or political fallout. The emergency past, "the activities of the military component of UNAMIR .shifted from providing security to assisting in the normalisation of the country" (UN, 1995a, para. 19).

On the negative side, in the wake of the decision to phase down the operation, UNAMIR had fewer resources to offer to the reconstruction challenge and became more preoccupied with its own wind-down. Rather than structured collaboration with aid personnel, an informal understanding prevailed. "If you need us, we are here. Let us know". For their part, aid agencies turning their attention to the reconstruction challenges which would carry them well into the period after UNAMIR's departure saw less to be gained from enlisting in UNAMIR's help.

Addressing the Regional Context

"The sense of security and confidence that is needed to persuade refugees to return", observed the Secretary-General in June 1995, reiterating observations made by many observers for many months, "depends not only on improved conditions inside the country but also on better relations among the countries of the Great Lakes region" (UN, 1995b, para. 6). During the first six months of 1995, however, developments throughout the region threatened to undermine rather than reinforce whatever progress emerged within Rwanda.

One problem involved rising Hutu-Tutsi tensions in Burundi itself. A series of incidents in early 1995 there, including assassinations and kidnappings, demonstrated the growing power of hard-liners in each party and the waning standing of those committed to power sharing. Tutsis from both Burundi and Rwanda were among the targets of attack in a country with a Hutu majority but a

Tutsi-controlled army. "In an all-too familiar pattern", one reporter noted, "rising levels of violence in Burundi are the mark of ethnic extremists bent on using bloodshed and terror to destroy Burundi's fragile coalition government just as Rwanda's was destroyed"[11]. As the months passed, governments and humanitarian organisations monitored developments with growing alarm. Visiting Burundi as part of his July 1995 trip to the region, the Secretary-General appealed for tolerance and reconciliation.

A related problem concerned the closing of various borders around the region to prevent spillover effects from the Rwanda crisis. In March, Tanzania closed its border with Burundi, limiting the entry of Rwandese refugees fleeing violence against them in Burundi. Burundi also discouraged refugees from Rwanda from crossing its border in the wake of the camp closures in the south-west, allegedly forcing some persons back into Rwanda. Rwanda closed its borders with Zaire, ostensibly for security reasons, but impeding the movement of relief supplies and of refugees as well.

> "The times call for thinking afresh, for striving together and for creating new ways to overcome crises. This is because the different world that emerged when the cold war ceased is still a world not fully understood. The changed face of conflict today requires us to be perceptive, adaptive, creative and courageous, and to address simultaneously the immediate as well as the root causes of conflict, which all-too often lie in the absence of economic opportunities and social inequities. Perhaps above all it requires a deeper commitment to co-operation and true multilateralism than humanity has ever achieved before."
>
> UN Secretary-General Boutros Boutros-Ghali
> Supplement to *An Agenda for Peace: Position Paper of the Secretary-General on the Occasion of the Fiftieth Anniversary of the United Nations.* Document A/50/60, S/1995/1, p. 24.

Responding to the interconnected nature of the problems, several efforts were mounted to tackle the region's problems on a regional basis. A conference co-sponsored by UNHCR and the OAU took place in Bujumbura in February. Discussions there resulted in a series of trilateral agreements among Rwanda, various Great Lakes countries, and UNHCR. The Security Council and the Secretary-General also encouraged a regional conference on security, stability and development. "There was clear consensus", the Secretary-General reported from his visit to the region, "that instability in any state in the area could have a dramatic effect on all its neighbours" (UN, 1995a, para. 45)

At a Great Lakes Economic Community meeting in Bujumbura June 10, Burundi, Rwanda, and Zaire decided to organise joint patrols to control their common borders and prevent "armed gangs" of Hutu refugees from destabilizing the region. Grand-Admiral Mavua Mudima, Zairean Defence Secretary, said nonetheless that the real solution would lie in the return of Rwandese refugees to their own country (*Le Monde*, 1995). Once again, the interconnectedness of problems — political, social, and humanitarian as well as of the region as a whole — was demonstrated.

The Continuing Dilemmas of International Action

In the Rwanda crisis in 1995 as in other complex emergencies, a number of fundamental dilemmas played themselves out. One concerned the difficulties of addressing immediate problems which are rooted in decades of social, political, and economic interactions. The high-visibility suffering in the Rwanda crisis attracted resources — many of them military — to immediate needs. Meanwhile, the underlying and more intractable dimensions of the problem received inadequate attention. Unaddressed, however, these promised to create new humanitarian crises and new calls for emegency assistance.

A second dilemma involved the reality that in major emergencies such as Rwanda's, there are many moving parts over which the international community has little control. Staff at UN headquarters in New York recall an early cable from the first Special Representative of the Secretary-General, Cameroonian diplomat Jacques-Roger Booh-Booh. Before the April events, he anticipated that the UN peace-keeping operation would represent one of the great success stories in UN history. Reflecting on the decision not to pass on the diplomat's optimism to the Security Council, a secretariat official mused in May 1995, "You never know what will happen, even when the situation looks promising. Every turn in the road gets more complicated. Where we are today, nothing has yet been resolved. Nothing".

Even more frustrating than unexpected twists and turns in the road is the reality that the choices faced by the international community are often not between "good" and "evil" but rather between competing goods or between lesser evils. The imperative of feeding Rwandan refugees conflicted with the necessity of bringing to justice those among them who had been the architects and perpetrators of genocide. As the Rwandan experience amply demonstrated, well-intended humanitarian action can help lay the groundwork for the next Chapter in the suffering. While the lack of international political will can be a problem, so, too, can the choices made with available resources.

A final dilemma concerns the extent to which outside resources should continue to be committed in the absence of meaningful progress. On the one hand, low levels of international aid flows in the latter part of 1994 and in 1995 had, by most accounts, delayed progress on reconstruction and reconciliation. On the other hand, failing such progress, international resources were likely to become even less available. "Given the multiplicity of conflicts" around the world, the Secretary-General pointedly reminded the Rwandan parliament in July 1995, "the international community's assistance, interest, and attention is being directed toward countries where the situation is improving"[12].

In the Rwanda crisis, as elsewhere, effective international action involved breaking a vicious cycle, turning negative spirals into positive synergisms. While serious problems associated with sending soldiers to the rescue were apparent, the presence of international troops also conveyed solidarity and succor to those in disastrous circumstances.

Thoughtfully conceived and creatively managed, international personnel — military and humanitarian alike — can represent a bridge across the divides of ethnic group and ideology, race and religion, caste and class. To achieve their full potential, however, military assets, no less than humanitarian resources themselves, need to serve effective strategies not only of relief and rehabilitation but also of conflict prevention and conflict resolution, development and peace.

Notes

1. Alex Belida, Voice of America broadcast, Feb. 16, 1995.

2. This concern was expressed by Amsterdam University Professor and former UNHCR official Guy Goodwin-Gill in an interview on the British Broadcasting Corporation June 21, 1995.

3. Associated Press, "133 000 Flee Zaïre's Efforts at Deportation", August 23, dateline Goma.

4. Aidan Hartley, "UN Force in Rwanda under Fire Over Massacre", Reuters. April 26, 1995.

5. One of those critical of UNAMIR's performance in the Kibeho incident was Jacques de Milliano, director of MSF-Holland. He expressed his views in a panel discussion on Humanitarian Law in Civil War and the Right to Humanitarian Assistance at a meeting on "Contemporary International Law Issues: Conflicts and Convergence", the Third Joint Conference of the American Society of International Law and the Nederlandse Vereniging voor Internationaal Recht in the Hague, July 14, 1995.

6. "Rwanda Killing Seen as Setback", Associated Press, dateline Nairobi, April 25, 1995.

7. The Commission was established April 27 and completed its report May 18, 1995. Its 10 members represented France, Canada, Belgium, Germany, the United Kingdom, the USA, the Netherlands, Rwanda, the OAU and the United Nations.

8. In addition, some of the $152.4 million commited in 1994 to work in the subregion but unexpended at year's end was also available for use in Rwanda in 1995. For the 1995 data, cf. UN 1995d.

9. UN Department of Public Information, "Secretary-General Invites Rwandan Parliament and Government to Promote National Reconciliation to Help Encourage Refugees' Return", Press Release SG/SM/5687, July 20, 1995, p. 1.

10. UNDPI, *ibid*.

11. Gretchen Lang, "Strife in Burundi Raises Fear of Another Rwanda," *Boston Globe*, March 22, 1995, p. 2.

12. UNDPI, *op. cit.*

Glossary of Acronyms

AICF	*Action internationale contre la faim*
AIDAB	Australian International Development Assistance Bureau
BRITCON	British contingent (UNAMIR)
BBTG	Broad Based Transitional Government (Rwanda)
CDR	Rwandan Coalition for the Defence of the Republic
CIVPOL	Civilian Police (UN)
CIDA	Canadian International Development Agency
CLADHO	Rwandan Human Rights Coalition
CMOC	Civil Military Operations Centre (US)
DAC	Development Assistance Committee (OECD)
DART	Disaster Assistance Relief Team (US)
DHA	Department of Humanitarian Affairs (UN)
DOD	Department of Defense (US)
EMMIR	*Élément médical militaire d'intervention rapide*
FRAFBAT	French-speaking African Battalion
GAO	General Accounting Office (US)
ICRC	International Committee of the Red Cross
ICVA	International Council of Voluntary Agencies
IDF	Israeli Defence Forces
IFRC	International Federation of the Red Cross and Red Crescent Societies
IRC	International Rescue Committee
MCDA	Military and Civil Defence Assets
MDM	*Médecins du monde*
MDR-*Parmehutu*	*Mouvement démocratique républicain — Parti du mouvement de l'émancipation des Bahutu*
MRND	*Mouvement républicain national pour le développement*
MSF	*Médecins sans frontières*
NATO	North Atlantic Treaty Organisation
NGO	Non-governmental Organisation
OAU	Organisation of African Unity
ODA	Official Development Assistance
OECD	Organisation for Economic Co-operation and Development
ONUMOZ	United Nations Operation in Mozambique
ONUSAL	United Nations Observer Mission in El Salvador
PDC	Christian Democratic Party (Rwanda)
PL	Liberal Party (Rwanda)
PDD	Presidential Decision Directive (US)
PSD	Social Democratic Party (Rwanda)
RANU	Rwandese Alliance for National Unity
RENP	Rwanda Emergency Normalisation Plan
RPA	Rwandese Patriotic Army

RPF	Rwandese Patriotic Front
ROWPU	Reverse Osmosis Water Purification Unit
RTLM	*Radio-télévision libre des mille collines*
RwAF	Rwandan Armed Forces
SRSG	Special Representative of the Secretary-General (UN)
UNAMIR	United Nations Assistance Mission for Rwanda
UNAR	*Union nationale rwandaise* (Rwandese National Union)
UNDHA	United Nations Department of Humanitarian Affairs
UNDP	United Nations Development Programme
UNDPI	United Nations Department of Public Information
UNHCR	United Nations High Commissioner for Refugees
UNICEF	United Nations Children's Fund
UNOSOM	United Nations Observation Mission in Somalia
UNPROFOR	United Nations Protection Force in the Former Yugoslovia
UNITAF	Unified Task Force (in Somalia) (US)
UNTAC	United Nations Transitional Authority in Cambodia
UNTAG	United Nations Transition Assistance Group in Nambia
UNOMUR	United Nations Observer Mission in Uganda-Rwanda
UNREO	United Nations Rwanda Emergency Office
UPRONA	*Union pour le progrès national*
USAID	United States Agency for International Development
WFP	World Food Programme (UN)
ZHS	*Zone humanitare sûre* (humanitarian safe zone)

Annex 1a
Chronology of Major Events of 1994 in the Rwanda Crisis

	Political Events	Military Events	Humanitarian Events
Apr. 5	UNAMIR mandate extended for six months		
Apr. 6	President Habyarimana's plane shot down; acting President, National Assembly Speaker, and President of Constitutional Court assassinated	10 Belgian UN peacekeepers murdered by Presidential Guards UNAMIR, its strength at about 2 000, attempts joint patrols with *Gendarmerie*	Genocide begins New wave of displaced persons into Kigali prefecture following resumed RPF offensive
Apr. 7	SC meets, takes no action		
Apr. 8	SC meets, takes no action	French and Belgian soldiers in Operations *Amaryllis* and Silver Back evacuate expatriates and selected others	
Apr. 9	UN Special Rep. Jacques-Roger Booh-Booh fails to set up transitional national authority without RPF representation. Acting Pres. Théodore Sindikubwabo appoints interim government		
Apr. 10	RwAF offers a cease-fire, RPF refuses	RPF orders UNAMIR's Ghanaian Battalion out of Buyumba	
Apr. 11	SC meets, takes no action	RPF at Kigali's edge	UNAMIR gathers and protects 8 000 civilians in stadium and 2 000 in hospital compound
Apr. 12	Interim govt. flees Kigali, apart from Minister of Defence	RPF warns French and Belgian troops to leave	
Apr. 13			ICRC stops transporting wounded after six civilians taken from ICRC vehicle and shot
Apr. 14		French and Belgian troops withdraw; Belgium withdraws UNAMIR contingent	Over 200 000 Rwandese refugees on Burundi border. MSF arrives in Kigali to visit hospital, leaves for security reasons. UN creates the Rwandan Emergency Office (UNREO), based in Nairobi, to co-ordinate relief efforts

Annex 1b

	Political Events	Military Events	Humanitarian Events
Apr. 18	Defence Minister sets up interim govt. in Gitarama		ICRC estimates casualties in hundreds of thousands
Apr. 19	Rwandan Govt. representative at the UN urges UNAMIR's reinforcement	UNAMIR turns down RwAF proposal to co-administer Kigali airport	Massacres reach Butare. *Préfet* who had been maintaining calm in the city arrested and killed
Apr. 21	SC adopts Res. 912 reducing approved troop levels from 2 500 to 270		
Apr. 23			UN Emergency Relief Co-ordinator arrives in Kigali with advance humanitarian team
Apr. 24			UNDHA appeals for $11.6 million for co-ordinated relief programme
Apr. 26			Canada promises $5million humanitarian aid
Apr. 27		UNAMIR strength at 459	
Apr. 29	RPF demands UNSG's Special Representative Jacques-Roger Booh-Booh's resignation		250 000 refugees cross into Tanzania in two-day period
May 2			US begins $15 million humanitarian aid programme
May 3		Heavy fighting in Kigali	More refugees flee into Tanzania
May 6	SC meets: takes no action		
May 10		Ghanian peacekeeper killed by RwAF in Amahoro stadium shelling	Refugees in Tanzania reach 262 000. US announces $38 million in aid
May 12	SC meets: takes no action		
May 13	UNSG reports on situation in Rwanda		
May 17	SC adopts Res. 918 authorising 5 500 troops and imposing arms embargo on Rwanda		
May 19			UN Human Rights Commissioner Lasso, on visit to Kigali, issues report on human rights situation

Annex 1c

	Political Events	Military Events	Humanitarian Events
May 24			UN Commission on Human Rights appoints Special Rapporteur on Rwanda
May 25		UNAMIR strength at 471	UN SG uses the term genocide
May 31	UNSG reports on Rwanda		Over 300 000 refugees in Ngara
June 3		RPF controls 60 per cent of Rwanda UNAMIR continues to protect civilians *in situ*	Major ethnic massacres in RwAF-held territory; reprisals in RPF-held areas. IFRC and USAID recover and bury 40 000 bodies from Lake Victoria; ICRC reports Kigali authorities have buried 67 000
June 7	SC convenes, takes no action		
June 8	SC adopts Res. 925 extending UNAMIR until December 9, 1994		
June 9	Ugandan Pres. Museveni encourages RPF to declare cease-fire	Kigali airport closed for security amid heavy fighting in capital	UNREO moves co-ordination base from Nairobi to Kabale (Uganda). NGOs in the field number 12
June 13		RPF takes control of Gitarama; Interim Govt. flees to Gisenyi	
June 16	French Foreign Secretary indicates French willingness to intervene in Rwanda. RPF declares French troops would be considered "hostile forces"		
June 18	President Mitterrand declares France ready to intervene		
June 22	SC adopts Res. 929 endorsing stopgap "multilateral operation" in Rwanda by France		
June 23		600 French troops airlifted to Goma and enter Rwanda (Gisenyi and Cyangugu)	
June 28			Special Rapporteur René Degni Ségui recommends international tribunal for perpetrators of genocide
July 1	SC adopts Resolution 935 to establish Expert Commission to investigate and compile evidence of grave violations of international humanitarian law in Rwanda, including		

Annex 1d

	Political Events	Military Events	Humanitarian Events
July 3		France sets up Secure Zone (ZHS) in southwestern Rwanda	
July 4		RPF takes Kigali and Butare	
July 6	Twagiramungu agrees to RPF proposal to form National Union Government		
July 7	France emphasizes intention to begin withdrawal of troops at the end of July, completing it by end of August	*Opération Turquoise* strength at 2 555 (incl. African Battallion). RFP controls two-thirds of Rwanda; RwAF maintains control of NW	An estimated 1.6 million displaced persons in ZHS
July 11	French Prime Minister Balladur in New York urges UN to reinforce UNAMIR on France's departure		
July 14		RPF seizes Ruhengeri	Mass refugee exodus begins as 800 000 refugees arrive in Goma; three-day total reaches c.1.2 million.
July 16		RPF seizes Gisenyi	
July 17	Bizimungu (an RPF member and a Hutu) appointed Rwandese President		UNHCR starts, then suspends airlift as mortar rounds fall on Goma airport; 400 000 more refugees reach Zaire
July 18	RPF declares cease-fire		
July 19	Formation of a Broad Base Govt. of National Union; Rwanda's UN Rep. Jean Damascène Bizimana resigns		UNHCR reports 1.2 million refugees Goma, 200 000 in Bukavu, 200 000 in Uvira; 600 000 displaced persons in Gikongoro, 500 000 in Cangugu; and 100 000 new arrivals from Burundi back in Rwanda.
July 20	US suspends recognition of former Rwandan Govt., closes Kigali Embassy, and expels Rwandan diplomats from the US		
July 21			President Clinton announces major aid contribution of $100 m. and 3 000-troop Operation Support Hope, including lift capacity into Bukavu and Goma
July 22		US troops deployed	
Aug. 2			UN Human Rights Commission appeals for $2.1m. to finance an extra 20 human-rights monitors
Aug. 3	UNSG reports on situation in Rwanda and on problems encountered in increasing UNAMIR troop strength to approved levels		

Annex 1e

	Political Events	Military Events	Humanitarian Events
Aug. 10		UNAMIR strength at 1 257	
Aug. 12			Rapporteur Degni Ségui's new report on human-rights abuses released
Aug. 21		French troops in *Opération Turquoise* withdraw from Rwanda; French-speaking African troops join UNAMIR	
Aug. 27			Commission of Experts propose Plan of Action to examine grave violations of humanitarian law
Sept. 13		Japan to provide 480 military troops to help Rwandan refugees in Goma following French withdrawal	
Sept. 30		French withdraw from Goma	
Oct. 6	UNSG reports on Rwanda situation		
Oct. 13			SRSG Shaharyar Khan presents RENP
Oct. 30			First talks between Rwanda and Zaire on refugee return
Nov. 8	SC adopts Res. 955, approving international tribunal to prosecute alleged genocide perpetrators		
Nov. 15			MSF exits Zaire refugee camps
Nov. 18	UNSG reports on growing insecurity in refugee camps	Over 2 000 *Interahamwe* reported to drill in Ngara, Tanzania	
Nov. 21	UNSG reports lack of commitments from govts. of troops to police Zaire camps		
Nov. 25	SG gives progress report on situation in Rwanda		
Nov. 30	SC extends UNAMIR mandate until June 9, 1995		

Annex 1f

	Political Events	Military Events	Humanitarian Events
Dec. 18			Upon UN request, Rwandan Govt. renounces decision to close displaced persons' camps in former ZHS (140 000 persons)
Dec. 21			Public Prosecutor R. Goldstone of International Tribunal visits Rwanda
Dec. 28			10 persons killed in Kibungo by Hutu Power extremists
Dec. 31		SRSG Sharharyar Khan declares UN peacekeepers will not be sent to refugee camps in Zaire	

Annex 2

Excerpts from United Nations Security Council Resolutions Related to Rwanda

Resolution 812 March 12, 1993

The Security Council encouraged establishment of a UN peacekeeping operation in support of the OAU-sponsored peace process. The Council called on the government of Rwanda and the Rwandan Patriotic Front to respect the cease-fire which had taken effect several days earlier and "to allow the delivery of humanitarian supplies and the return of displaced persons".

Resolution 846 June 22, 1993

The Security Council established the UN Observer Mission Uganda-Rwanda (UNOMUR) to monitor the Rwandan-Ugandan border, urged conclusion of a comprehensive peace settlement, and called on the protagonists to respect international humanitarian law. UNOMUR was extended for six months by **Resolution 891** of December 20, 1993 and for a final period of three months through September 21 by **Resolution 928** of June 20, 1994.

Resolution 872 October 5, 1993

The Security Council created the UN Assistance Mission for Rwanda (UNAMIR) to monitor observance of the cease-fire agreement, security throughout Rwanda, and the process of repatriation and resettlement and "assist in the coordination of humanitarian assistance activities in conjunction with relief operations". UNAMIR was extended for six months by **Resolution 909** of April 5, enacted a day before the outbreak of violence.

Resolution 912 April 21, 1994

The Council expressed shock at the "large-scale violence in Rwanda, which has resulted in the death of thousands of innocent civilians, including women and children, the displacement of a significant number of the Rwandese population, including those who sought refuge with UNAMIR, and the significant increase in refugees to neighbouring countries".

Condemning "the ongoing violence", the Council adjusted UNAMIR's mandate, charging it "(a) To act as an intermediary between the warring parties in an attempt to secure their agreement to a cease-fire; (b) To assist in the resumption of humanitarian relief operations to the extent feasible; and (c) To monitor and report on developments in Rwanda, including the safety and security of the civilians who sought refuge with UNAMIR". The Council also reduced UNAMIR's approved troop strength from 2 500 to 270.

Resolution 918 May 17, 1994

The Council authorised expansion of UNAMIR strength to 5 500 troops, adding to its mandate several additional responsibilities, including: "(a) To contribute to the security and protection of displaced persons, refugees and civilians at risk in Rwanda, including through the establishment and maintenance, where feasible, of secure humanitarian areas; (b) To provide security and support for the distribution of relief supplies and humanitarian relief operations". Determining that "the situation in Rwanda constitutes a threat to peace and security in the region", the Council, acting under Chapter VII of the UN Charter, imposed an arms embargo on Rwanda.

Resolution 925 June 8, 1994

The Council endorsed the Secretary-General's detailed proposal of May 31 for expanding UNAMIR to the already approved strength of 5 500 troops. In extending its mandate for six months until December 9, the Council noted that "UNAMIR's expanded military component will continue only as long as and to the extent that it is needed to contribute to the security and protection of displaced persons, refugees and civilians at risk in Rwanda and to provide security, as required, to humanitarian relief operations".

Resolution 929 June 22, 1994

The Council endorsed the proposal by France to establish "a temporary operation under national command and control aimed at contributing, in an impartial way, to the security and protection of displaced persons, refugees and civilians at risk in Rwanda". The undertaking would be "a multinational operation ... set up for humanitarian purposes in Rwanda until UNAMIR is brought up to the necessary strength".

Resolution 935 July 1, 1994

The Council establishes a Commission of Experts to review "evidence of grave violations of international humanitarian law", including genocide.

Resolution 955 November 8, 1994

The Council decided "to establish an international tribunal for the sole purpose of prosecuting persons responsible for genocide and other serious violations of international humanitarian law committed in the territory of Rwanda and Rwandan citizens responsible for genocide and other such violations committed in the territory of neighbouring States, between 1 January and 31 December 1994".

Resolution 965 November 30, 1994

In extending the mandate of UNAMIR through June 9, 1995, the SC reaffirmed that UNAMIR will "(a) Contribute to the security and protection of displaced persons, refugees and civilians at risk in Rwanda including through the establishment and maintenance, where feasible, of secure areas; (b) Provide security and support for the distribution of relief supplies and humanitarian relief operations". UNAMIR tasks were expanded to include establishment and training of "a new, integrated, national police force".

Resolution 997 June 9, 1995

The Council expressed concern about "reports of military preparations and increasing incursions into Rwanda by elements of the former regime", stressed the need for accelerated efforts by the government to promote "a climate of stability and trust in order to facilitate the return of Rwandan refugees in neighbouring countries", and urged donor governments to accelerate aid for rehabilitation and reconstruction.

The Council extended the mandate of UNAMIR until December 8, 1995, reducing its troop strength to 2 330 within three months and 1 800 within four months. It adjusted UNAMIR's mandate to assist the government in facilating the return of refugees, "support the provision of humanitarian aid, and of assistance and expertise in engineering, logistics, medical care and demining", contribute to the security of humanitarian agencies and personnel in case of need, and co-ordinate UN activities in Rwanda.

Annex 3

About the Humanitarianism and War Project and the Authors

Philippe Ch. A. Guillot, is currently Lecturer at the University of Rouen's Faculty of Law. He has a Masters Degree in International Conflict Analysis from the University of Kent at Canterbury and a doctorate (Doctor Juris Communitatis Europae) from the University of Rouen. Since completing military service in the UN Interim Force in Lebanon (UNIFIL) in 1985, he has specialised in peacekeeping studies and in international humanitarian law. He has monitored developments in Rwanda and Burundi since 1988. He is currently Secretary-General of the International Association of Soldiers for Peace.

Larry Minear has served as co-director and principal researcher for the Humanitarianism and War Project since 1991. In that capacity, he has led or been a member of teams which have carried out research in many of the world's major complex emergencies. He is author or co-author of a number of books and case studies. He has worked on humanitarian and development issues since 1972, both as an official of two US non-governmental organisations (Church World Service and Lutheran World Relief) and as a consultant to UN organisations, the US government, and private relief groups. He was a consultant to the OECD Development Centre's informal meeting in 1994 on Development within Conflict: The Challenge of Man-made Disasters.

The Humanitarianism and War Project is a policy research initiative launched in 1991 to review recent experience in complex emergencies and to recommend improved strategies to humanitarian practitioners. To date the Project has conducted case studies in the Persian Gulf, the Horn of Africa, Central America, South-East Asia, the Balkans, and the Newly Independent States. In addition to a series of monographs presenting country-specific findings, the Project has published a number of books and training materials for practitioners and articles and books for the policy and academic communities and for the concerned international public.

The Project is based at the Thomas J. Watson Jr. Institute for International Studies of Brown University in Providence, Rhode Island. It enjoys support from a wide range of organisations and institutions. To date funds have come from:

— governments (Australia, France, the Netherlands, the United Kingdom, and the United States);

— international organisations (UNICEF, UNHCR, UNDP, UNDRO/DHA, WFP, UN Special Program for the Horn of Africa, the UN Volunteers, and the International Organisation for Migration);

— non-governmental organisations (the American Red Cross, Catholic Relief Services, Danish Refugee Council, the International Center for Human Rights and Democratic Development [Canada], International Federation of the Red Cross and Red Crescent Societies, International Orthodox Christian Charities, International Rescue Committee, Lutheran World Federation, Lutheran World Relief, Mennonite Central Committee, Norwegian Refugee Council, Oxfam-UK, Save the Children UK and US, Trocaire, World Vision, and the Red Cross Societies of Denmark, Finland Norway, Sweden); and

— foundations (The Pew Charitable Trusts, the McKnight Foundation, the Rockefeller Foundation, the Arias Foundation, and the US Institute of Peace).

Bibliography

ABDELMALKI, L. and D. DUFOURT (eds.) (1994), *La Nouvelle coexistence des nations*, Édition de l'Épargne, Paris.

ABI-SAAB, G. (1993), "La deuxième génération des opérations de maintien de la paix", *Le Trimestre du Monde*, Vol. IV, No. 20.

ACTIONAID (1995), *The Reality of Aid 1995*, Earthscan, London.

AFRICA WATCH (1992), *Rwanda. Talking Peace and Waging War, Human Rights since the October 1990 Invasion*, Human Rights Watch Arms Project, Vol. IV, No. 3.

AFRICA WATCH (1994), *Who Is Arming Rwanda?*, Washington D.C., January.

AFRICAN RIGHTS (1994), *Rwanda: Death, Despair and Defiance*, privately printed, London.

AFRICAN RIGHTS (1995), "Humanitarianism Unbound", privately printed, London.

AGIR ICI and SURVIE (1995), *L'Afrique à Biarritz. Mise en examen de la politique française*, Karthala, Paris.

AJELLO, A. (1996), "The Coordination of Humanitarian Assistance in Mozambique in the Context of ONUMOZ", in J. WHITMAN and D. POCOCK, *op. cit.*

AKEHURST, M. (1986), "Humanitarian Intervention", in H. BULL (ed.), *op. cit.*

ANDERSON, M.B. and P. WOODROW (1989), *Rising from the Ashes: Development Strategies in Times of Disaster*, Westview, Boulder, CO.

ASSOCIATION DROIT DES GENS (1993), *À la recherche du nouvel ordre mondial : l'ONU, mutations et défis*, Complexe, Brussels.

AYOUB, M. (1995), "The New-Old Disorder in the Third World", in T. WEISS (ed.), *op. cit.*

BADIE, B. et A. PELLET (eds.) (1993), *Les Relations internationales à l'épreuve de la science politique*, Economica, Paris.

BARRET-DUCROCQ, F. (ed.) (1994), *Intervenir ? Droits de la personne et raisons d'État*, Académie universelle des cultures, Paris.

BAYART, J.-F. (1993), "Fin de partie au sud du Sahara ? La politique africaine de la France", in S. MICHAÏLOF (ed.), *op. cit.*

ter BEEK, A.L. and W. KOK (1994), "Rwanda: Report Aan de Voorzitter van de Tweede Kamer der Staten-Generaal", July 27.

BERTHÉLEMY, J.-C., R.S. McNAMARA and S. SEN (1994), "The Disarmament Dividend: Challenges for Development Policy", OECD Development Centre, Policy Brief No. 8, Paris.

BETTATI, M. (1993), "Action humanitaire d'État et diplomatie", in Betrand BADIE et Alain PELLET (eds.), *op. cit.*

BETTATI, M. (1994), "Intervention : ingérence ou assistance ?", *Revue Trimestrielle des Droits de l'Homme*, No. 19, July.

BIJARD, L. (1994), "Turquoise, l'opération sans boussole", *Le Nouvel Observateur*, June 30.

BOLTON, S. (1994), "Carnet de Bord", *Le Nouvel Observateur*, MSF, Goma, July 26.

BOUTROS-GHALI, B. (1995), *Supplement to an Agenda for Peace, Position Paper of the Secretary-General on the Occasion of the Fiftieth Anniversary of the United Nations*, document A/50/60, S/1995/1, January.

BRAECKMAN, C. (1994), *Rwanda : histoire d'un génocide*, Fayard, Paris.

BRAUMAN, R. (1994), *Devant le mal : Rwanda, un génocide en direct*, Arléa, Paris.

BREAD FOR THE WORLD (1995), *A World in Crisis: Hunger 1996*, Silver Spring, MD.

BROCHE, F. (1994), *Au Bon Chic humanitaire*, Première Ligne, Paris.

BULL, H. (ed.) (1986), *Intervention in World Politics*, Oxford University Press, Oxford.

BUNDESMINISTERIUM DER VERTEIDIGUNG (1995), "Informationen zur Sicherheitspolitik: Beteiligung der Bundeswehr an Missionen der Vereinten Nationen, 1992 bis 1994", Ministry of Defence, Bonn, February.

BUREAU OF INTELLIGENCE AND RESEARCH, US DEPARTMENT OF STATE (1994), "Improving Coordination of Humanitarian and Military Operations", Report of a Conference June 23.

BUSH, K.D. (1995), "Unhappy Marriages of Convenience: Military-NGO Collaboration in Humanitarian Crises", *Security Dialogue*, Vol. 26 (1).

CANADIAN INTERNATIONAL DEVELOPMENT AGENCY (1995), "Rwanda: Emergency Assistance", April.

CHOPRA, J. (1995), "Peacekeeping's Uncertain Future", *Bulletin of Atomic Scientists*, March/April.

CHOPRA, J. and T.G. WEISS (1992), "Sovereignty Is No Longer Sacrosanct: Codifying Humanitarian Intervention", *Ethics & International Affairs*, Vol.VI.

CHRÉTIEN, J.-P. (1981), "Du Hirsute au Hamite : les variations du cycle de Ntare Rushati, fondateur du royaume de Burundi", *History in Africa*.

CHRÉTIEN, J.-P. (1992), "Pluralisme politique et équilibre au Rwanda et au Burundi", in A. GUICHAOUA (ed.), *op. cit.*

CHRÉTIEN, J.-P. (1994a), "Un nazisme tropical", *Libération*, April 26.

CHRÉTIEN, J.-P. (1994), "L'Histoire des 'Tutsi civilisateurs' est une vaste mystification", *Le Temps Stratégique*, No. 61, December.

de CLERZAC, J. (1994), "L'armée, SAMU du monde : faut-il repenser l'humanitaire?", *Revue universelle des faits et des idées*, No. 178, June-October.

COMMISSION ON GLOBAL GOVERNANCE (1995), *Our Global Neighbourhood*, Oxford University Press, Oxford.

COQ, B. and M. FLOQUET (1994), *France, ton armée fout le camp*, Albin Michel, Paris.

D'HERTEFELT, M. (1964), "Mythes et idéologies dans le Rwanda ancien et contemporain", in J. VANSINA, R. MAUNY & L.V. THOMAS (eds.) *op. cit.*

DALLAIRE, Major-General R.A (1996), "The Changing Role of UN Peacekeeping Forces: The Relationship between UN Peacekeepers and NGOs in Rwanda", in J. WHITMAN and D. POCOCK (eds.), *op. cit.*

DAMROSCH, L.F. and D.J. SCHEFFER (eds.) (1991), *Law & Force in the New International Order*, Westview Press, Boulder, CO.

DANIEL, D. (1995), *Beyond Traditional Peacekeeping*, Macmillan, London.

DAUDET, Y. (ed.) (1995), *Les Nations Unies et la restauration de l'État*, Recontres internationales de l'I.E.P. d'Aix-en-Provence, Pédone, Paris.

DEGUINE, H. and R. MÉNARD (1995), "Les extrémistes de Radio Machette", *Le Monde diplomatique*, March.

DEL PERUGIA, P. (1994), "Comment le Rwanda construisit l'une des civilisations les plus subtiles d'Afrique", *Le Temps Stratégique*, No. 61, December.

DENG, F.M. and L. MINEAR (1992), *The Challenges of Famine Relief: Emergency Operations in the Sudan*, The Brookings Institution, Washington, D.C.

DES FORGES, A. (1995), "Face au génocide, une réponse désastreuse des États-Unis et des Nations Unies", in A. Guichaoua (ed.), *op. cit.*

DESTEXHE, A. (1994), *Rwanda : essai sur le génocide*, Complexe, Brussels.

DONINI, A. (1995), *UN Coordination in Complex Emergencies: Lessons from Afghanistan, Mozambique and Rwanda*, Occasional Paper No. 22, Watson Institute, Providence, RI.

DONINI, A. and N. NILAND (1994), "Rwanda: Lessons Learned. A Report on the Coordination of Humanitarian Activities", DHA, New York, November.

ERNY, P. (1994), *Rwanda 1994. Clés pour comprendre le calvaire d'un peuple*, L'Harmattan, Paris.

EVANS, G. (1993), *Cooperating for Peace: The Global Agenda for the 1990s and Beyond*, Allen and Unwin, St. Leonards, Australia.

FAES, G. (1994), "Zaire : Le retour du dinosaure", *Jeune Afrique*, Vol. XXXIV, No. 1759, 22-28, September.

FALANDRY, L. (1994), "Les médecins militaires au service des populations civiles", in F. BARRET-DUCROCQ (ed.), *op. cit.*

FÉDÉRATION NATIONALE DES ANCIENS DES MISSIONS EXTÉRIEURES (1994), *Infos Extérieures*, No. 6, December.

FONTANEL, J. (1994), "Le désarmement et ses incidences sur les pays en voie de développement", in L. ABDELMALKI and D. DUFOURT (eds.), *op. cit.*

GAHAMA, J. (1983), *Le Burundi sous administration belge*, Karthala, Paris.

GAYDOS, J.C. and G.A. LUZ (1994), "Military Participation in Emergency Humanitarian Assistance", *Disasters*, Vol. 18, No. 1.

GLASER, A. and S. SMITH (1994), *L'Afrique sans Africains. Le rêve blanc du continent noir*, Stock, Paris.

GOMA EPIDEMIOLOGY GROUP (1995), "Public Health Impact of Rwandan Refugee Crisis: What Happened in Goma, Zaire in July, 1994?", *The Lancet*, Vol. 345, Feb. 11.

GORDON, R. (1994), "Article 2(7) Revisited: The Post-Cold War Security Council", *ACUNS [Academic Council on the United Nations System]Reports & Papers No. 5*.

GOVERNMENT OF CANADA (1995), "Towards a Rapid-Reaction Capability for the United Nations", Canada Communications Group, Ottawa.

GOVERNMENT OF JAPAN, Ministry of Foreign Affairs (1994), "Building Peace: Japan's Participation in United Nations Peace-keeping Operations", Ministry of Foreign Affairs, July, Tokyo.

GOY, R. (1991), "Quelques accords récents mettant fin à des guerres civiles", *Annuaire français de droit international*, Vol XXXVIII.

GUICHAOUA, A. (ed.) (1992), *Enjeux nationaux et dynamiques régionales dans l'Afrique des Grands Lacs*, URA-CNRS, Université de Lille I, Karthala, Paris.

GUICHAOUA, A. (ed.) (1995), *Les crises politiques au Burundi et au Rwanda (1993-1994)*, Université de Lille I, Karthala, Paris.

GUILLOT, P. (1994a), "France, Peacekeeping and Humanitarian Intervention",*International Peacekeeping* (London), Vol. 1, No. 1.

GUILLOT, P. (1994b), "Promoting Western Standards of Democracy through Multi dimensional Peace Support Operations", *ELSA [European Law Students' Association] Law Review*, No. 2.

de HEUSCH, L. (1994), "Anthropologie d'un génocide : le Rwanda", *Les Temps Modernes*, Vol. XLIX, No. 579, December.

HONKE, G. (1990), *Au plus profond de l'Afrique, le Rwanda et la colonisation allemande, 1805-1919*, Peter Hammer Verlag, Wuppertal.

HUMAN RIGHTS WATCH (1992), *Rwanda: Talking Peace and Waging War: Human Rights since the October 1990 Invasion*, Vol. 14, No. 3, New York.

HUMAN RIGHTS WATCH (1993), *The Lost Agenda: Human Rights and UN Field Operations*, Human Rights Watch, New York.

HUMAN RIGHTS WATCH (1994), *Arming Rwanda. The Arms Trade and Human Rights Abuses in the Rwandan War*, January, New York.

ICRC (1988), *Annual Report*, Geneva.

ICRC (1990), *Annual Report*, Geneva.

ICRC (1992), *Annual Report*, Geneva.

ICRC (1994), *Annual Report*, Geneva.

INTERACTION (1993), *NGO After-Action Review of the US Army's Joint Readiness Training Center's Exercise in Peace Enforcement*, Interaction, Washington, D.C., November.

INTERNATIONAL COUNCIL OF VOLUNTARY AGENCIES (1993), "NGO Views and Recommendations on Refugees and Displaced Persons", ICVA Statement to the 44th Session of the Executive Committee of the UN High Commissioner for Refugees' Programme, ICVA, Geneva.

INTERNATIONAL FEDERATION OF RED CROSS AND RED CRESCENT SOCIETIES (1994), *World Disaster Report*, Geneva.

INTERNATIONAL FEDERATION OF RED CROSS AND RED CRESCENT SOCIETIES (1995), *Under the Volcanoes: Rwanda's Refugee Crisis*, IFRC, Geneva.

JONAH, J.O.C. (1993), "Humanitarian Intervention", in T.G. WEISS and L. MINEAR (eds.), *op. cit*.

JONGMAN, A. (1995), "War and Political Violence", in *Dutch Yearbook on Peace and Security*, Nijmegan, University of Nijmegan, the Netherlands.

KENT, R. (1996), "The Integrated Operations Centre in Rwanda: Coping with Complexity", in J. WHITMAN and D. POCOCK (eds.), *op. cit*.

KOUCHNER, B. (1991), *Le Malheur des autres*, éditions Odile Jacob, Paris.

LAKE, A. et al. (1990), *After the Wars: Reconstruction in Afghanistan, Indochina, Central America, Southern Africa, and the Horn of Africa*,Transaction Publishers, New Brunswick.

LANXADE, A.J. (1995), "L'Opération Turquoise", *Défense nationale*, February.

LAROSE-EDWARDS, P. (1994), "The Rwandan Crisis of April 1994: The Lessons Learned", International Human Rights, Democracy & Conflict Resolution, Ottawa.

LAROSE-EDWARDS, P. (1995), "United Nations Internal Impediments to Peace-keeping Rapid Reaction", International Human Rights, Democracy, & Conflict Resolution, April 2, 1995, Ottawa. [A report prepared for the Regional Security and Peace-keeping Division, International Security, Arms control, and CSCE Affairs Bureau, Dept. of Foreign Affairs and International Trade].

Le Bolchévik (1994), No. 129, July-August.

L'Interdépendant (1994), "Rwanda : des parlementaires et des ONG approuvent l'appel de La Haye", bulletin n° 28 et supplément spécial sur le Rwanda, novembre.

Le Monde, (1995), June 13.

Le Nouvel Afrique-Asie (1994), No. 58-59, July-August.

Le Prolétaire (1994), No. 427, July-August.

Le Temps Stratégique (1994), No. 61, December.

LEMARCHAND, R. (1970), *Rwanda & Burundi*, Praeger Press, New York.

LEYMARIE, P., "Litigieuse intervention française au Rwanda", *Le Monde Diplomatique*, No. 484, July 1994.

Libération (1995), 3 juin.

LINDEN, J. (1977), *Church & Revolution in Rwanda*, M.U.P., Manchester.

LOUIS, R. (1960), *Ruanda-Urundi (1884-1919)*, Clarendon Press, Oxford.

LUCKHAM, R. (1995), "Dilemmas of Military Disengagement and Democratization in Africa", IDS Bulletin, Vol. 26, No. 2.

LUGAN, B. (1995), *Afrique : de la colonisation philanthropique à la recolonisation humanitaire*, Christian de Bartillat, Courtry.

MacFARLANE, N., L. MINEAR, and S. SHENFIELD (1995), *Armed Conflicts in Georgia: A Case Study in Humanitarian Action and Peacekeeping*, Watson Institute, Providence.

MacKINLAY, J. (1993), "Armed Relief", in T.G. WEISS and L. MINEAR (eds.), *op. cit.*

MacKINLAY, J. (1995), "Military Response to Complex Emergencies", in T.G. WEISS (ed.), *op. cit.*

McCULLUM, H. (1995), *The Angels Have Left Us*, World Council of Churches, Geneva.

MÉDECINS SANS FRONTIÈRES (1994), "MSF dénonce le retrait des Nations Unies", April 22, Bruxelles.

MÉDECINS SANS FRONTIÈRES (1995), *Populations en danger, 1995. Rapport annuel sur les crises majeures et l'action humanitaire*, La Découverte, Paris.

MEYER, D. (1995), "La participation du Japon aux opérations de restauration de l'État", in Y. DAUDET (ed.), *op. cit.*

MICHEL, J. H. (1995), *Development Co-operation: 1994 Report on the Efforts and Policies of the Members of the Development Assistance Committee*, OECD, Paris.

MICHAÏLOF, S. (ed.) (1993), *La France et l'Afrique — Vade-mecum pour un nouveau voyage*, Karthala, Paris.

MINEAR, L. (1988), *Helping People in an Age of Conflict: Toward a New Professionalism in U.S. Voluntary Humanitarian Assistance*, InterAction, New York and Washington.

MINEAR, L. (1988-89), "The Forgotten Human Agenda", *Foreign Policy*, No. 73, Winter.

MINEAR, L. et al. (1991), *Humanitarianism under Siege: A Critical Review of Operation Lifeline Sudan*, Red Sea Press, Trenton, NJ.

MINEAR, L. et al. (1994), *Humanitarian Action in the Former Yugoslavia: The U.N.'s Role 1991-93*, Watson Institute and the Refugee Policy Group, Providence, RI.

MINEAR, L. and T. G. WEISS (1993), *Humanitarian Action in Times of War: A Handbook for Practitioners*, Lynne Rienner, Boulder, CO. [Also available in French and Spanish.]

MINEAR, L. and T. G. WEISS (1995), *Humanitarian Politics*, Foreign Policy Association, New York.

MOONEY, T. (ed.) (1995), *The Challenge of Development within Conflict*, OECD Development Centre, Paris.

MORRIS, N. (1995), "Military Support for Humanitarian Aid Operations", *Strategic Comments*, International Institute for Strategic Studies, No. 2, Feb. 22.

MORTIMER, E., "High Price of Dallying: The World Should Not Have to Improvise a Response to Each Crisis", *Financial Times*, July 27.

MULTIDONOR EVALUATION OF EMERGENCY ASSISTANCE TO RWANDA (1994), "Terms of Reference", 20 December.

MUNYARUGERERO, F.-X. (1995), "Tutsi Power : un an de régime FPR", *Africa International*, No. 282, April.

NAHIMANA, F. (1993), *Le Rwanda. Émergence d'un État*, L'Harmattan, Paris.

NATSIOS, A.S. (1994), "Food Through Force: Humanitarian Intervention and U.S. Policy", *The Washington Quarterly*, Winter (17:1).

NATSIOS, A.S. (1996), "Illusions of Influence: The CNN Effect in Complex Emergencies", in R.I. ROTBERG and T.G. WEISS (eds.), *op. cit.*

NETHERLANDS MINISTRY OF FOREIGN AFFAIRS (1994), Operations Review Unit (1994), *Humanitarian Aid to Somalia*, Ministry of Foreign Affairs, The Hague.

NEWBURY, C. (1988), *The Cohesion of Oppression. Clientship & Ethnicity in Rwanda 1860-1960*, Columbia University Press, New York.

NGUYEN QUOC, D., P. DALLIER and A. PELLET (1994), *Droit international public*, LGDJ, 5th edition, Paris.

OGATA, S. (1994), *The State of the World's Refugees: The Challenge of Protection*, Penguin Books, New York.

OTANI, Y. (1993), "Les problèmes juridiques posés par la participation du Japon à des opérations conduites par les Nations Unies", *Annuaire français de droit international*, Vol. XXXIX.

PAYE, O. (1993), "Les opérations de maintien de la paix et les nouveaux désordres internationaux", in ASSOCIATION DROIT DES GENS, *op. cit.*

PEASE, K.K. and D.P. FORSYTHE (1993), "Humanitarian Intervention and International Law", *Austrian Journal of Public & International Law*, Vol. XLV.

PERRY, W.I. (1995), "The Rules of Engagement", *Defense Issues*, Vol. 9, No. 84.

POINCARÉ, N. (1995), *Rwanda : Gabriel Maindron, un prêtre dans la tourmente*, Les éditions de l'Atelier, Les éditions ouvrières, Paris.

PRESS, R.M. (1994), "Rwandans Speak of Openness to Reconciliation", *Christian Science Monitor*, Aug. 17.

PRONK, J.P. (1994), "Verslag reis Goma", Report Aan Voorzitter van de Tweede Kamer, July 25.

PRUNIER, G. (1993), "Éléments pour une histoire du Front Patriotique Rwandais", *Politique Africaine*, No. 51, October.

RANDEL, J. (1994), "Aid, The Military and Humanitarian Assistance: An Attempt to Identify Recent Trends", *Journal of International Development*, Vol. 6, No. 3.

RANDEL, J. and T. GERMAN (eds.) (1994), *The Reality of Aid 1994: An Independent Review of International Aid*, Actionaid, London.

RANDEL, J. and T. GERMAN (eds.) (1995), *The Reality of Aid 1995: An Independent Review of International Aid*, Actionaid, London.

REFUGEE POLICY GROUP (1994), *Hope Restored? Humanitarian Aid in Somalia 1990-1994*, Refugee Policy Group, Washington, D.C.

RENNER, M. (1994), *Budgeting for Disarmament: The Costs of War and Peace*, Worldwatch, Washington, D.C.

REYNTJENS, F. (1994), *L'Afrique des Grands Lacs en crise, Rwanda, Burundi : 1988-1994*, Karthala, Paris.

Rivarol (1994), No. 2 209, July 29-Sept.

ROTBERG, R.I. and T. G. WEISS (eds.) (1996), *From Massacres to Genodice: The Media, Public Policy, and Humanitairan Crises*, Brookings Institution, Washington, D.C.

ROUGIER, A. (1910), "La théorie de l'intervention d'humanité", *Revue Générale de Droit International Public*.

RUMIYA, J. (1992), *Le Rwanda sous le régime du mandat belge (1916-1931)*, L'Harmattan, Paris.

RUPESINGHE, K. (1992), "The Disappearing Boundaries Between Internal and External Conflicts", in R. KUMAR (ed.), *Internal Conflict and Governance*, The Macmillan Press Ltd, London.

SANDOZ, Y. (1992), " 'Droit' or 'devoir d'ingérence' and the Right to Assistance: the Issues Involved", *International Review of the Red Cross*, May-June.

SAPIR, D. G. and H. DECONINCK (1995), "The Paradox of Humanitarian Assistance and Military Intervention in Somalia", in T.G. WEISS (ed.), *op. cit.*

SCHENKENBERG VAN MIEROP (1995), "Collaboration between Humanitarian Organizations and Military Personnel", MSF-Holland, May.

SCHROEDER, General D. (1994), *After Action Review: Operation Support Hope*, US European Command, Frankfurt.

SENATE ARMED SERVICES COMMITTEE (1994), "Department of Defense Briefing on the Situation in Rwanda", Transcript of Hearing of July 25, U.S. Government Printing Office, Washington, D.C.

SHIRAS, P. (1996), "Humanitarian Emergencies and the Role of NGOs", in J. WHITMAN and D. POCOCK (eds.), *op. cit.*

SICILIANOS, L. A. (1990), *Les réactions décentralisées à l'illicite. Des contre-mesures à la légitime défense*, Librairie Générale de Droit et de Jurisprudence, Paris.

SIDDIQUE, A.K., A. SALAM, M.S. ISLAM, K. AKRAM, R.N. MAJUMDAR, K. ZAMAN, N. FRONCZAK and S. LASTON (1995), "Why Treatment Centres Failed to Prevent Cholera Deaths among Rwandan Refugees in Goma, Zaire", *The Lancet*, Vol. 345, Feb. 11.

SMITH, S. (1995), "France-Rwanda : Lévirat colonial et abandon dans la région des Grands Lacs", in A. Guichaoua (ed.), *op. cit.*

SMITH, S. and J. GUISNEL (1994), "L'impossible mission militaro-humanitaire", *Libération*, July 19.

Socialisme International (1994), No. 73, July-August.

SOUNALET, M. (1994), *Vivre jusqu'à demain : une mission au Rwanda*, L'Anabase, L'Esprit des Péninsules, Paris.

STEERING COMMITTEE OF THE JOINT EVALUATION OF EMERGENCY ASSISTANCE TO RWANDA (1996), *The International Response to Conflict and Genocide: Lessons from the Rwanda Experience*, Copenhagen, Steering Committee.

TANCA, A. (1993), *Foreign Armed Intervention in Internal Conflict*, Martinus Nijhoff Publishers or Kluwer Academic Publishers, Dordrecht or Boston.

TERNON, Y. (1995), *L'État criminel : les génocides au XXe siècle*, Seuil, Paris.

TESON, F.R. (1993-94), "International Abductions, Low Intensity Conflicts and State Sovereignty: Oral Inquiry", *Columbia Journal of Transnational Law*, Vol. XXI, No.3.

THAROOR, S. (1996), "The Future of Peacekeeping", in J. WHITMAN, *op. cit.*

THORNBERRY, C. (1996), "Peacekeepers, Humanitarian Aid, and Civil Conflicts", in WHITMAN and POPOCK, *op. cit.*

TOMUSCHAT, C. (1993), "Les opérations des troupes allemandes à l'extérieur du territoire allemand", *Annuaire français de droit international*, Vol. XXXIX.

UNITED NATIONS (1994a), Document, S/1994/1405.

UNITED NATIONS (1994b), Document S/1994/1305, Nov. 17.

UNITED NATIONS (1994c), Progress Report of the Secretary-General on the United Nations Assistance Mission for Rwanda (S/1994/1344, Nov. 25).

UNITED NATIONS (1994d), Report of the Secretary-General on Security in Rwandese Refugee Camps (S/1994/1308, Nov. 18).

UNITED NATIONS (1994e), Progress Report of the Secretary-General on the United Nations Assistance Mission for Rwanda (S/1994/1133, October 6).

UNITED NATIONS (1995a), Progress Report of the Secretary-General on the United Nations Assistance Mission for Rwanda, (S/1995/678), August 8.

UNITED NATIONS (1995b), Report of the Secretary-General on the United Nations Assistance Mission for Rwanda, S/1995/457, June 4.

UNITED NATIONS (1995c), *Consolidated Inter-Agency Appeal for Persons Affected by the Crisis in Rwanda*, January-December, Vol.I.

UNITED NATIONS (1995d), *Consolidated Inter-Agency Appeal for Persons Affected by the Crisis in Rwanda*, (Updated Financial Summary as of August 7, 1995).

UNITED NATIONS DEPARTMENT OF PUBLIC INFORMATION (1994), *The United Nations & the Situation in Rwanda*, Reference Paper, August 1994, DPI/1484/AFR/PKO. An update by the same name was published in April 1995.

UNITED NATIONS DEPARTMENT OF HUMANITARIAN AFFAIRS (1994), "Guidelines on the Use of Military and Civil Defence Assets in Disaster Relief", DHA, Geneva, May.

UNITED NATIONS DEPARTMENT OF HUMANITARIAN AFFAIRS (1995a), *United Nations Consolidated Inter-Agency Appeal for Persons Affected by the Crisis in Rwanda*, January-December, Vol. I.

UNITED NATIONS DEPARTMENT OF HUMANITARIAN AFFAIRS (1995b), *Consolidated Inter-Agency Humanitarian Assistance Appeals: List of Appeals Launched or Ongoing for 1992/1993/1994/1995*.

UNITED NATIONS DEPARTMENT OF HUMANITARIAN AFFAIRS (1995c), "The Detention Crisis in Rwanda", Aug. 4.

UNITED NATIONS DEPARTMENT OF HUMANITARIAN AFFAIRS (1995d), "Protection of Humanitarian Mandates in Conflict Situations".

UNITED NATIONS DEVELOPMENT PROGRAMME (1994), *Human Development Report 1994*, Oxford University Press, New York and Oxford.

UNITED NATIONS HIGH COMMISSIONER FOR REFUGEES (1995a) "Refugees at a Glance", August.

UNITED NATIONS HIGH COMMISSIONER FOR REFUGEES (1995b), *Zairean Camp Security Operation*, Briefing Note of July 7.

UNITED NATIONS HIGH COMMISSIONER FOR REFUGEES (1995c), *Zairean Camp Security Operation*, Briefing Note of June 9.

UNITED NATION HIGH COMMISSIONER FOR REFUGEES (1995d), "Humanitarian Emergencies and Refugees: Concept Paper", prepared for an Informal Consultation on Service Packages, April 3, Geneva.

UNITED NATIONS HIGH COMMISSIONER FOR REFUGEES (1995e), "A UNHCR Handbook for the Military on Humanitarian Operations", UNHCR, January, Geneva.

UNREO (1994a), *Humanitarian Situation Report*, Sept. 30.

UNREO (1994b), *Situation Report No. 69*, Aug. 17.

UNREO (1994c), *Situation Report No. 68*, Aug. 16.

UNREO (1994d), *Situation Report No. 63*, Aug. 10.

USAID (1995), "Rwanda-Civil Strife/Displaced Persons", Situation Report No. 3 Fiscal Year 1995, January 30.

UNITED STATES COMMITTEE FOR REFUGEES (1994), "Genocide in Rwanda: Documentation of Two Massacres during April 1994", Washington, D.C.

UNITED STATES DEPARTMENT OF NATIONAL DEFENSE (1995), Backgrounder, BG-94-008 (revised), Jan. 12.

UNITED STATES DEPARTMENT OF STATE and UNITED STATES MARINE CORPS FIRST EXPEDITIONARY FORCE (1995), "Integrating Military & Civilian Efforts in Humanitarian Assistance and Peace Operations", [Report of a Conference Sponsored by the Bureau of Intelligence and Research of the Department of State and the U.S. Marine Corps' First Expeditionary Force], US Marine Corps, Camp Pendleton, CA.

UNITED STATES GENERAL ACCOUNTING OFFICE (1995a), "Peace Operations: Heavy Use of Key Capabilities May Affect Response to Regional Conflicts", US Government Printing Office, Washington, D.C.

UNITED STATES GENERAL ACCOUNTING OFFICE (1995b), Peace Operations: Estimated Fiscal Year 1995 Costs to the United States, Report GAO/NSIAD-95-138BR, May.

UNITED STATES GENERAL ACCOUNTING OFFICE (1995c), "Peace Operations: Information on U.S. and U.N. Activities", GAO/NSIAD-95-102BR, February.

VAITER, M. (1995), *Je n'ai pas pu les sauver tous*, Plon, Paris.

VANSINA, J. (1964), *Les anciens Royaumes de la Savane*, Université de Louvain, Louvain.

VANSINA, J., R. MAUNY and L.V. THOMAS (eds.) (1964), *The Historian in Tropical Africa*, London.

VASSALL-ADAMS, G. (1994), *Rwanda: An Agenda for International Action*, Oxfam Publications, Oxford.

VERSCHAVE, F.-X. (1994) *Complicité de génocide ? La politique de la France au Rwanda*, La Découverte, Paris.

VINACKE, H.M. (1934), *International Organization*, F.S. Crofts & Co., New York.

de WAAL, A. and R. OMAAR (1994), "Can Military Intervention be Humanitarian?", *Middle East Report*, Vol. 24, No. 2-3, March-June.

WALLENSTEEN, P. and K. AXELL (1994), "Major Armed Conflicts", *SIPRI Yearbook*.

WATROUS, S. (1994), "Nobody Here But Us Roadbuilders", *The Progressive*, Vol. 58, No. 10, October.

WEISS, T. G. (ed.) (1995), *The United Nations and Civil Wars*, Lynne Rienner, Boulder, CO and London.

WEISS, T. G. and L. MINEAR (eds.) (1993), *Humanitarianism Across Borders: Sustaining Civilians in Times of War*, Lynne Rienner Publishers, Boulder, CO and London.

WEISS, T.G. and K.M. CAMPBELL (1992), "Military Humanitarianism", *Survival*, Vol. 33, No. 5 [Sept./Oct.].

WHITE, N. (1994), "UN Peacekeeping: Development or Destruction?", *International Relations*, Vol. XII, No. 1.

WHITMAN, J. (1996), "The Political Limits of Humanitarian Assistance", in WHITMAN and POCOCK, *op. cit.*

WHITMAN, J. and D. POCOCK (eds.) (1996), *After Rwanda: The Coordination of United Nations Humanitarian Assistance*, MacMillan, London.

WILLIAME, J.-C. (1995), "Aux sources de l'hécatombe rwandaise", *Cahiers Africains*, No. 14, Institut Africain-CEDAFC, L'Harmattan, Brussels and Paris.

WRIGHT, N. (1996), "The Hidden Costs of Better Coordination", in J. WHITMAN and D. POCOCK (eds.), *op. cit.*

MAIN SALES OUTLETS OF OECD PUBLICATIONS
PRINCIPAUX POINTS DE VENTE DES PUBLICATIONS DE L'OCDE

AUSTRALIA – AUSTRALIE
D.A. Information Services
648 Whitehorse Road, P.O.B 163
Mitcham, Victoria 3132   Tel. (03) 9210.7777
                          Fax: (03) 9210.7788

AUSTRIA – AUTRICHE
Gerold & Co.
Graben 31
Wien I   Tel. (0222) 533.50.14
          Fax: (0222) 512.47.31.29

BELGIUM – BELGIQUE
Jean De Lannoy
Avenue du Roi, Koningslaan 202
B-1060 Bruxelles   Tel. (02) 538.51.69/538.08.41
                    Fax: (02) 538.08.41

CANADA
Renouf Publishing Company Ltd.
1294 Algoma Road
Ottawa, ON K1B 3W8   Tel. (613) 741.4333
                      Fax: (613) 741.5439

Stores:
61 Sparks Street
Ottawa, ON K1P 5R1   Tel. (613) 238.8985
12 Adelaide Street West
Toronto, ON M5H 1L6   Tel. (416) 363.3171
                       Fax: (416)363.59.63

Les Éditions La Liberté Inc.
3020 Chemin Sainte-Foy
Sainte-Foy, PQ G1X 3V6   Tel. (418) 658.3763
                          Fax: (418) 658.3763

Federal Publications Inc.
165 University Avenue, Suite 701
Toronto, ON M5H 3B8   Tel. (416) 860.1611
                       Fax: (416) 860.1608

Les Publications Fédérales
1185 Université
Montréal, QC H3B 3A7   Tel. (514) 954.1633
                        Fax: (514) 954.1635

CHINA – CHINE
China National Publications Import
Export Corporation (CNPIEC)
16 Gongti E. Road, Chaoyang District
P.O. Box 88 or 50
Beijing 100704 PR   Tel. (01) 506.6688
                     Fax: (01) 506.3101

CHINESE TAIPEI – TAIPEI CHINOIS
Good Faith Worldwide Int'l. Co. Ltd.
9th Floor, No. 118, Sec. 2
Chung Hsiao E. Road
Taipei   Tel. (02) 391.7396/391.7397
          Fax: (02) 394.9176

DENMARK – DANEMARK
Munksgaard Book and Subscription Service
35, Nørre Søgade, P.O. Box 2148
DK-1016 København K   Tel. (33) 12.85.70
                       Fax: (33) 12.93.87

J. H. Schultz Information A/S,
Herstedvang 12,
DK – 2620 Albertslung   Tel. 43 63 23 00
                         Fax: 43 63 19 69
Internet: s-info@inet.uni-c.dk

EGYPT – ÉGYPTE
Middle East Observer
41 Sherif Street
Cairo   Tel. 392.6919
         Fax: 360-6804

FINLAND – FINLANDE
Akateeminen Kirjakauppa
Keskuskatu 1, P.O. Box 128
00100 Helsinki

Subscription Services/Agence d'abonnements :
P.O. Box 23
00371 Helsinki   Tel. (358 0) 121 4416
                  Fax: (358 0) 121.4450

FRANCE
OECD/OCDE
Mail Orders/Commandes par correspondance :
2, rue André-Pascal
75775 Paris Cedex 16   Tel. (33-1) 45.24.82.00
                        Fax: (33-1) 49.10.42.76
                        Telex: 640048 OCDE
Internet: Compte.PUBSINQ@oecd.org

Orders via Minitel, France only/
Commandes par Minitel, France exclusivement :
36 15 OCDE

OECD Bookshop/Librairie de l'OCDE :
33, rue Octave-Feuillet
75016 Paris   Tél. (33-1) 45.24.81.81
               (33-1) 45.24.81.67

Dawson
B.P. 40
91121 Palaiseau Cedex   Tel. 69.10.47.00
                         Fax: 64.54.83.26

Documentation Française
29, quai Voltaire
75007 Paris   Tel. 40.15.70.00

Economica
49, rue Héricart
75015 Paris   Tel. 45.75.05.67
               Fax: 40.58.15.70

Gibert Jeune (Droit-Économie)
6, place Saint-Michel
75006 Paris   Tel. 43.25.91.19

Librairie du Commerce International
10, avenue d'Iéna
75016 Paris   Tel. 40.73.34.60

Librairie Dunod
Université Paris-Dauphine
Place du Maréchal-de-Lattre-de-Tassigny
75016 Paris   Tel. 44.05.40.13

Librairie Lavoisier
11, rue Lavoisier
75008 Paris   Tel. 42.65.39.95

Librairie des Sciences Politiques
30, rue Saint-Guillaume
75007 Paris   Tel. 45.48.36.02

P.U.F.
49, boulevard Saint-Michel
75005 Paris   Tel. 43.25.83.40

Librairie de l'Université
12a, rue Nazareth
13100 Aix-en-Provence   Tel. (16) 42.26.18.08

Documentation Française
165, rue Garibaldi
69003 Lyon   Tel. (16) 78.63.32.23

Librairie Decitre
29, place Bellecour
69002 Lyon   Tel. (16) 72.40.54.54

Librairie Sauramps
Le Triangle
34967 Montpellier Cedex 2   Tel. (16) 67.58.85.15
                             Fax: (16) 67.58.27.36

A la Sorbonne Actual
23, rue de l'Hôtel-des-Postes
06000 Nice   Tel. (16) 93.13.77.75
              Fax: (16) 93.80.75.69

GERMANY – ALLEMAGNE
OECD Bonn Centre
August-Bebel-Allee 6
D-53175 Bonn   Tel. (0228) 959.120
                Fax: (0228) 959.12.17

GREECE – GRÈCE
Librairie Kauffmann
Stadiou 28
10564 Athens   Tel. (01) 32.55.321
                Fax: (01) 32.30.320

HONG-KONG
Swindon Book Co. Ltd.
Astoria Bldg. 3F
34 Ashley Road, Tsimshatsui
Kowloon, Hong Kong   Tel. 2376.2062
                      Fax: 2376.0685

HUNGARY – HONGRIE
Euro Info Service
Margitsziget, Európa Ház
1138 Budapest   Tel. (1) 111.62.16
                 Fax: (1) 111.60.61

ICELAND – ISLANDE
Mál Mog Menning
Laugavegi 18, Pósthólf 392
121 Reykjavik   Tel. (1) 552.4240
                 Fax: (1) 562.3523

INDIA – INDE
Oxford Book and Stationery Co.
Scindia House
New Delhi 110001   Tel. (11) 331.5896/5308
                    Fax: (11) 332.5993
17 Park Street
Calcutta 700016   Tel. 240832

INDONESIA – INDONÉSIE
Pdii-Lipi
P.O. Box 4298
Jakarta 12042   Tel. (21) 573.34.67
                 Fax: (21) 573.34.67

IRELAND – IRLANDE
Government Supplies Agency
Publications Section
4/5 Harcourt Road
Dublin 2   Tel. 661.31.11
            Fax: 475.27.60

ISRAEL – ISRAËL
Praedicta
5 Shatner Street
P.O. Box 34030
Jerusalem 91430   Tel. (2) 52.84.90/1/2
                   Fax: (2) 52.84.93

R.O.Y. International
P.O. Box 13056
Tel Aviv 61130   Tel. (3) 546 1423
                  Fax: (3) 546 1442

Palestinian Authority/Middle East:
INDEX Information Services
P.O.B. 19502
Jerusalem   Tel. (2) 27.12.19
             Fax: (2) 27.16.34

ITALY – ITALIE
Libreria Commissionaria Sansoni
Via Duca di Calabria 1/1
50125 Firenze   Tel. (055) 64.54.15
                 Fax: (055) 64.12.57
Via Bartolini 29
20155 Milano   Tel. (02) 36.50.83

Editrice e Libreria Herder
Piazza Montecitorio 120
00186 Roma   Tel. 679.46.28
              Fax: 678.47.51

Libreria Hoepli
Via Hoepli 5
20121 Milano　　　　　　　Tel. (02) 86.54.46
　　　　　　　　　　　　　Fax: (02) 805.28.86

Libreria Scientifica
Dott. Lucio de Biasio 'Aeiou'
Via Coronelli, 6
20146 Milano　　　　　　　Tel. (02) 48.95.45.52
　　　　　　　　　　　　　Fax: (02) 48.95.45.48

JAPAN – JAPON
OECD Tokyo Centre
Landic Akasaka Building
2-3-4 Akasaka, Minato-ku
Tokyo 107　　　　　　　　Tel. (81.3) 3586.2016
　　　　　　　　　　　　　Fax: (81.3) 3584.7929

KOREA – CORÉE
Kyobo Book Centre Co. Ltd.
P.O. Box 1658, Kwang Hwa Moon
Seoul　　　　　　　　　　Tel. 730.78.91
　　　　　　　　　　　　　Fax: 735.00.30

MALAYSIA – MALAISIE
University of Malaya Bookshop
University of Malaya
P.O. Box 1127, Jalan Pantai Baru
59700 Kuala Lumpur
Malaysia　　　　　　　　　Tel. 756.5000/756.5425
　　　　　　　　　　　　　Fax: 756.3246

MEXICO – MEXIQUE
OECD Mexico Centre
Edificio INFOTEC
Av. San Fernando no. 37
Col. Toriello Guerra
Tlalpan C.P. 14050
Mexico D.F.　　　　　　　Tel. (525) 665 47 99
　　　　　　　　　　　　　Fax: (525) 606 13 07

Revistas y Periodicos Internacionales S.A. de C.V.
Florencia 57 - 1004
Mexico, D.F. 06600　　　　Tel. 207.81.00
　　　　　　　　　　　　　Fax: 208.39.79

NETHERLANDS – PAYS-BAS
SDU Uitgeverij Plantijnstraat
Externe Fondsen
Postbus 20014
2500 EA's-Gravenhage　　　Tel. (070) 37.89.880
Voor bestellingen:　　　　　Fax: (070) 34.75.778

**NEW ZEALAND –
NOUVELLE-ZÉLANDE**
GPLegislation Services
P.O. Box 12418
Thorndon, Wellington　　　Tel. (04) 496.5655
　　　　　　　　　　　　　Fax: (04) 496.5698

NORWAY – NORVÈGE
NIC INFO A/S
Bertrand Narvesens vei 2
P.O. Box 6512 Etterstad
0606 Oslo 6　　　　　　　Tel. (022) 57.33.00
　　　　　　　　　　　　　Fax: (022) 68.19.01

PAKISTAN
Mirza Book Agency
65 Shahrah Quaid-E-Azam
Lahore 54000　　　　　　　Tel. (42) 735.36.01
　　　　　　　　　　　　　Fax: (42) 576.37.14

PHILIPPINE – PHILIPPINES
International Booksource Center Inc.
Rm 179/920 Cityland 10 Condo Tower 2
HV dela Costa Ext cor Valero St.
Makati Metro Manila　　　Tel. (632) 817 9676
　　　　　　　　　　　　　Fax: (632) 817 1741

POLAND – POLOGNE
Ars Polona
00-950 Warszawa
Krakowskie Przedmieácie 7　Tel. (22) 264760
　　　　　　　　　　　　　Fax: (22) 268673

PORTUGAL
Livraria Portugal
Rua do Carmo 70-74
Apart. 2681
1200 Lisboa　　　　　　　Tel. (01) 347.49.82/5
　　　　　　　　　　　　　Fax: (01) 347.02.64

SINGAPORE – SINGAPOUR
Gower Asia Pacific Pte Ltd.
Golden Wheel Building
41, Kallang Pudding Road, No. 04-03
Singapore 1334　　　　　　Tel. 741.5166
　　　　　　　　　　　　　Fax: 742.9356

SPAIN – ESPAGNE
Mundi-Prensa Libros S.A.
Castelló 37, Apartado 1223
Madrid 28001　　　　　　Tel. (91) 431.33.99
　　　　　　　　　　　　　Fax: (91) 575.39.98

Mundi-Prensa Barcelona
Consell de Cent No. 391
08009 – Barcelona　　　　　Tel. (93) 488.34.92
　　　　　　　　　　　　　Fax: (93) 487.76.59

Llibreria de la Generalitat
Palau Moja
Rambla dels Estudis, 118
08002 – Barcelona
　　　(Subscripcions) Tel. (93) 318.80.12
　　　(Publicacions) Tel. (93) 302.67.23
　　　　　　　　　　　　　Fax: (93) 412.18.54

SRI LANKA
Centre for Policy Research
c/o Colombo Agencies Ltd.
No. 300-304, Galle Road
Colombo 3　　　　　　　　Tel. (1) 574240, 573551-2
　　　　　　　　　　　　　Fax: (1) 575394, 510711

SWEDEN – SUÈDE
CE Fritzes AB
S–106 47 Stockholm　　　　Tel. (08) 690.90.90
　　　　　　　　　　　　　Fax: (08) 20.50.21

Subscription Agency/Agence d'abonnements :
Wennergren-Williams Info AB
P.O. Box 1305
171 25 Solna　　　　　　　Tel. (08) 705.97.50
　　　　　　　　　　　　　Fax: (08) 27.00.71

SWITZERLAND – SUISSE
Maditec S.A. (Books and Periodicals - Livres
et périodiques)
Chemin des Palettes 4
Case postale 266
1020 Renens VD 1　　　　　Tel. (021) 635.08.65
　　　　　　　　　　　　　Fax: (021) 635.07.80

Librairie Payot S.A.
4, place Pépinet
CP 3212
1002 Lausanne　　　　　　Tel. (021) 320.25.11
　　　　　　　　　　　　　Fax: (021) 320.25.14

Librairie Unilivres
6, rue de Candolle
1205 Genève　　　　　　　Tel. (022) 320.26.23
　　　　　　　　　　　　　Fax: (022) 329.73.18

Subscription Agency/Agence d'abonnements :
Dynapresse Marketing S.A.
38, avenue Vibert
1227 Carouge　　　　　　　Tel. (022) 308.07.89
　　　　　　　　　　　　　Fax: (022) 308.07.99

See also – Voir aussi :
OECD Bonn Centre
August-Bebel-Allee 6
D-53175 Bonn (Germany)　　Tel. (0228) 959.120
　　　　　　　　　　　　　Fax: (0228) 959.12.17

THAILAND – THAÏLANDE
Suksit Siam Co. Ltd.
113, 115 Fuang Nakhon Rd.
Opp. Wat Rajbopith
Bangkok 10200　　　　　　Tel. (662) 225.9531/2
　　　　　　　　　　　　　Fax: (662) 222.5188

TRINIDAD & TOBAGO
SSL Systematics Studies Limited
9 Watts Street
Curepe
Trinadad & Tobago, W.I.　　Tel. (1809) 645.3475
　　　　　　　　　　　　　Fax: (1809) 662.5654

TUNISIA – TUNISIE
Grande Librairie Spécialisée
Fendri Ali
Avenue Haffouz Imm El-Intilaka
Bloc B 1 Sfax 3000　　　　Tel. (216-4) 296 855
　　　　　　　　　　　　　Fax: (216-4) 298.270

TURKEY – TURQUIE
Kültür Yayinlari Is-Türk Ltd. Sti.
Atatürk Bulvari No. 191/Kat 13
Kavaklidere/Ankara
　　　　　　　　　　　　　Tel. (312) 428.11.40 Ext. 2458
　　　　　　　　　　　　　Fax: (312) 417 24 90
Dolmabahce Cad. No. 29
Besiktas/Istanbul　　　　　Tel. (212) 260 7188

UNITED KINGDOM – ROYAUME-UNI
HMSO
Gen. enquiries　　　　　　Tel. (0171) 873 0011
Postal orders only:
P.O. Box 276, London SW8 5DT
Personal Callers HMSO Bookshop
49 High Holborn, London WC1V 6HB
　　　　　　　　　　　　　Fax: (0171) 873 8463
Branches at: Belfast, Birmingham, Bristol,
Edinburgh, Manchester

UNITED STATES – ÉTATS-UNIS
OECD Washington Center
2001 L Street N.W., Suite 650
Washington, D.C. 20036-4922 Tel. (202) 785.6323
　　　　　　　　　　　　　Fax: (202) 785.0350
Internet: washcont@oecd.org

Subscriptions to OECD periodicals may also be placed through main subscription agencies.

Les abonnements aux publications périodiques de l'OCDE peuvent être souscrits auprès des principales agences d'abonnement.

Orders and inquiries from countries where Distributors have not yet been appointed should be sent to: OECD Publications, 2, rue André-Pascal, 75775 Paris Cedex 16, France.

Les commandes provenant de pays où l'OCDE n'a pas encore désigné de distributeur peuvent être adressées aux Éditions de l'OCDE, 2, rue André-Pascal, 75775 Paris Cedex 16, France.

5-1996

OECD PUBLICATIONS, 2, rue André-Pascal, 75775 PARIS CEDEX 16
PRINTED IN FRANCE
(41 96 08 1) ISBN 92-64-14917-1 – No. 48857 1996